THE COUP AT CATHOLIC UNIVERSITY

PETER M. MITCHELL

THE COUP AT CATHOLIC UNIVERSITY

~

The 1968 Revolution in Catholic Education

IGNATIUS PRESS   SAN FRANCISCO

Cover design by Milo Persic

ISBN 978-1-58617-756-0
Library of Congress Control Number 2014905851
Printed in the United States of America ♾

*To Monsignor Eugene Kevane
and all Catholic educators,
especially my parents,
Robin and Susan Mitchell*

Today must mark a beginning and not an end.
Let us pledge ourselves to that goal.

—Charles Curran, April 24, 1967

What is the real meaning, value, validity and importance of being pontifical in today's America?
It is an albatross around the University's neck.

—Middle States Association Evaluation,
October 1967

For if the plan succeeds to capture this official National
Catholic University of the American Hierarchy, there
will be incalculable future results. The seeds of religious
doubt, doctrinal confusion, and outright crisis in Faith
will be sown over the entire United States through the
very schools and colleges operated by and in the name of
the Church. . . .
   I shall tremble for the future of the Church in this
country.
                              —Eugene Kevane, January 18, 1968

Contents

I. The Curran Affair

II. The School of Theology Takes Control of CUA

III. The Triumph of Dissent

Appendices

Preface

The protagonists of the story recounted in these pages were part of the generation that came of age in the summer of 1968. Their actions indicated a deep frustration with authoritarianism in the Church, that is, with a culture of Church authority that was often unjust and arbitrary, sometimes grievously so, in its attitudes and actions. They were of the generation that lived through the dramatic years and changes of the Second Vatican Council and, as a result, were passionately committed to their cause of renewing the Church so that it would be more pastoral, human, and loving in its living out of the gospel of Jesus Christ. Their generation remains with us and continues to have a great influence on the Church and on American culture in the early twenty-first century.

I am of a different generation, one that came of age twenty-five years later, in the summer of 1993. In Denver, Colorado, Pope John Paul II challenged us at World Youth Day with his words, "This is no time to be ashamed of the Gospel. It is time to preach it from the rooftops." We went forth from Denver proud to be Catholic and convinced that the "Gospel of Life" as expressed in the fullness of the Church's spiritual and moral teaching was good news that the world needed to hear. We too were and are passionate.

There has been, to say the least, some tension between these two generations within the Catholic Church in the United States. Much of that tension is the fruit of both generations' failure to understand fully how powerfully each has been shaped by its own experiences. The goal of my research and writing has been to shed light on the historical truth of the experiences of the generation that imbibed the atmosphere of euphoria and genuine hope in a renewed Church that surrounded the Second Vatican Council. It is often difficult for my generation to appreciate fully what it was like to have lived through the years before, during, and immediately following Vatican II. Many of those who lived then still have a remarkable amount of emotional investment in the events of those tumultuous years. The Catholic Church in this country became divided—often bitterly so—over the questions raised by Charles Curran and others who embraced the theology of dissent. His frustration with the leadership of the institutional Church was real. As a result of his vocal opposition, the theological authority of the Magisterium came to be seen by many Catholics as an outdated obstacle to openness and progress in the Church.

Having grown up in post-*Roe v. Wade* America, my generation has personally experienced the destructive effects of the moral permissiveness heralded in the 1960s as the way of freedom and love. We sense that a certain injustice occurred in the way the teaching authority of the Church was rejected by many during a historical moment in which the long-term consequences of such rejection may not have been readily apparent. We have become convinced that the Magisterium's consistent teaching is not an obstacle to the Holy Spirit but rather an instrument of the wisdom and love of the Holy Spirit, offering enduring moral clarity to a culture that is often confused in its search for truth. Our gratitude for the teaching of the Magisterium, however, should not be interpreted to mean that we naïvely desire to return to the legalism, clericalism, and stifling censorship that was all too common in the preconciliar years. We are too young to remember the supposedly good old days before the Council. The fact that those who do remember them personally often respond so emotionally and negatively when those days are recalled should give my generation pause. It is possible to accept the theological teaching authority of the shepherds of the Church without necessarily supporting every attitude held and practical decision made by those shepherds over the years.

Both Charles Curran's generation and my own have been formed by the vastly different historical contexts in which we came of age. It follows that our interpretations of the events surrounding 1968 are at times vastly different. I hope that his generation will at least respect the fact that my generation's experiences and insights are no less valid than theirs. Curran showed me great respect when I interviewed him and shared the findings of my research with him. Listening to him talk about his experiences led me to do a great deal of reflecting on what really happened at CUA in the late 1960s. It is my hope that this book may lead others to do the same.

I want to thank all those without whose help and encouragement this book would never have been begun or finished: Father Marcel Chappin, S.J., who directed my original thesis at the Pontifical Gregorian University; Father James Conn, S.J.; Bishop Fabian Bruskewitz; Bishop John Folda, with whom I was privileged to work for many years as a seminary professor and who patiently encouraged me in my writing; my brother priests too numerous to mention; the seminarians of St. Gregory the Great Seminary; the many faithful laity at all the parishes where I have served; and last but definitely not least my parents, Robin and Susan, heroic Catholic educators, and my siblings, Elizabeth, Anne, Father John Paul, and Maria.

"*Tout est grace*", said Saint Thérèse of the Child Jesus. Remembering Monsignor Eugene Kevane's confident devotion to the Little Flower, I thank Jesus in his Divine Mercy for the gift of my priesthood, enabling me to persevere and to bring this work to its completion. May it bring unity and healing to the Catholic Church in the United States.

FATHER PETER MITCHELL
May 22, 2014
Feast of Saint Rita of Cascia, Saint of the Impossible
Fifteenth Anniversary of My Priestly Ordination

Introduction

This book tells the story of a crucial and defining moment in the history of Catholic identity in the United States—namely, the controversy that occurred in the late 1960s at the Catholic University of America[1] in Washington, D.C., over the precise meaning of academic freedom vis-à-vis the role of the Magisterium in Catholic higher education. The cultural upheavals that occurred during those tumultuous years in American society, combined with the rapid and dramatic changes that occurred within the Catholic Church in the immediate aftermath of the Second Vatican Council (1962–1965), contributed to a volatile and contentious atmosphere in Catholic higher education. On the one hand, the American educational tradition placed a high value on freedom of inquiry and research, as well as the right of professors to carry out their academic work without interference from higher authorities. On the other hand, the Catholic Tradition held the role of the Magisterium (the teaching authority of the pope and the bishops) as central to the educational enterprise, a necessary safeguard to ensure that the teaching given by professors at Catholic universities is orthodox, in agreement with defined Catholic teaching on faith and morals. Many Catholic institutions of higher education were caught between the expectations of the bishops who governed them, that they be fully Catholic in preserving orthodoxy, and the expectations of their faculties, that they be fully American in respecting absolute academic freedom. The result was a battle for control of Catholic academia not lacking in drama and controversy.

---

[1] Throughout this work, the Catholic University of America is referred to as "Catholic University" or "CUA" in keeping with the prevailing custom on its campus.

At its foundation in 1889, Catholic University was consciously designed by the bishops of the United States to play a central and influential role in the system of Catholic education that has always been one of the defining marks of the Church in the United States.[2] As a pontifical university, established by and directly under the authority of the Holy See, CUA was founded to further the mission of the Church by teaching Catholic doctrine, particularly in its ecclesiastical faculties: the Schools of Sacred Theology, Philosophy, and Canon Law. These schools were intended to have an extraordinary impact not only on the Catholic Church but also on the wider American society by forming scholars who would in turn teach others at Catholic institutions throughout the country.

The great American principle of freedom of religion formed the foundation of CUA's right to exist as an institution of higher education with a specifically religious commitment and orientation. From its foundation until the 1960s, Catholic University enjoyed a relatively peaceful existence, as did many other religiously affiliated colleges and universities in the United States, under the direct oversight of a religious authority: the CUA board of trustees, which was composed entirely of American bishops.

Beginning in the spring of 1967, however, this direct religious oversight of the American bishops was challenged and effectively overthrown, in the name of academic freedom, by the faculty of CUA's School of Theology. The wide-ranging national debate then occurring within the Catholic Church over what role, if any, the Magisterium should have in the oversight of Catholic institutions of higher education was played out in microcosm at CUA during the tumultuous years 1967 to 1969. The confrontation at CUA was closely watched throughout the country, for if the practical oversight of the Magisterium could be eliminated at the bishops' own pontifical university, it would follow that other Catholic universities, less directly overseen by the pope and the bishops, would not need to heed the teaching of the Magisterium either.

---

[2] Pope Leo XIII in his 1887 letter of foundation instructed James Cardinal Gibbons, archbishop of Baltimore, to establish a pontifical Catholic university in the United States, "that youth be nourished more carefully with sound doctrine, and that those young men especially who are being educated for the Church, should be fully armed to fit them for the task of defending Catholic truth".

The rapidity with which Catholic higher education was transformed during the years immediately following the Second Vatican Council may have caught some onlookers by surprise, particularly among the American hierarchy. The upheaval, however, had been long in the making, and what is more surprising is that it took so long for it to happen. The Catholic intellectual world in the United States on the eve of the Council was marked by a growing frustration with the lack of encouragement of authentic intellectual development by the institutional Church, a frustration particularly acute at Catholic University due to an extremely poor relationship between its faculty and its administration.[3] This frustration occasioned an ever louder call throughout the country for a new generation of lay leadership to replace the clerically dominated authority structure of Catholic higher education, so that Catholic colleges and universities could achieve some level of credible competence in the eyes of their secular peers. This clerical authority was perceived, not without good reason, as extremely controlling and fearful of genuine academic debate, often resorting to censorship in an effort to prevent any semblance of unorthodoxy from existing within the walls of Catholic academia.

The immediate aftermath of Vatican II saw an unprecedented and largely unexpected release of these tensions in the form of the wholesale rejection by Catholic intellectuals of traditional theology and the authoritative role of the Magisterium. Postconciliar theology was marked by a desire for openness that equated the pronouncements of the Magisterium with a narrow-mindedness that was to be eschewed for the sake of a supposedly more relevant and modern approach to faith and truth.

The postconciliar revolution in theology found a willing and powerful ally in the American Association of University Professors (AAUP), whose principles had developed during the course of the twentieth century into a quasi-religious ideology of academic freedom in opposition to any and all creedal statements of a priori dogmatic truth. Throughout the 1960s, the AAUP waged an aggressive attack on religious institutions of higher education and demanded that they renounce any

---

[3] In 1955, John Tracy Ellis lamented the "ghetto mentality" espoused by the Catholic hierarchy and thus by Catholic institutions of higher education in his landmark essay, "American Catholics and the Intellectual Life", *Thought* 30 (1955): 351–88.

former commitment to so-called denominational interests for the sake of the supposedly greater and more unifying common good of doing research in which the only constraint would be "truth itself". Religious bodies that governed institutions of higher education were put into an entirely defensive posture by the AAUP, which threatened to have federal funding of their institutions taken away if they did not radically change them. Churches generally found themselves unsuccessfully attempting to defend the existence of objective religious truth in an almost entirely hostile atmosphere. The absolutist position of academic freedom named religious truth its avowed enemy and ridiculed as incompetent and out of touch with modernity those who tried to cling to dogma. This hostility to ecclesiastical authority, embraced by many Catholic educators in the name of being fully American, was given formal expression in the 1967 "Land O' Lakes Statement", which declared the absolute independence of Catholic universities from the juridical oversight of the American hierarchy.

These factors collectively set the stage for the showdown at Catholic University in the spring of 1967. The dismissal of Charles Curran, the campus-wide strike, and the swift reinstatement of Curran during the week of April 17 to 24 became the pivotal moment on which all subsequent developments depended in the debate over academic freedom at CUA. Though often overshadowed in the historiography of the period by the more prominent dispute of 1968 at the time of the release of *Humanae Vitae*, the 1967 strike was the essential precondition for the July 30, 1968, "Statement of Dissent". In the words of Samuel J. Thomas:

> Indeed, the outcome of the 1967 affair not only determined the locus of the 1968 conflict over the dissent from *Humanae Vitae*; it also contributed to the resolution of that conflict and, in turn, helped prolong Curran's tenure at the university well beyond what his opponents had hoped for.[4]

The CUA board of trustees hoped for an end to controversy and a restoration of stability when they decided to reinstate Curran to his teaching position. Such a hope for an end to their troubles, however,

---

[4] Samuel J. Thomas, "A 'Final Disposition . . . One Way or Another': The Real End of the First Curran Affair", *Catholic Historical Review* 91 (October 2005): 718.

could not have been more completely misplaced. In more ways than anyone (perhaps least of all the bishops) could have imagined at that moment, Charles Curran was correct in declaring that April 24, 1967, marked a beginning and not an end. The victory of Curran marked a permanent shift in the position of the American bishops vis-à-vis Catholic universities: the bishops had temporarily restored tranquility at CUA at the expense of the permanent loss of their practical authority over all Catholic higher education. The dissenting professors became fully confident that they could teach at CUA in open disagreement with the Magisterium and that the American bishops would not and could not effectively do anything about it. In the name of being fully American, the Catholic identity of CUA was definitively rejected by the ascendant postconciliar theologians. The practical redefinition of the nature of Catholic higher education that occurred through Curran's victory in April 1967 was an explosion in the history of the Catholic Church in the United States, and its effects remain normative in American Catholic higher education to the present day.

Abbreviations

AAB   Archives of the Archdiocese of Baltimore

AALA   Archives of the Archdiocese of Los Angeles

AAUP   American Association of University Professors

ACK   Archives of Cardinal Krol

ACP   Archives of Father Carl J. Peter

ACUA   Archives of the Catholic University of America

AMK   Archives of Monsignor Eugene A. Kevane

CTSA   Catholic Theological Society of America

IFCU   International Federation of Catholic Universities

NCCB   National Conference of Catholic Bishops

NCEA   National Catholic Educational Association

I

THE CURRAN AFFAIR

I

The Catholic University Strike:
April 17–24, 1967

The Dismissal of Charles Curran

On Monday morning, April 17, 1967, the rector of the Catholic University of America, Bishop William J. McDonald, summoned Father Charles Curran, associate professor of CUA's School of Sacred Theology, to his office.[1] Having given Curran no notice, McDonald held a letter informing him that, at a meeting one week earlier, the CUA board of trustees had voted "that your services as a member of our Faculty be terminated with the expiration of your present appointment on August 31, 1967."[2]

---

[1] The meeting was also attended by Monsignor Joseph McAllister, executive vice-rector of the university; Monsignor James Magner, vice-rector for business and finance; and Dean Walter Schmitz of the School of Theology. The basic chronology of this week given here follows that found in Albert Pierce's *Beyond One Man*, a pamphlet produced in 1967 compiling various statements and documents pertinent to the case. It is held in the special collection of the Mullen Library of the Catholic University of America. Charles Curran's perspective is taken from his account in *Loyal Dissent: Memoir of a Catholic Theologian* (Washington: Georgetown University Press, 2006), 35–37. The account of the actions of the School of Theology relies on the minutes of the School of Sacred Theology (hereafter cited as Minutes, School of Theology), April 18, 1967, "School of Sacred Theology Minutes" box, "School of Sacred Theology Minutes" folder, Archives of the Catholic University of America (hereafter cited as ACUA), American Catholic History Research Center and University Archives, Catholic University of America, Washington, D.C. The account of the actions of the individual members of the CUA board of trustees during the week of April 17–24, 1967, comes from the report submitted by Archbishop Krol to the CUA board of trustees on May 5, 1967, on behalf of his committee charged with investigating Father Curran (box 34a, Archives of Cardinal Krol [hereafter cited as ACK], Philadelphia Archdiocesan Historical Research Center, Philadelphia, Pennsylvania).

[2] McDonald to Curran, April 15, 1967, box 34a, ACK.

The spirit in the room, as described immediately afterward by McDonald to board of trustees member Archbishop John Krol of Philadelphia, was tense and confrontational. In Krol's words:

> On Monday, April 17, the Most Reverend Rector telephoned me to report that in the presence of others he had advised Father Curran that his contract would not be renewed. He [McDonald] said Father Curran's reaction was strong. He [Curran] said he would immediately give out the information to the newspapers and that he would open the way to a real storm. In fact, he told the Rector that unless he had word by the following noon, he would make the release. He is also reported as having told the Rector that even if the order was rescinded, he would not give any assurances about disclosing the matter to the newspapers.[3]

Curran's own account of the meeting relates his frustration over being handed a decision about which he had been given no notice, no explanation, and no opportunity to defend himself:

> After hearing McDonald out, I responded that the whole process was dishonest and that dishonesty in the church had to stop. I had a right to a full and fair hearing and had not received one. I threatened to make the whole situation public but finally agreed to do nothing for twenty-four hours. McDonald was apparently so flustered by my response that he never gave me the letter he had prepared.[4]

Despite Curran's threat to take the matter to the press, Krol reminded McDonald as they spoke by telephone of his firm conviction that no public explanation of Curran's dismissal would be necessary:

> I suggested to the Rector that he immediately call the public relations man, advise him of the facts, and if Father Curran appealed to the press, a statement should be issued stating the facts. There was no dismissal and there was no tenure—it was simply allowing a contract to lapse—and there was no charge of unorthodoxy or any question of academic freedom.[5]

Any statement of explanation made by the board of trustees, said Krol, "should constantly repeat the simple fact that this was merely a non-

---

[3] Krol's report to the board of trustees, May 5, 1967, box 34a, ACK.

[4] Curran, *Loyal Dissent*, 36.

[5] Krol's report to the board.

renewal of the contract for a professor who had no tenure". Krol was willing to attend a meeting with Curran proposed for April 26—nine days later—but was emphatic that any such meeting must not include discussion of Curran's theological views. Krol believed the trustees' decision, and especially any theological concern underlying that decision, was not open to discussion, not even with Curran himself.[6]

News of Curran's dismissal flashed across the CUA campus that afternoon, and by the following morning, Tuesday, April 18, the faculty of the School of Theology called an "emergency meeting" in Caldwell Lounge.[7] A review was made of the unanimous support that had been given by the School of Theology to Curran in October 1966, in response to an inquiry about Curran's integrity and orthodoxy that had been made by McDonald. The school's dean, Father Walter J. Schmitz,[8] spoke to the faculty in Curran's defense, criticizing the board's decision to dismiss Curran as an entirely arbitrary action that lacked proper charges, a proper hearing, or any due process, all of which were required according to the standards of the American Association of University Professors (AAUP), of which CUA was a proud member. Schmitz asked if anyone had been consulted by the board before Curran's dismissal, and the response was negative. Emphasizing the grave nature of the crisis, Schmitz called for immediate action on the part of the School of Theology.

Schmitz's remarks met with "spontaneous applause" on the part of the faculty, and various letters and words of support from other members of the university community were shared. Curran himself addressed his fellow theology professors, declaring that he was asking

---

[6] The meeting was never held because, according to Krol, "Father Curran was not interested in attending such a meeting" (Krol's report to the board). Indeed, Curran relates that he rejected McDonald's offer of a meeting with the board as "too little and too late" (*Loyal Dissent*, 36). It is understandable that Curran would not have been greatly inclined to attend a meeting during which he would have no opportunity to defend his position. At any rate, events progressed so swiftly that by April 26, Curran had already been reinstated. The swift and overwhelming success of the campaign mounted by the School of Theology in defense of Curran and academic freedom was not foreseen by the board of trustees.

[7] Minutes, School of Theology.

[8] Walter J. Schmitz, S.S. (1907–1994) joined the CUA faculty in 1950 and was dean of the School of Sacred Theology from 1961 to 1973. He remained at CUA as professor emeritus and senior lecturer until 1986.

not merely for a hearing before the board but for his categorical rein-statement, which he considered the only just solution to the crisis that the board of trustees had brought upon the university.

The School of Theology unanimously agreed that what had happened to Curran was an outrageous injustice that had not followed even a semblance of due process and the only possible resolution to the matter was to reinstate him as a professor. To pressure the administration to reinstate Curran, the professors decided to take their list of grievances to the press. Even though this was perhaps regrettable, because it would bring the divisions at CUA into the public forum, it was nevertheless necessary if they were to obtain the public sympathy essential to the success of their cause. Their argument supporting Curran was to be based entirely on the principles of academic freedom and would *not* in any way address Curran's theological position. They rallied not for the acceptance of Curran's theological views but for basic justice: the right of a professor to hear his accusers and to defend himself accordingly.

That night Schmitz sent a telegram to the board of trustees protesting the "serious injustice" of their decision:

> The members of the faculty of the School of Theology of the Catholic University of America are most profoundly disturbed with the Board of Trustees' failure to renew the contract of Father Charles Curran. In the present context this decision cannot be interpreted by the public as other than indicating some deficiency in his teaching performance or in his doctrinal or personal integrity. Under these circumstances a serious injustice has been done him, given the fact that he had no opportunity to learn what reasons may have motivated the Trustees. The spirit of *Integrae Servandae* of the Congregation of the Doctrine of the Faith[9] is not being preserved. We are most anxious to pre-serve and improve the public image of the university which adverse publicity in this instance could not but damage further. Respectfully with the deepest conviction and concern we urge that this decision be rescinded immediately and that subsequently a meeting be held to clarify the issues involved. Real assurance that such a meeting will be held at the nearest possible date and within the current semester is most important if really damaging publicity is to be avoided.[10]

---

[9] This Motu Proprio of Pope Paul VI (December 7, 1965) renamed and reorganized the Holy Office as the Congregation for the Doctrine of the Faith.

[10] Schmitz to Krol, telegram, April 19, 1967, box 34a, ACK.

The School of Theology's ultimatum was unmistakable: either reinstate Curran immediately, or the faculty would turn public opinion against the board of trustees by declaring that its actions were absolutely unacceptable, un-American, and an embarrassment to the entire Catholic Church in the United States. This basic strategy would form the rationale for the actions of the School of Theology for the remainder of the tumultuous week.

The Investigation of Curran

Who exactly was this Father Charles Curran, and how had he come to find himself at the center of such controversy? He had first come to national prominence in the fall of 1966, when the *National Catholic Reporter* ran an article on the thirty-three-year-old priest-professor, describing him as "one of the bright young men coming in on the winds of change" that had begun to blow in the Church as a result of the Second Vatican Council.[11] Curran, a priest of the Diocese of Rochester, New York, traveled the country giving lectures advocating that "the Church must stop . . . the habit of handing down absolutist decrees on morality to an unquestioning people." Dressed in "slacks and a knit sport shirt", the "boyish" Father Curran used colloquial speech to explain to ordinary Catholic laypeople that soon they would need to rely more on their own consciences than on their unquestioning acceptance of pronouncements of the Magisterium. "The Christian people will have to stand on their own", he declared. "People will have to make their own decisions."

Just as the Church had developed her teaching on the relationship of Church and state at the Second Vatican Council, led by the pioneering work of John Courtney Murray, so now Curran proposed to undertake the same service in the field of moral theology. He boldly offered new, more permissive positions on questions of sexual ethics, such as birth control, sex outside of marriage, and masturbation, formulated in the light of what Curran called the experience of the Christian people, because "the Church's magisterium will always be a little bit behind the times." In defense of this development in moral teaching, Curran

---

[11] "Curran—'No Monopoly on the Spirit'", *National Catholic Reporter*, September 21, 1966, 1–2.

pointed to the fact that Pope Paul VI had called a study commission on the question of the morality of birth control. Regardless of what it might eventually decide, Curran reasoned, the very existence of such a commission was an admission by the Holy Father that classical moral theology as it was handed down and taught in seminaries could not provide a satisfactory answer to the questions posed by the rapid changes in modern society.

What was the essence of the new moral sense that Curran discerned within the consciences of the faithful? It considered the greatest source of moral knowledge to be "the experience of Christian people" and understood, in Curran's words, that "no one in the Church has a monopoly on the Holy Spirit, be he pope or bishop or priest or peasant." This new moral sense focused not on condemning specific acts, but rather on taking the whole moral situation into account, so that an individual in any given setting would be able to see his moral life in a more positive light as a part of God's covenant. "I mean, even the Boy Scout oath sounds more positive than the Ten Commandments", Curran joked. With his characteristically disarming humor and popular way of expressing himself, Curran sought to move moral theology away from the lists of negative proscriptions contained in the classical manuals and instead make moral teaching relevant and appealing to men and women of the late twentieth century.

Curran was not alone in his desire to renew theology, and particularly moral theology, in the post-Vatican II Church. He was part of a significant movement of self-consciously "postconciliar" theology emphasizing the competence and relevance of theologians, especially young theologians, in contrast with the relative, if not total, incompetence of the Church's Magisterium in pronouncing on theological matters. Postconciliar theology dismissed obedience to the Magisterium as simplistic and unworthy of the autonomous modern man, and it declared all that had been taught by the Magisterium before the Second Vatican Council to be contingent and historically conditioned. The Tradition of the Church regarding faith and morals was declared to be subject to change when it no longer accorded with the experience of the Christian faithful. Curran joined prominent American theologians such as Walter Burghardt and Richard McCormick in asserting that Vatican II had called the laity to instruct the pastors of the Church, because divine revelation was to be found in the sense of faith of the entire People of God more than in the teaching of Tradition and the Magisterium.[12]

While many of his peers advocated similar ideas, Curran garnered particular attention because his field of expertise was sexual morality. He was not proposing changes to some obscure matter of dogmatic theology or addressing some purely academic question; rather, his teachings directly addressed the Catholic Church's stance toward what was perhaps the most significant cultural development of the mid- to late 1960s: the sexual revolution. Just at the moment that the media-fed popular culture became preoccupied with sex, a young, congenial, photogenic priest was proposing, directly and unapologetically, that the Catholic Church should relax her teachings in this area of morality. Curran's proposals received prominent and sympathetic coverage in both the Catholic and the secular press, and he rapidly became known throughout the country.

The *National Catholic Reporter* article on Curran certainly attracted the attention of the Executive Committee of the CUA board of trustees. At its October 20, 1966, meeting, McDonald related that Curran had told him in a recent conversation that the *Reporter* article did not accurately reflect his views. Kindly and cordially, Curran had assured McDonald that the article had been neither written nor approved by him. Even if the article had been accurate, Curran maintained it would be preposterous to judge someone's theological position based on a newspaper article: "It is impossible", Curran wrote to McDonald, "for any teacher to explain his entire teaching in just a few paragraphs. . . . And for the very same reason I cannot now explain my teaching fully in a one-page

---

[12] A 1966 symposium on Catholic higher education held at Notre Dame declared in the name of Vatican II that postconciliar Catholics had come far beyond the simplistic docility and blind obedience of the preconciliar years and could no longer be expected to accept traditional faith uncritically and unquestioningly (Edward Manier, Introduction to Edward Manier and John W. Houck, eds., *Academic Freedom and the Catholic University* [Notre Dame, Ind.: Fides Publishers, 1967], 1). See also Richard A. McCormick, "The Teaching of the Magisterium and the Theologians", *CTSA Proceedings* 24 (1969): 239–54 and Walter J. Burghardt, "American Church and American Theology: Response to an Identity Crisis", *CTSA Proceedings* 28 (1973): 13. Robert Hunt went so far as to declare that the Magisterium was "simply incompetent in theology" (Robert E. Hunt, "Panel Discussion," *CTSA Proceedings* 23 [1968]: 266).

memo."[13] He had offered to be judged by a panel of his peers if they would listen to the entire content of his five lectures on tape. Curran had further pointed out to McDonald that his book *Christian Morality Today* held an imprimatur from the bishop of Fort Wayne, Indiana.[14]

In comments to the Executive Committee, McDonald described Curran as "a controversial figure", noting that a number of bishops regarded Curran as a good theologian while others did not. After some discussion on the matter, Archbishop Patrick O'Boyle of Washington, D.C., chancellor of CUA, asked McDonald to instruct Curran not to make any statements on birth control until the pope gave further instruction on the matter.[15]

At the next board meeting, in November 1966, O'Boyle asked that a committee be appointed to investigate Curran's writing and theological positions. The board named a three-man investigative committee consisting of McDonald, Archbishop Philip Hannan of New Orleans, and Archbishop John Krol of Philadelphia, commissioning it to determine "the exact views of Father Charles Curran, and to recommend appropriate action".[16] At that time, it seemed to the board that the matter was urgent, because the theology faculty had recommended that Curran be promoted to the rank of associate professor, and the Promotions Committee of the CUA academic senate was in the process of approving that recommendation. The rector thus asked that the committee give Curran's teaching their immediate attention.[17]

The bishops entrusted with the task of investigating Curran's writings were in many ways typical of the post-World War II American episcopacy, formidable men each in his own way. O'Boyle (1896–1987), a native of Scranton, Pennsylvania, had been ordained a priest of the Archdiocese of New York in 1921. Appointed archbishop of Washington in 1947, O'Boyle had gained fame in the 1950s for de-

---

[13] Curran to McDonald, October 21, 1966, "School of Sacred Theology" box 2, "School of Sacred Theology Minutes, 1962–1967" folder, ACUA.

[14] Leo Pursley (1902–1998) was bishop of Fort Wayne from 1957 to 1976.

[15] Minutes of the CUA board of trustees Executive Committee, October 20, 1966, box 30a, ACK.

[16] Minutes of the CUA board of trustees (hereafter cited as Minutes, board of trustees), November 13, 1966, 16, quoted in Krol's report to the board.

[17] McDonald to Krol, January 16, 1967; quoted in Krol's report to the board.

segregating Catholic schools in Washington three years before the 1954 U.S. Supreme Court decision *Brown v. Board of Education*, which outlawed segregation in schools. In many ways, until the events of 1967 to 1969 at CUA, O'Boyle had the reputation of being a progressive on social issues.[18] Hannan (1913–2011) had been ordained a priest of the Archdiocese of Washington in 1939 and had served as an army chaplain in the Second World War in the Eighty-Second Airborne Division. Consecrated auxiliary bishop of Washington in 1956, Hannan became archbishop of New Orleans in 1965.[19] Krol (1910–1996), the son of Polish immigrants, had been ordained a priest of the Diocese of Cleveland in 1937 and served as auxiliary bishop there from 1953 until 1961, when he had been named archbishop of Philadelphia.[20]

All three men had been present at Vatican II as Council fathers. They had spent their entire lives as priests within the seemingly stable, organized, and largely obedient American Catholic Church of the mid-twentieth century. Their training and experience had prepared them to be "brick-and-mortar" pastors and administrators: opening schools, founding parishes, and fundraising for hospitals, orphanages, and other institutions essential to the mission of serving the vast numbers of immigrants in the American Church. The role of bishops as administrators overseeing this vast organizational complexity had in many ways been taken for granted by several generations of American Catholics. In the mid-1960s, however, American culture and the Church these men were commissioned to shepherd rapidly became, in an almost entirely unforeseeable way, unstable, disorganized, and rebellious. By 1967, many in Catholic education, influenced by the ascendant ideology of the AAUP, saw the direct clerical oversight of the bishops at CUA, the nation's premier pontifical university, as at best an embarrassment and at worst an outrageous affront to intelligent Catholic thought. The bishops of the board of trustees perceived the threat to their authority embodied in the marriage of AAUP principles with postconciliar

---

[18] For the life of O'Boyle, see Morris J. MacGregor, *Steadfast in the Faith: The Life of Patrick Cardinal O'Boyle* (Washington: Catholic University of America Press, 2006).

[19] For the life of Hannan, see his autobiography, *The Archbishop Wore Combat Boots* (Huntington, Ind.: Our Sunday Visitor, 2010).

[20] To date the only published work examining Krol's life is that of E. Michael Jones, *John Cardinal Krol and the Cultural Revolution* (South Bend, Ind.: Fidelity Press, 1995).

theology, but they seem to have underestimated the frustration among Catholic intellectuals with the way Catholic higher education was perceived by their secular peers. Throughout the 1960s, intellectuals who had felt constricted during the preconciliar years began more assertively to advance theological views that were in opposition to the definitive teaching of the Magisterium. Because the majority of bishops had been trained primarily not as scholars but as pastors and administrators, the authority of theologians—and not that of bishops—was assumed to be the most competent voice on doctrinal matters. In that divide between theologians and bishops (a distinction entirely foreign to the ancient Church but one that had become accepted in the twentieth-century Church both in America and throughout the world) lies one of the keys to understanding the events that transformed CUA and thus the landscape of American Catholic higher education. The theologians led by Curran claimed that American educational standards of academic freedom gave them the right to speak and teach without interference from any outside authority, including the bishops who composed the CUA board of trustees. The bishops, however, claimed that their role as guardians of the Catholic faith obliged them to intervene whenever they believed that the teaching of a particular professor compromised the Catholic identity of the university. Two conflicting groups emerged: theologians emphasizing the importance of fully embracing the American educational tradition and bishops seeking to keep CUA faithful to Catholic teaching. In the anti-authoritarian cultural milieu that came to be defined by the tumultuous year 1968, "Catholic" identity was hard pressed to defend itself against the "American" values of "absolute freedom" set forth by the AAUP. The 1967–1969 revolution at CUA was to be quite simply, from the point of view of the American hierarchy, a disaster.

During the spring semester of 1967, McDonald, Hannan, and Krol read Curran's *Christian Morality Today* and solicited opinions about Curran from various other theologians. Hannan, judging the work negatively, wrote to Krol and McDonald: "The book would disqualify him from holding a position at the Catholic University of America."[21] Hannan suggested that the Doctrinal Committee of the National Conference of Catholic Bishops investigate Curran's writing. Krol similarly

---

[21] Hannan to Krol, January 19, 1967, in Krol's report to the board.

judged Curran's moral position to be clearly "some form of situationism", while noting that Curran denied his position was "absolute situationism."[22] Krol saw Curran's teaching position at CUA as problematic: "It was obvious that he was a controversial person—that he came to the University because his own diocese found him troublesome and, to quote one of his superiors: 'They had to give him the "axe" for disobedience.' "[23] Krol also noted that a certain doublespeak in Curran's words was the most pernicious aspect of his teaching:

> He says he is not advocating in practice a norm "different from the prevailing norm." He says as a confessor and guide he must continue to uphold the present teaching of the Church. But before he completes this section, he states: "There are times when contraception might be necessary for an individual couple. I have counseled couples along these lines." . . . Throughout the book Father Curran artfully jumps from one to a[nother] contrary position.

Krol recommended in March 1967 that the committee not attempt to pass judgment on the orthodoxy of Curran's writing, because he was concerned that the board of trustees would get entangled in what could be a long and complicated disputation over the intricacies of Curran's teaching.[24] Rather, Krol proposed what seemed to him a simpler and safer solution: a committee recommendation to the board of trustees that Curran's contract be allowed to expire at the end of August. Krol reasoned that this course of action would spare the board from having either to pass judgment on Curran's orthodoxy or to explain its action publicly. Hannan gave a summary of Krol's position at the March meeting of the board:

> Archbishop Krol . . . was convinced that it was sufficient to state, if asked, that Father Curran had failed to teach and write with clarity. . . . It was decided that the least controversial manner of handling the matter was simply to notify him that his appointment would not be renewed.

---

[22] Krol's report to the board. Situationism denies the existence of absolute moral norms, maintaining instead that, because no two situations are ever exactly alike, a unique and unrepeatable moral judgment must be formed in every situation.

[23] Curran had taught theology at St. Bernard Seminary in Rochester, New York, for two years before being sent by Bishop James E. Kearney to teach at CUA.

[24] At a meeting on March 17, 1967, in Krol's report to the board.

At one point, I asked the Rector if he thought that this mode of procedure would cause trouble. He replied that it would but that he was willing to do whatever was necessary. The Rector asked if he should give a reason to Father Curran for the non-renewal of the contract. Archbishop Krol was strongly of the opinion that it was not necessary since the statutes clearly stated that the board of trustees was empowered not to renew a contract. I had the hope that the Rector could take care of the matter in the manner of his approach since he would be speaking with Father Curran.[25]

Krol's opinion prevailed, despite the evident misgivings of McDonald that such a decision would cause controversy; the committee accordingly recommended to the board the nonrenewal of Curran's contract.

On April 10, 1967, the board of trustees, meeting at the Conrad Hilton in Chicago, took up consideration of the committee's recommendation.[26] McDonald, the one tasked with informing Curran of his fate, asked how he should announce or convey the decision. Because Curran had received the unanimous recommendation of the faculty of Sacred Theology as well as the approval of the academic senate for promotion to the rank of associate professor, McDonald warned the board that "the action now proposed . . . may result in serious campus repercussions."[27] Despite McDonald's warning, a resolution was passed on the motion of Krol, seconded by Archbishop Cody of Chicago, that Curran's contract be terminated on August 31, 1967.[28] The resolution passed by a vote of fourteen to one. Archbishop Paul Hallinan of Atlanta cast the lone dissenting vote, stating his belief that Curran had a right to be informed of the precise reason for this action.[29] He requested that the minutes record his opposition to the resolution.

---

[25] Hannan to O'Boyle, May 5, 1967, box 34a, ACK.

[26] Minutes, board of trustees, April 10, 1967, 10, box 32c, ACK.

[27] Hannan later mentioned to O'Boyle that at the April 10 meeting, McDonald had remarked to Cardinal Spellman that "the decision would rock the University" (Hannan to O'Boyle, May 5, 1967).

[28] John Patrick Cody (1907–1982) was archbishop of Chicago from 1965 to 1982 and was named a cardinal by Pope Paul VI in 1967.

[29] Paul John Hallinan (1911–1968) was archbishop of Atlanta from 1962 to 1968. He attended the Second Vatican Council and was the only American to serve on the liturgical commission. For the life of Hallinan, see Thomas J. Shelley, *Paul J. Hallinan, First Archbishop of Atlanta* (Wilmington, Del.: M. Glazier, 1989).

As the vote was taken, O'Boyle, chairman of the board of trustees, commented that in making the decision, the board was guided by "what is right" and not by "fear of reaction".[30] Perhaps some of the board members thought that their decision would mark the end of the controversy surrounding Curran. They could not have been more mistaken. The dismissal of Curran ignited a tinderbox of frustration and anger that had existed among the faculty at CUA for many years.

The Roots of Dissatisfaction at CUA

Throughout the 1960s, a simmering resentment had existed between the faculty and the administration of CUA due to dissatisfaction with inadequate resources, leadership, and facilities, as well as acts of censorship by the administration during the conciliar years.[31] The School of Canon Law had been frustrated in 1963 by the dismissal of a professor without warning, presumably for ideological reasons.[32] Many alumni thought CUA was not keeping pace with other American

---

[30] Krol's report to the board.

[31] For example, during the preparatory phase of the Second Vatican Council, the CUA School of Canon Law discovered that the recommendations it had submitted after being consulted by the Holy See had been censored by the rector and had not been sent to Rome. In 1963, the university administration banned four well-known Catholic theologians (Godfrey Diekman, O.S.B.; John Courtney Murray, S.J.; Hans Küng; and Gustave Weigel, S.J.) from speaking on the CUA campus. The reason proffered for the ban was that the four theologians were all involved closely in the issues then being debated at the Second Vatican Council, and the administration maintained that it wanted to avoid taking a side in those debates. The outcry against this censorship was quite significant for its time, although to a later generation, the 1963 protests would seem quite mild and overly deferential to the authority of the board. For a discussion of the atmosphere at CUA, see C. Joseph Nuesse, *The Catholic University of America: A Centennial History* (Washington, D.C.: 1990), 392–96.

[32] See Robert B. Townsend, "Culture, Conflict, and Change: The '67 Strike at Catholic University", unpublished paper written in 1990. In January 1963 McDonald dismissed Reverend Edward Siegmann, C.PP.S., associate professor of Scripture in the School of Theology. Townsend writes: "[Siegmann] had become associated with progressives at the Council. When pressed, McDonald cited unspecified (and apparently nonexistent) 'health concerns.' In response the faculty of the school offered only a written protest, and did not seek the support of faculty in other schools" (p. 12). Townsend's study proposes that the worldview of the "faculty subculture" evolved during the 1960s through various frustrating experiences with the university administration to the point where it was no longer willing to submit unquestioningly to the sacral authority of

universities and was failing to attract top talent and individuals of academic and professional excellence. In 1966 national alumni president Leo A. Daly wrote McDonald that "a dedicated, well-trained, and paid faculty" was an academic necessity for the future health and growth of the university. There was a growing concern, Daly wrote, that the administration of the university had become excessively centralized. In the strong opinion of the majority of the faculty, there was a serious need for the rector to delegate his administrative and academic duties so that he would have greater freedom to focus on matters of policy and the urgent need of fundraising.[33]

The student body at CUA was also dissatisfied with the atmosphere on campus, and many students wrote to the board of trustees to protest Curran's treatment.[34] One typically frank and frustrated letter written to Krol came from an undergraduate who demanded to know why the bishops had fired the "most well-known, sought after theologian in the country".[35] The student related in no uncertain terms how she and her fellow students felt about the entire CUA administration: "Do you know that about 70% of the student body have never laid eyes on the Rector? Do you know that the funniest joke on campus is: We have a Rector?!?" The young woman presented a long list of grievances: the absence of a theater on campus (due, she said, to the incompetence of the board and the rector), the departure from CUA of more than fifty competent professors, and the desire of many CUA students to transfer to other universities. She and many of her friends had never recommended CUA to any prospective student, she said, "because its curriculum is too stifled, too controlled and too cramped". She went on to explain how frustrating it was to be a CUA student:

[A] student comes to Catholic University with a strong faith and looks for an atmosphere where that faith can grow and where she

the "ecclesial subculture" that governed the university. The fruit of this evolution, according to Townsend, was seen in the organized strike of April 1967 supporting Curran, which united the entire "faculty subculture" in an unprecedented and ultimately successful show of resistance to the never-before-challenged authority of the "ecclesial subculture".

[33] Daly to McDonald, April 27, 1966, box 30b, ACK.

[34] The Krol archives contain numerous personal letters of this nature written to Krol during the week of the strike (box 34a).

[35] Letter of Kathy O'Toole, addressed "Dear Bishop," April 1967, box 34a, ACK.

at the same time can be truly educated. Instead, she is thrown up against a blank wall of authoritarianism, of stilted courses which have no relation either to her major or to her liberal education, of a board of trustees who prove again and again either their unwillingness or their inability to govern this "university." As a result she looses [*sic*] her faith, her respect for the Church as a whole and the hierarchy in particular, her respect in Catholic education, and faces the possibility of herself being incompetent as a result of a poor education. This tends to make me *very* bitter.

In addition to those who held academic concerns, a large number of priests and religious at CUA were deeply dissatisfied with their living situation and benefits. In November 1966, the Conference of Clerical and Religious Faculty Members sent a confidential letter to the chancellor, the rector, and the board of trustees that decried the serious injustice being committed against its members, who were forced to endure a substandard housing situation with no provision for their pension, social security, or other insurance needs: "The facts are that the interests of the clerical and religious faculty members are not being looked after." While lay salaries had increased regularly, their salaries had not changed at all for years.[36] A position paper sent by the same conference to the board of trustees in the spring of 1967 lamented that CUA was the only school in the country and perhaps even the world where such glaring disparity existed. The paper presented itself as an expression of the consensus of many longtime members of the faculty, who believed that the poor morale among their peers impeded academic excellence and hindered the mission of the university.[37]

The faculty had requested a new rector during the 1966–1967 academic year. On February 24, an assembly of 103 ordinary professors from all schools of the university declared that "it is critical for the future of the university that the rector be an outstanding person nationally known", a clear vote of no confidence in Bishop McDonald, who was seen by many of the faculty as the immediate cause of much of the university's inefficiency and lack of academic luster.[38] The

---

[36] Conference of Clerical and Religious Faculty Members to CUA's chancellor, rector, and board of trustees, November 4, 1966, box 30a, ACK.

[37] Box 30a, ACK.

[38] Henderson to Krol, March 10, 1967, box 30b, ACK. Professor Henderson of the Department of Physics served as the president of the Assembly of Ordinary Professors.

assembly hoped that a new rector would be both Catholic and American, about fifty years old (experienced but not on the verge of retirement; McDonald was then sixty-three), and would possess a "high degree of administrative achievement, courage in making decisions, . . . [the] ability to organize, to select able assistants, to delegate responsibility, and to recognize talent and leadership". Each of these qualities indicated that the faculty thought McDonald lacked both the administrative skills and the personal qualities necessary to give CUA dynamic leadership at a crucial moment in its history. Furthermore, although the statutes of the university required both the rector and the vice-rector to be clerics, the faculty were emphatic that the "serious crisis" the university was facing demanded a lay rector. The faculty assumed that the search for a rector would be undertaken by a collaborative effort of both the board of trustees and the faculty, taking into account the opinions of other interested parties, in accord with the procedural standards of the American Council on Education, the Association of Governing Boards of Universities and Colleges, and the AAUP.[39]

The movement in favor of a lay rector and the greater level of collaboration between the board of trustees and the faculty was a reflection of the changing nature of Catholic University and of the environment of American higher education. The decade from 1956 to 1965 had seen more growth in the faculty and enrollment at CUA than in the entire period between its founding in 1889 and 1956.[40] By 1966, 520 of the 600 faculty at CUA were laypeople, as were 75 percent of its 6,600 undergraduate and graduate students. Although founded primarily as a graduate school for the education of clergy and religious in the ecclesiastical sciences, the university had expanded to include a diverse range of schools, degrees, and programs that appealed to numerous laypeople and a significant number of non-Catholic students. The faculty believed a lay rector would better reflect the changing nature of education at CUA and the makeup of its faculty and student body. Perhaps even more importantly, the faculty feared that the ongoing presence of a bishop-rector who had direct oversight of the university sent the wrong message to those who wielded influence in American higher education and that such a direct link to the hierarchical Church could threaten the amount of federal funding CUA received. The faculty ad-

---

[39] Henderson to Krol, March 10, 1967.
[40] Daly to McDonald, April 27, 1966, box 30b, ACK.

monished the bishops on the board of trustees that it was imperative that "we do everything in our power to emphasize the predominantly secular character of the education we offer."[41]

Making a favorable impression on the leaders of secular higher education was also a concern of the CUA chapter of the AAUP. On March 31, 1967, a few weeks before the faculty strike, AAUP chapter president Alexander Giampietro wrote Krol that CUA "should unquestionably be the most respected Catholic university in the country and should rival the best secular institutions in scholarship".[42] The letter lamented that CUA was not considered the best Catholic college in the nation or even comparable to second-rate secular institutions, and it strongly recommended that CUA follow the example of Johns Hopkins University, which had recently held an extensive search for a new president that expressly sought to find not just an "acceptable" person but the very best candidate available. The importance of this position at CUA could not be overestimated, Giampietro wrote, because the rector was required not only to address theological problems but also to serve as the head of a university whose high-profile nature meant it was constantly being scrutinized. "In times such as these," Giampietro urged, "neither the Church nor the University can afford a second-rate man in such an influential position." The negative publicity the university had received regarding its present state and especially the condition of its administration was "completely devastating to every aspect of university operation". Bright students were discouraged from applying, talented professors were not attracted, benefactors were discouraged, and the morale of the entire institution was being undermined. It was, all in all, a most grievous state of affairs for the nation's flagship Catholic university.

The CUA faculty also saw an urgent need for greater vision and planning in the way decisions were made within the university administration. In a memorandum sent to the board on March 16, 1967, the faculty expressed its concern that, because the rector was a bishop, the faculty perceived him to be more concerned with ecclesiastical pressures than with academic matters in the life of the university. Excessive centralization had led to poor decisions that could have been better

---

[41] Henderson to Krol, March 10, 1967. The phrase "to emphasize the predominantly secular character of the education we offer" was underlined in pen by Krol.

[42] Giampietro to Krol, March 31, 1967, box 30b, ACK.

made at lower levels.[43] The lack of collaboration between schools was not in accord with recent developments in American higher education. Several public controversies in recent years over various speakers on campus were seen as a sign of "a certain desperation on the part of the Faculty". Low morale among both professors and students was leading to apathy, cynicism, and extremism, and indeed many faculty had either left or were seriously considering leaving due to the lack of academic freedom at CUA. The memorandum declared that there was a grave and urgent need for consultation and planning about the future of the university, a process in which the faculty had both the right and the obligation to be involved.

Aware of this discontent and pressure for change, and also in light of the upcoming accreditation visit from the Middle States Association in the fall of 1967, the board of trustees established a Long Range Planning Committee, chaired by Krol, to consider what reevaluation of the role and purpose of Catholic University was necessary within the current educational situation in the United States. This committee included prominent lay alumni, many of whom were deeply concerned about the present situation and the future of CUA. Andrew P. Maloney of the Bankers Trust Company of New York wrote to Krol in March 1967 to accept a position on the Long Range Planning Committee, "since I am so firmly convinced that the University is at a very critical crossroads".[44]

The statutes of the university, which had been revised in 1937, underlined the explicitly doctrinal mission given to Catholic University at the time of its founding by Pope Leo XIII in 1889.[45] Leo's apostolic letter that had founded CUA, *Quod in Novissimo Conventu*, expressed hope that the university would always be a place where the truths known by both revelation and reason were taught in harmony under the watchful guidance of the American bishops.[46] In 1890 the founding

---

[43] CUA faculty to the board of trustees, memorandum, March 16, 1967, box 30a, ACK.

[44] Maloney to Krol, March 21, 1967, box 30a, ACK.

[45] "Wherefore it is necessary that youth be nourished more carefully with sound doctrine, and that those young men especially who are being educated for the Church, should be fully armed to fit them for the task of defending Catholic truth" (Leo XIII, *Quod in Novissimo Conventu*, April 10, 1887).

[46] "But in order that this noble institute may be happily established and conducted to ever increasing prosperity, it must remain under the authority and protection of all the

rector of CUA, Bishop John Joseph Keane, described three essential attributes at the heart of the university's mission: faithfully Catholic through obedience to the Holy See, thoroughly American and in harmony with other institutions of higher education, and adapted to the intellectual requirements of the modern age.[47] This founding vision of Pope Leo XIII and Bishop Keane had guided CUA since its inception.

The great question facing CUA at this moment of its history, however, was whether these founding principles could still be considered feasible in the face of current developments. The determination to be both fully Catholic *and* fully American had in the spring of 1967 reached a critical juncture, and many of the members of the university community believed that what had been the status quo for much of CUA's seventy-eight-year history would not suffice to provide for its future in the turbulent and dramatically changing atmosphere of American higher education. Even the 1937 revision of the university's statutes, which had declared that "the aim of the Catholic University of America is to search out truth scientifically", left many questions unresolved, in light of CUA's pontifical status.[48] The commitment to the scientific method of the empirical sciences, which was the cornerstone of modern developments in American higher education, seemed difficult if not impossible to reconcile with the conviction that in the theological sciences truth was known by divine revelation, which was concretely expressed in the authoritative teaching of the Magisterium of the Catholic Church.

Bishops of the country, in such a way that its whole administration shall be directed by them through certain Bishops selected for that purpose, whose right and duty it shall be to regulate the system of study, to make rules of discipline, to select the professors and other officials of the University, and to ordain whatever else pertains to its best government" (Leo XIII, *Quod in Novissimo Conventu*).

[47] "First, it was laid down the paramount principle that the teaching of the University should be faithfully Catholic, conformed in all things to the creed of the Church and the decisions of the Holy See. Secondly, it was decreed with no less heartiness that the spirit and action of the University must be thoroughly American, cordially in harmony with our country's institutions. Thirdly, it was emphatically agreed that, in all the teaching of the Professors, and all the moulding of the students, regard must be had to the actual needs of our age and country, so that the character and work of the University may not only embody the wisdom of the past, but be eminently adapted to the intellectual requirements of the present" ("The Catholic University of America—Statement of Purpose", from the March 1967 meeting of the board of trustees, box 30a, ACK).

[48] The Pontifical Statutes of 1937, article I.

All of this deeply rooted dissatisfaction among faculty, alumni, and students, which had existed at CUA long before Father Charles Curran's arrival in the fall of 1965, helped to create a situation in which near-unanimous support was given to Curran by the university community in his showdown with the board of trustees. Curran, keenly aware of these tensions within the university, understood that they could be effectively used to promote his cause. Both faculty and students united together in an unprecedented display of solidarity as they protested what they felt to be the unjust treatment of one of their own and demanded that CUA be remolded according to the vision of the AAUP as modeled by successful and influential secular universities.

A Campus in Chaos

On Tuesday evening, April 18, 1967, a mere two weeks away from final exams and the end of the spring term, an overflow crowd of several hundred CUA students and faculty filled McMahon Auditorium for a rally in support of Curran. Many at this meeting signed a resolution demanding that the board of trustees renew Curran's contract immediately. The resolution declared that Curran had been treated unjustly, especially given the fact that he had been allowed no hearing before his meeting with McDonald. It further declared that the "arbitrary" action of the board of trustees amounted to "a repudiation of the professional judgment and integrity of the Faculty of the School of Theology, as well as of the professional judgment of the Academic Senate".[49] Both the School of Theology (the previous November) and the academic senate (four weeks earlier) had unanimously recommended that Curran's contract be renewed. Declaring that the board of trustees had committed an offense not only against CUA but against "truth itself", the student-signers of the resolution, led by Albert C. Pierce and several priests, stated that the board's removal of Curran had violated both the standards of American higher education and the renewal of the Church called for by Vatican II:

> An action of this sort is anathema in the intellectual world. The fact that the Trustees have taken such an action has cast the name of the

---

[49] Albert C. Pierce, *Beyond One Man*, 38.

University into disrepute among its fellow institutions. If this action stands unrescinded the Catholic University of America will become the laughing stock of American academia. The value of any degree issued in the name of this university will be decimated.

The action is further in blatant opposition to the spirit of the Second Vatican Council. If this situation is not reversed, the Catholic University of America . . . will stand as an institutionalized repudiation of the best of the heritage of the Catholic Church, as developed in Vatican II.[50]

The resolution concluded by calling for a general boycott of all classes at the university until the renewal of Curran's contract. In addressing the assembly that evening, Father Daniel Maguire[51] of the Religious Education Department summarized the position of those supporting Curran with a catchy phrase that became the slogan of the strikers during the following days: "If there is no room for Father Charles Curran in The Catholic University *of* America, then there is no room for Catholic University *in* America."[52] It was simply unacceptable, said Maguire, for a professor at an American institution of higher education to be subject to judgment by any supposedly higher authority of a religious nature, a position that perfectly embodied the stated principles of the AAUP with regard to church-related institutions.[53]

The following morning, April 19, an assembly of some two thousand students and faculty, all boycotting their classes, assembled outside the Mullen Memorial Library and demanded that the rector meet with them. McDonald declined the invitation, though he did speak with two student leaders in his office.[54] The demonstration continued outside the library throughout the day. That afternoon, an additional "emergency meeting" of the theology faculty was convened.

---

[50] Ibid., 38–39.

[51] Daniel Maguire, a priest of the Archdiocese of Philadelphia, joined the CUA faculty in 1963. In 1969 he sought laicization. He resigned from CUA in 1971 after a dispute with the university administration in which he sought to retain tenure as a professor of theology even after being laicized. He has taught moral theology and ethics at Marquette University since 1971.

[52] Pierce, *Beyond One Man*, 4.

[53] *Report of the Special Committee on Academic Freedom in Church-Related Colleges and Universities*, in *Bulletin of the American Association of University Professors* 53 (1967): 369.

[54] Curran, *Loyal Dissent*, 37.

After commending all parties involved for their "dignity, restraint, . . . [and] decorous manner of protest", Schmitz presided over a discussion on the essential need to avoid any mention of religious or theological matters in the debate at hand; the words *purely academic* were twice inserted into the discussion of the nature of the problem.[55]

The faculty drafted and approved a resolution supporting Curran and calling for the suspension of all university activities.[56] Made public at a press conference that afternoon, it stated unequivocally that the nonrenewal of Curran's contract threatened the stability of the entire university: "The academic freedom and the security of every professor of this university is [*sic*] jeopardized. We cannot and will not function until Father Curran is reinstated." The resolution also invited the other schools of the university to join the protest.

The press conference ended with a statement by Curran himself, noting larger implications than simply the future of his own teaching career: "The issues involved in this dismissal are greater than any one man. Both Catholic theology in America and Catholic university education are in question."[57] Saying that he in no way denied the need for the authority and guidance of bishops in the Church, Curran declared that the question of his dismissal was an academic affair in which the board of trustees had trampled on the autonomy of the School of Theology, the academic senate, and the entire university. It was a grievous violation of proper procedure that he had never been given a hearing to defend himself against any charges. For this reason he felt forced to protest the decision not to renew his contract. By keeping the argument limited to the question of academic freedom, Curran and the School of Theology hoped to garner wide support from the academic community both at CUA and elsewhere.[58]

That same evening, one by one the other schools of the university, including the Schools of Philosophy, Law, and Music, joined ranks with the School of Theology in passing resolutions of solidarity with Cur-

---

[55] Minutes, School of Theology, April 18, 1967, ACUA.

[56] "Resolution of the School of Theology concerning Father Charles Curran", April 19, 1967, box 12, folder 1, Archives of Monsignor Eugene A. Kevane (hereafter cited as AMK), St. Gregory the Great Seminary Library, Seward, Nebraska.

[57] "Statement of Father Charles E. Curran", April 19, 1967, box 12, folder 1, AMK.

[58] Curran, *Loyal Dissent*, 37.

ran.[59] The outcry on behalf of Father Curran grew even stronger on Thursday, April 20, when the entire CUA faculty passed a resolution supporting their colleague.[60] By a vote of 400 to 18, the Assembly of Ordinary Professors resolved that the decision of the board of trustees was "tantamount to a rejection of the entire faculty of the school [of Theology] and its teaching". The board's decision had placed Catholic University "outside of the American Academic Community" and raised "grave questions for the continuation of Catholic Higher Education in America". The CUA faculty declared that "the academic freedom of the man, of the Faculty of the school, and of the whole University is jeopardized to the peril of its reputation, accreditation, and academic standing." They declared themselves in support of the School of Theology's resolution of the previous day and declared, using identical language, "We cannot and will not function as members of our respective faculties unless and until Father Charles Curran is reinstated." By this declaration, every school of Catholic University, with the exception of the School of Education, joined the unprecedented strike. The boycott continued for the remainder of the week. Protesting students and faculty kept a continual presence on the mall outside the National Shrine of the Immaculate Conception and held rallies on Friday, Saturday, and Sunday, April 21 through 23. Support came in from all over the country as Curran and his supporters spoke to news reporters and picketed in front of cameras from newspapers across the United States.

Speakers at these demonstrations placed responsibility for the controversy at the feet of the board of trustees. Typical of their reasoning were the words of Father Robert Hunt[61] of the School of Theology:

---

[59] Various resolutions, April 19–20, 1967, "Minute Book" folder, "Faculty Assembly 1965–1978" box, ACUA.

[60] "Resolution of the Assembly of Ordinary Professors", April 20, 1967, in Pierce, *Beyond One Man*, 40. Although the resolution was entitled "Resolution of the Assembly of Ordinary Professors", it was in fact a vote of the entire university faculty, as the total number of 418 votes makes clear. This helpful clarification was made by Curran in his interview with the author (April 15, 2009).

[61] Robert Hunt (1934–1999) was ordained a priest of the Archdiocese of Newark in 1957, having studied theology with Charles Curran at the Gregorian University in Rome. He taught dogmatic theology at CUA from 1961 to 1969. After the controversy over *Humanae Vitae*, Hunt left the priesthood, married, and pursued a career in real estate. With Curran he coauthored *Dissent in and for the Church* (New York: Sheed

"The responsibility is not ours. Primarily . . . the responsibility for all the inconveniences . . . is squarely with the action of the board of trustees."[62] Also prominent in the speakers' defense of their position was the argument that the board of trustees was punishing Curran for seeking the truth. As Father Carl Peter,[63] also of the School of Theology, said in his address to the crowd on Sunday afternoon, April 23: "History offers ample precedents to warrant this assertion that the cause of truth is not served by the suppression of scientific opinion. . . . We claim but this right: let us be what by calling us university professors you demand that we be—free men devoted to a never-ending search for the truth that will make man's future better than his past."[64] Peter, who in 1968 would disagree with Curran over dissent against the encyclical *Humanae Vitae*, here expressed the frustration felt by many within Catholic higher education with the stifling atmosphere at their institutions. Curran's dismissal became a lightning rod for the great dissatisfaction among many professors at Catholic universities, not only in theological schools but in many other disciplines as well.

Other academic institutions, both Catholic and secular, also brought pressure to bear on the bishops by declaring their support for Curran. Faculty from Villanova University wrote to Krol, their local ordinary, demanding that he support academic freedom "by repudiating the manner in which the Rev. Charles J. [*sic*] Curran was dismissed with no specific charges given and no public hearing held before his peers". They made this petition not simply to defend Curran but also because they felt it necessary to defend their own prestige in the American academic community:

> Not only for the sake of justice to Father Curran, the faculty and students of Catholic University, but also for the sake of strengthening the freedom to search for and disseminate the truth in all Catholic

---

and Ward, 1970). His brother John F. Hunt, a lawyer with Cravath, Swain, and Moore of New York, represented the dissenting theologians in their dispute with the board of trustees in 1969.

[62] Pierce, *Beyond One Man*, 14.

[63] Carl J. Peter (1932–1991) was a member of the CUA School of Theology from 1964 until his death in 1991.

[64] Pierce, *Beyond One Man*, 19.

education in America, and finally, that we, as members of the academic community, be not further embarrassed before our non-Catholic colleagues.[65]

Krol's secretary responded by reiterating Krol's position and disputing the accuracy of the Villanova petition: Curran had not been dismissed, nor had any accusation of wrongdoing been made against him.[66] The Villanova faculty likely found the response unconvincing.

The tremendous pressure now being exerted against the board of trustees started to show its effects as cracks appeared in the unity of the bishops. Individual bishops began to make public criticism of the board's action, most notably Cardinal Shehan[67] of Baltimore and Archbishop Hallinan. Shehan, in Rome the week of April 17, issued a statement that Curran should be "restored to his former status" and that the entire board of trustees should reconsider the matter.[68] Noting Curran's academic competence and the recommendation he had received from his peers, Hallinan said, "It was unwise for the trustees to act in a situation in which faculty members were not heard."[69] Cardinal Cushing[70] of Boston declared that he did not have any right to judge Curran's status and would not condemn him. "He [Curran] must teach all sides. It makes no sense to appoint people to a university board who know absolutely nothing about running a university."[71] His blunt criticism of his fellow bishops implied that they were not competent to make decisions regarding academic matters that were essential to effective university administration.

---

[65] Villanova faculty to Krol, petition, April 1967, box 34a, ACK.

[66] James Connelly to the Villanova faculty, April 1967, box 34a, ACK.

[67] Patrick Shehan (1898–1984) was Archbishop of Baltimore from 1961 to 1974. He attended the Second Vatican Council and was named a cardinal by Pope Paul VI in 1965. For his life see his autobiography, *A Blessing of Years* (South Bend, Ind.: University of Notre Dame Press, 1982).

[68] "Shehan Backs Fired Priest-Professor", *Baltimore Evening Sun*, April 21, 1967. All newspaper and periodical articles are found in the ACUA and the AMK.

[69] "Shehan Backs Fired Priest-Professor".

[70] Richard Cushing (1895–1970) was archbishop of Boston from 1944 to 1970. He was named a cardinal by Pope Pius XII in 1958. Cushing attended the Second Vatican Council, where he played a vital role in drafting *Nostra Aetate*. He had close connections with the Kennedy family. For an informal account of his life see Joseph Dever, *Cushing of Boston: A Candid Portrait* (Boston: Bruce Humphries Publishers, 1965).

[71] "Time for Boy Scouts?" *Time*, April 28, 1967, 62.

Curran and his supporters were certainly aware of the growing divisions between the bishops of the board and felt increasingly confident that they would win Curran's reinstatement. Curran recalled that on Friday, April 21, 1967, Father Robert Hunt, his colleague in the School of Theology, spoke by telephone with Father Harry Darcy, who worked in the office of the apostolic delegate in Washington. Hunt and Darcy were priests of the Archdiocese of Newark who knew each other well. Darcy gave a blunt assessment of the situation to Hunt: "You got 'em by the short hairs!"[72] This encouragement renewed hope among Curran's exhausted supporters during the tense weekend of April 22 and 23 that if they could just hold on a bit longer, they would achieve their goal to have Curran reinstated.

A further factor that may have contributed to the bishops' view of the way events were developing on the CUA campus was an anonymous letter sent to the apostolic delegate to the United States, Archbishop Egidio Vagnozzi, on Saturday, April 22, 1967, alleging that academic favors had been offered to students in exchange for their active support of the strike. The unknown author of the letter purported to be a student in the School of Theology and alleged that Curran had called him and asked him to help take action against Curran's dismissal. "Having been closely associated with Father Curran both as a friend and as a student," the author wrote, "I can tell you that the situation is much more serious than is actually known."[73] The anonymous student described Curran as careful in his teaching but outspoken with his friends in criticizing Rome and the Church's teaching on birth control. At a meeting the student claimed he had attended that week, he alleged that Curran had offered clear academic benefits to those students who would strike in his support and specifically encouraged them to enlist other students in the effort:

> Realizing that the success of the strike would depend largely on the student role, it was decided to do everything possible to encite [sic] the students to protest. At this meeting students from surrounding colleges and universities were called and asked to sent [sic] delegations of students to help fill the ranks of those from Catholic University so

---

[72] Author's interview with Curran, April 15, 2009.

[73] "A student of theology" to Vagnozzi, who forwarded it to Krol on April 22, 1967, protocol no. 1540/67, box 34a, ACK.

that the action would have the appearance of being larger than it really was. In order to induce more students to participate it was agreed with members of other departments, among them the History and Philosophy Departments, to insure [*sic*] the students that they would not be required to take comprehensive exams or other final examinations if they would cooperate with the strike. I am a student of theology and when I expressed concern about my examinations he [Curran] assured me that regardless of the outcome he would see to it that I would receive a high grade for my efforts to help him.[74]

Curran vehemently denies that he ever made any such offer to any student or anyone else at any time.[75] The letter's anonymity raises significant doubts about the credibility of the allegations. Yet the fact that Vagnozzi forwarded the letter to Krol shows that it likely played some role, however small, in the formulation of the bishops' understanding and judgment of the events surrounding the April 1967 strike.

As the week unfolded Archbishop O'Boyle confidentially sought permission from the other bishops on the board of trustees to negotiate with the School of Theology. As early as Thursday, April 20, O'Boyle sent a telegram to the various bishops, asking them to approve a press release stating that the board had reversed its decision and was going to meet with Curran and other professors of the School of Theology.[76]

O'Boyle asked for an immediate reply, which would be kept confidential. While there is no known record of how each bishop replied, it seems a majority of bishops on the board accepted O'Boyle's statement, effectively "voting" to rescind Curran's dismissal.[77] Cardinal McIntyre[78] of Los Angeles and Krol did not approve of O'Boyle's statement.[79] However, O'Boyle's consultation via telegram with the

---

[74] "A student of theology" to Vagnozzi.

[75] Author's interview with Curran, April 15, 2009.

[76] O'Boyle to McIntyre, telegram, April 20, 1967, Mc 5309 (1967), Archives of the Archdiocese of Los Angeles (hereafter cited as AALA), San Fernando Mission, Mission Hills, California.

[77] O'Boyle wrote to McIntyre the following week (April 28, 1967): "The board . . . voted to rescind the dismissal of Father Curran" (Mc 5309 [1967], AALA).

[78] James McIntyre (1886–1979), a priest and then auxiliary bishop of New York under Cardinal Spellman from 1941 to 1948, was archbishop of Los Angeles from 1948 to 1970 and was named a cardinal in 1953 by Pope Pius XII.

[79] McIntyre sent a telegram to O'Boyle on Monday, April 24, 1967, calling the action

rest of the board gave him sufficient confidence to move toward Curran's reinstatement.

On the morning of April 24, Krol telephoned Hannan to confer. Since the strike began, Krol had been in frequent telephone contact with O'Boyle, Hannan, and other members of the board of trustees, and he had continued to advocate holding the line of their decision to allow Curran's contract to lapse without any further explanation. To his surprise, however, Krol discovered that Hannan was in Washington in a meeting with O'Boyle, McDonald, and Schmitz. Although they were meeting without having informed him, Krol spoke with them by telephone and remained constant in his opinion that yielding to Curran would only make matters worse. Krol was convinced that a decision to reinstate Curran at this point, while alleviating the immediate pressure on the board of trustees, would in the long run serve only to undermine its authority, as he explained in a letter to the board shortly after the strike ended:

> After talking with Archbishop O'Boyle and Archbishop Hannan, it appeared that they and Bishop McDonald felt that the decision of the Trustees had to be rescinded. At this point I repeated the argument that if the Board of Trustees was obliged to follow the recommendations of the Academic Senate, then it no longer had any authority; that if it could not even allow a contract of a professor who lacked tenure to lapse, then it was no longer a Board of Trustees.

Krol was confident that if the bishops could remain strong and united for just a short while longer, Curran would recognize the futility of his protest and agree to back down:

> I also explained that in a brief meeting with Cardinal Spellman[80] and Archbishop Dearden[81] on the previous Friday, there was a consensus of opinion that time was on the side of the University and of the Trustees. One of the reasons for this was that two of the priest

---

of the School of Theology "emphatically reprehensible" and continuing to maintain that Curran's contract should be canceled (Mc 5309 [1967], AALA). Krol was unaware of how events were proceeding.

[80] Francis Spellman (1889–1967) was archbishop of New York from 1939 to 1967 and was named a cardinal by Pope Pius XII in 1946.

[81] John Dearden (1907–1988) was archbishop of Detroit from 1959 to 1980 and was named a cardinal by Pope Paul VI in 1969.

friends of Father Curran had called the United States Catholic Conference offices alleging that Father Curran was worried and that if Archbishop Dearden would enter into the controversy on behalf of the Conference of Bishops, Father Curran was willing to declare a thirty day truce or moratorium.[82]

Curran denies ever having proposed or even considered such a "truce", recalling a phone call of quite a different nature during those same crucial days, which emboldened rather than worried his supporters.[83] Krol was perhaps out of touch with how events and opinions had progressed and developed since the beginning of the strike. He remained unchanged in his position, while O'Boyle, Hannan, and McDonald had radically changed theirs. These three, under the weight of immense pressure, now felt that reinstating Curran would be the best way to bring the nightmare of the strike to an end. Krol's confidence that the trustees had time on their side was decidedly not shared by his colleagues:

> Nevertheless, it was clear that those attending the meeting in Washington felt there was no alternative [but to reinstate Curran]. It was the lesser of two evils. I again said that I believed that the great evil would be to yield, since it would only invite a constant flow of similar problems. Nevertheless, I agreed that I would not take any exception to the decision of the majority and I would not express any public dissent.
>
> It may be added that there were communications from laity, insisting that the Trustees stand their ground—that a yielding would have an adverse effect on the support of the University. It was also pointed out that in another instance where there was disturbance at the University, the authorities held firm.[84]

O'Boyle described his five-hour meeting with Hannan, McDonald, and Schmitz as one in which he came to realize fully the difficulty of the position in which the board had put itself. O'Boyle described the factors considered at the meeting in a letter written to McIntyre the same week: "When he [Curran] was informed by the Rector that the

---

[82] Krol's report to the board.

[83] Author's interview with Curran, April 15, 2009.

[84] Krol to the board. It is not clear exactly which other "disturbance" Krol was referring to in his report.

board voted to dismiss him, he was at the same time informed that there were no charges against him. This left us pretty much tied up." Even though technically the board had the power to dismiss Curran without a hearing, O'Boyle observed, accurately if a bit too late, "this just doesn't go down today with the public when a man is being dismissed." The committee that had examined Curran's teaching had not presented any substantive charges against Curran to the board. Thus, during the course of their long meeting on Monday, April 24, O'Boyle, Hannan, and McDonald, in consultation with Dean Schmitz, decided to appoint Curran associate professor of theology. While still at the meeting, O'Boyle telephoned various bishops on the board, informing them of his decision: "They went along with our decision but I presume reluctantly, which was our position also."[85]

O'Boyle, Hannan, and McDonald made their decision believing that, for the sake of victory in the greater struggle for control of Catholic University, they needed to admit defeat in this smaller battle over Curran's teaching position. Krol, on the other hand, remained emphatic to the end that the entire outcome of the struggle would hinge on *this* decision: if the bishops wavered now by accepting unorthodox teaching at the nation's premier pontifical university, there would be no end in sight to the demands that would be made by professors at CUA and elsewhere in the name of the "right to dissent" and academic freedom. In the end, Krol was outnumbered and essentially overruled by O'Boyle, Hannan, and McDonald. Yet, with characteristic loyalty, Krol promised to refrain from publicly criticizing the decision of his fellow bishops, and he remained faithful to that promise. The decision of O'Boyle and Hannan to reinstate Curran was announced as the decision of the entire board of trustees.

At the beginning of the April 24 meeting, O'Boyle and Hannan had at first intended to reinstate Curran without promotion to the rank of associate professor; that is, they had intended to send the question of Curran's promotion and tenure back to the regular academic process. However, over the course of what Curran describes as a "long, hard bargaining session" that day, they eventually agreed to give Curran not

---

[85] O'Boyle stated that he telephoned Krol, Dearden, and Bishop Wright. He regretted having been unable to reach Spellman (O'Boyle to McIntyre, April 28, 1967 [Mc 5311 (1967)], AALA).

only reinstatement but also promotion with tenure to the rank of associate professor.[86] O'Boyle and Hannan had likewise prepared a statement for the press, but Curran rejected it as unacceptable. This progression of events showed that Curran and his supporters were clearly in the driver's seat as the board of trustees desperately sought a way to bring about a swift end to the fiasco of the strike.

At 3:00 P.M. on April 24, 1967, O'Boyle summoned the entire faculty of the School of Theology to a meeting at the Mullen Library. At its conclusion, O'Boyle announced to the protesters assembled outside that their long week of rallies, marches, pickets, and press conferences had finally paid off: "The board of trustees has voted to abrogate its decision." McDonald then announced that Curran would be promoted to the rank of associate professor the following September, as had been previously recommended by the School of Theology and the academic senate. Finally, Curran himself spoke to the crowd, exhorting them to continue their efforts on behalf of justice, freedom, and truth: "Today must mark a beginning and not an end", he said. "Let us pledge ourselves to that goal."[87]

---

[86] Author's interview with Curran, April 15, 2009.
[87] Pierce, *Beyond One Man*, 22.

2

The Role of the Media in
Public Perception of the Strike

The victory of "Father Charlie" and his supporters was largely orchestrated through an astute and masterful use of print and television media to generate sympathy for Curran's cause and antagonism toward the authority of the bishops who composed the board of trustees. From the very beginning of the April 1967 faculty strike, Curran's supporters organized press conferences and highly visible public demonstrations on campus that portrayed Curran as the unjust victim of discrimination by an oppressive university administration. Their demand for rights from an authoritarian power structure resonated loudly with the media during the era when both the civil rights movement and the protests against the United States' involvement in Vietnam were at the forefront of the national consciousness. The extensive coverage that the Curran incident received in the university, Catholic, and secular press caused him to win substantial support from casual observers both within the Catholic Church and without.

Coverage in the *Tower*

The coverage of the Curran controversy in the Catholic University student newspaper, the *Tower*, manifested deep-seated resentment against the board of trustees for its perceived incompetence as well as embarrassment over the status and reputation of CUA within the American academic community. On Tuesday, April 25, 1967, the day after Curran was reinstated, the *Tower* editorial expressed approval that "an intelligently informed and individually resolute academic community" had "shoved [Curran] down [the] throats" of the board of trustees.[1] The piece unequivocally condemned the board for having made their decision to dismiss Curran based on "second-hand information, gross misinterpretation, and their own theological inadequacy", which had caused a grave violation of academic freedom and of the integrity of Catholic education in general. It declared that the board's rash authoritarianism had implications far beyond CUA or even Catholic higher education: "Their academic and professional incompetence has embarrassed the whole of academia." A certain spirit of triumphalism pervaded the condemnation of the board and the simultaneous vindication of Curran, which is unsurprising given the extraordinary and emotional nature of what had transpired.

Various articles and letters to the editor printed in the *Tower* during the strike and its aftermath reveal the overwhelming support for Curran among prominent individuals within the university community. The president of the class of 1969 wrote to express his pride that CUA had made "a positive contribution to the cause of academic freedom throughout the country", in contrast to more negative demonstrations at Berkeley and St. John's during the same period.[2] Dr. Manuel Cardozo, head of the Department of History, relayed the praise of Senator Williams[3] of Delaware for the "unmatched dignity and decorum" by which the student and faculty demonstrators "saved the honor of the Catholic University of America".[4] The group of faculty from the Catholic universities in Philadelphia who had written Cardinal Krol sent a copy of their telegram to the *Tower* and thus gave further voice to their demand that Curran be reinstated "for the sake of justice" and that as Catholic educators they "be not further embarrassed before our non-Catholic colleagues".[5] In what was perhaps the most scathing and total condemnation of all, one letter to the editor declared that the only hope for the successful future of CUA was the total elimination of the bishops' role in overseeing the university: "If and when 'this

---

[1] "The Jig Is Up", *Tower*, April 25, 1967, 2.

[2] Victor A. Capece, "Fight for Freedom", *Tower*, April 25, 1967, 4.

[3] John Williams (1904–1988) served in the U.S. Senate from 1947 to 1970.

[4] Manuel Cardozo, "With Dignity", *Tower*, April 27, 1967, 2.

[5] "Krol on Carpet", *Tower*, April 25, 1967, 4 (telegram sent to Archbishop Krol by Catholic administrators and faculty members at universities in the Philadelphia area).

place' divorces itself from its 'pontifical' status, if and when 'this place' has a body of responsible individuals for trustees, and if and when the Bishops of the United States relinquish their roles as Trustees, then will 'this place' be a University.'"[6]

The majority opinion within the academic community at CUA, as expressed in the *Tower*, was clearly one of outrage and embarrassment that was transformed into exuberance: outrage at Curran's dismissal without a hearing by the bishops on the board of trustees, embarrassment at CUA's status within the greater American academic community, and finally exuberance over the triumph of academic freedom and the pursuit of truth over the arbitrary authority of the board.

Coverage in the Catholic Press

The Catholic press throughout the United States was largely sympathetic to the boycotting faculty and students. Numerous writers maintained that the issue was *not* about Curran's theological positions or the authority of the Magisterium but was rather a strictly academic and procedural question. Curran had been summarily dismissed without any hearing by the board of trustees: "In essence, the immediate dispute was between the University's board of trustees and its Academic Senate", said a commentary written by the editor of the Archdiocese of Baltimore's *Catholic Review* that appeared in the *National Catholic Register*.[7] The true issue was not priests protesting against bishops but rather the academic rights of faculty vis-à-vis the board: "Academic justice and not religious obedience was the immediate issue." In the editor's opinion, the only matter that had been settled by the affair was that the rights of faculty, as defined by the AAUP, could not be blatantly violated by the bishops on the board of trustees. A Jesuit graduate student at CUA noted in *America* magazine that academic freedom had still not been defined, nor had any matter of theology been settled or even discussed: "The only issue that was clearly settled was one of procedure."[8] The lead story in the Diocese of Brooklyn's *Tablet* ran with

---

[6] Letter to the editor, *Tower*, April 20, 1967, 2.

[7] J.R. Schaefer, "These Were the Real Issues at C.U.", *Catholic Review*, April 28, 1967, 1; "Wrapup of Catholic U.—Curran Case", *National Catholic Register*, May 14, 1967, 3.

[8] D.M. Knight, "What Happened at Catholic U.", *America*, May 13, 1967, 725.

the headline "Birth Control Not Issue" and claimed that there was unanimous agreement on this point on the part of all those involved.[9] The Curran controversy was, according to much of the Catholic press, an entirely academic affair.

The Catholic press praised the protesters and Curran himself for their decorum, dignity, and respectfulness toward the authority of the CUA administration and toward the authority of the American bishops. The students who led the boycott were portrayed as unwilling heroes who had chosen such an extreme action only as a last resort. They were not dissenting but standing up for "civil rights, human rights, and academic freedom", and their demonstrations were "orderly, serious, and not irreverent".[10] In the midst of a highly volatile situation, the students of CUA kept events under control, "consciously avoided sensationalism", and were distinguished by their "clean-shaven faces, conventional haircuts, and tasteful clothes".[11] The *Catholic Review* described Curran as easygoing, approachable, wearing a T-shirt, youthful and jovial, one who was "happily harassed" and "constantly chuckling".[12] The "gangling, bespectacled, 33-year-old professor",[13] who gave the impression of being "a senior counselor at boys' camp",[14] was certainly no radical or liberal, but a "mildly controversial and modestly mannered theologian"[15] whose most radical idea was that "Catholics should talk to each other"[16] and who was located theologically in the "extreme center",[17] a "shrewd middle-of-the-roader".[18] Curran embodied "a combination of boyishness, outspokenness, scholarship, and a concern for the Living God rather than stereotypes", said an

---

[9] "Birth Control Not Issue", *Tablet*, April 27, 1967, 1.

[10] *Alert Catholic*, no. 193 (June–July 1967).

[11] Schaefer, "These Were the Real Issues at C.U.", 1; "Wrapup of Catholic U.—Curran Case", 3.

[12] A.E.P. Wall, "Fr. Curran Says Catholics Should Talk to Each Other", *Catholic Review*, April 28, 1967, 1.

[13] N.K. Herzfeld, "Blow Up at Catholic U.", *Commonweal*, May 5, 1967, 190.

[14] Wall, "Fr. Curran Says Catholics Should Talk to Each Other", 1.

[15] Schaefer, "These Were the Real Issues at C.U.", 1; "Wrapup of Catholic U.—Curran Case", 3.

[16] Wall, "Fr. Curran Says Catholics Should Talk to Each Other", 1.

[17] Albert C. Pierce, *Beyond One Man*, 10.

[18] Herzfeld, "Blow Up at Catholic U.", 190.

article in the *National Catholic Reporter*.[19] The same article went on to declare that the persecution Curran was undergoing made him akin to Thomas More; Stephen, the first martyr; or even Isaac as he was being sacrificed by Abraham. Throughout the vast majority of the coverage given the controversy in the Catholic press, the position of Curran and the faculty and students demonstrating on his behalf was portrayed as one of moderation, calmness, openness, and simple justice.

By contrast, the Catholic press portrayed the bishops on the board of trustees as out of touch with the situation at CUA, fearful of change, and clinging to control by an arbitrary use of their authority. *Commonweal* began its lead editorial on May 5, 1967, by bluntly stating that the action of the board "makes us wonder—and not for the first time, either—if a few of the American bishops might not be driven by some ecclesiastical version of a death wish."[20] *America* asked in astonishment how such a lack of foresight on the part of the bishops was possible: How could they not have realized that the dismissal of Curran by executive decision without any hearing would cause an uproar within the academic community?[21] The board of trustees was portrayed as intimidated by and fearful of Curran's youth and intelligence. One priest-student at CUA was quoted as saying, "The trustees who voted on Charlie Curran couldn't even pass one of his courses."[22] According to *Commonweal*, the bishops had foolishly tried to run Catholic University as if it were a seminary; however, the journal's lead editorial declared, a university could no longer be administered by the system of clericalism and ecclesiastical paternalism that had prevailed until then in American Catholic higher education. The board of trustees had the audacity to act in the way it did only because most of its members were bishops; in so doing they had attempted to squelch the "creative independent thought" that must be the hallmark of a university. The American academic community had always suspected (albeit unfairly, said *Commonweal*) that Catholic institutions of higher education were places where arbitrary authority made free inquiry impossible; the board's actions

---

[19] "Father Curran: Symbol of Bishops' Problem", *National Catholic Reporter*, April 26, 1967, 5.

[20] "This Time, Catholic U", *Commonweal*, May 5, 1967, 187.

[21] "Of Many Things", *America*, May 6, 1967, 663.

[22] Herzfeld, "Blow Up at Catholic U.", 190.

had seemed determined to prove this suspicion true, to the deep frustration of the Catholic intellectual world.[23]

An additional recurring theme in the Catholic press was the portrayal of Curran as the vanguard of a new, modern, postconciliar spiritual freedom that was being opposed by the narrow-minded and heads-in-the-sand American hierarchy. Heavily quoted was Curran's self-description as a man ushering in a new "responsibility", a new "opportunity", and a new "mandate and charge"; a man whose reinstatement as professor of theology marked "a beginning and not an end".[24] Curran was praised for being a man courageous enough to think for himself, who only reluctantly supported the boycott as "a positive action necessary to free the university from the shackles of another age".[25] For too long, said Curran, American Catholics had been unquestioningly obedient. The professors of CUA were now telling their bishops: "We respect your authority, but where we have special knowledge and competence, we share that authority."[26] Curran's dismissal was the flashpoint where these two differing visions of authority had made their stand in opposition to each other. The *National Catholic Reporter* explained Curran's significance this way, quoting an unidentified CUA theology professor: "Let's face it, Charley rolls up within himself—and well within the bounds of orthodoxy— the whole climate, spirit, way of thinking, and way of acting with openness and unequivocation that represents the problem for the bishops of the United States."[27] The Catholic media assessed Curran's "openness and unequivocation" as a phenomenon that the closed and equivocating bishops felt compelled to eliminate from the ecclesiastical scene, and for the most part this same Catholic press rejoiced that the bishops' efforts to do so had proven unsuccessful.

The new age that Curran stood for was said to entail a complete restructuring of Church authority. Just as society had in the past been structured monarchically but was now democratically organized, so must it be with the "new" Church. Curran was quoted extensively describing what the post-Vatican II Church would look like:

---

[23] "This Time, Catholic U", 188.
[24] Schaefer, "These Were the Real Issues at C.U.", 7; "Wrapup of Catholic U.—Curran Case", 3.
[25] Herzfeld, "Blow Up at Catholic U.", 190.
[26] *Alert Catholic*, no. 193 (June–July 1967).
[27] "Father Curran: Symbol of Bishops' Problem", 5.

I think there is a realization that authority will be exercised in a different way in the future. This is indicated by the organization of modern society, which does not operate from the top down. Each one contributes. We stimulate each other to contribute to the good of all. This sort of thing has to happen in the Church. . . . There's a difference today in the way we see reality.[28]

The realization of this new age in the Church had been powerfully advanced by the courageous stand Curran and his supporters had taken during their weeklong boycott. As the director of the Department of Education of the United States Catholic Conference wrote in his newsletter for Catholic school superintendents soon after the strike, Curran's reinstatement was "encouraging" and could "be regarded as a victory for Catholic education in America".[29] Catholics were being called upon to "grow up" as members of the Church. Just as growth could often involve discomfort, the present trials were inevitable but well worth it. A door of hope had been opened that the bishops had futilely attempted to slam shut.

In summary, the Curran incident was portrayed by the Catholic press as follows:

1. The debate was presented not as a theological or ecclesiastical matter but as a purely academic and procedural concern.

2. Curran and his supporters were depicted as moderate, youthful, easygoing victims of injustice.

3. The bishops were described as out of touch, grasping for power, and fearful of change or any independent thinking.

4. Curran was hailed as the herald of a new era of modernity and democracy in the Church that had been ushered in by the Second Vatican Council.

---

[28] Ibid.

[29] Charles Donahue, *Washington Perspective: A Newsletter for Superintendents*, reprinted and distributed on campus by Curran's steering committee, "CUA Controversies" box, "Curran Controversy, 1967" folder, ACUA.

Coverage in the Secular Press

In a marked contrast with the Catholic press, the secular press seemed more perceptive about what was at stake in the Curran controversy: the Church's teaching on sexual morality was on the line, and the outcome of the power struggle between bishops and theologians would have far-reaching implications for the entire Catholic Church. Similarly to the Catholic press, the secular media expressed sympathy for Curran and an interest in his cause as a victim of an unjust and oppressive authoritarian structure, but it emphasized that the controversy centered on Curran's position on issues of sexual morality, most notably birth control. Curran was identified universally as "a professor of moral theology who advocates a change in the Catholic position on birth control".[30] His fight for academic freedom was consistently presented in the context of the bigger picture of his fight to change Catholic moral teaching.[31]

Like their Catholic counterparts, secular reporters described Curran sympathetically as congenial, youthful, and open to the future, in contrast with an aging Church hierarchy hemmed in by the Church's outdated teaching. A photo of a smiling Curran in the *New York Times* ran with the caption: "He is eminently approachable."[32] The accompanying article described Curran as a humble, humorous professor who played golf and drove an old car without a muffler, a teacher loved by his students as "one of the greatest Christians on campus . . . eminently fair and highly respectable". The *Washington Post* referred to Curran as a professor having "a world-wide reputation as an author and lecturer" whose "personal integrity and dedication to the Catholic faith have brought him unparalleled respect from his colleagues".[33] Curran and

---

[30] Words of David Brinkley from the text of the *Huntley-Brinkley Report* broadcast on NBC Radio on April 19, 1967, "Faculty Assembly, 1965–1978" box, "Curran Case" folder, ACUA.

[31] See "Victory at C.U.", *Time*, May 5, 1967, 84; "Shehan Backs Fired Priest-Professor", *Baltimore Evening Sun*, April 21, 1967, 1; "Ouster of Liberal Priest Spurs CUA Boycott Threat", *Washington Post*, April 19, 1967, 1; "CU Classes are Empty", *Washington Daily News*, April 20, 1967, 2; "Multiple Efforts Under Way to End Catholic U. Shutdown", *Washington Evening Star*, April 22, 1967, 1.

[32] "Priest for Students: Charles Edward Curran", *New York Times*, April 25, 1967, 1.

[33] J.R. Hailey, "Catholic U. Rebellion Laid to Faculty", *Washington Post*, April 22, 1967, 1.

his supporters were fighting for "human dignity", said the *Post*, so that CUA could keep "its proper place in the academic world". Curran was portrayed as moderate and balanced, the victim of an outrageous crackdown by a reactionary and controlling board of trustees, which considered him dangerous "because he said five years ago what everyone is saying today on birth control".[34] He was "a strong man", said the *Post*, "confident in his belief that teachers must be free to explore the realms in which they teach". On the day after his reinstatement, a beaming, youthful Curran appeared on the front page of Washington's *Evening Star* beneath a photograph of a wrinkled and senile-looking Archbishop O'Boyle.[35] In the accompanying article, a "relaxed and happy" Curran reflected on the "marvelous community" created at CUA by the boycott and declared that "to stop our efforts . . . would be irresponsible."[36] Clearly, according to the secular press, Curran had succeeded in uniting the faculty and the students of CUA in supporting him because of his balanced position and the obvious injustice that had been committed against him by the board of trustees.

That same board of trustees was portrayed by the secular press as divided and largely incompetent. The press based this portrayal on the statements of Cardinal Shehan and Archbishop Hallinan criticizing the board's decision to remove Curran. Likewise, Cardinal Cushing's statement that the bishops were incompetent to run a university was promoted by the press as clear evidence that the board of trustees simply was not qualified to govern CUA competently and responsibly. O'Boyle was portrayed by *Time* magazine as having acted rashly and without full knowledge of the facts when he voted for Curran's dismissal, based on his own words at the time of Curran's reinstatement that the board had rescinded its decision based on "additional information".[37] *Time* interpreted O'Boyle's explanation as "meaning their [the board members'] belated and sudden embarrassed discovery that prior to the dismissal decision Curran had been unanimously recommended for promotion by both the [CUA] theology faculty and its academic

---

[34] Words of Reverend Daniel McGuire of the CUA School of Theology, quoted in J.R. Hailey, "Catholic U. Rebellion Laid to Faculty," *The Washington Post* (22 April 1967) 1.

[35] *Evening Star*, April 25, 1967, photographer Ken Heinen.

[36] J. Fialka, "CU Reinstates Father Curran, Shutdown Ends", *Evening Star*, April 25, 1967, 1.

[37] "Victory at C.U.", 84.

senate".[38] These out-of-touch bishops, according to the *Evening Star*, had not been "sufficiently sensitive to the changing climate in Catholic as well as non-Catholic educational circles".[39] The divided, incompetent, and defeated impression of the bishops conveyed by the secular press made a striking contrast to the united, professional, and triumphant image of the pro-Curran protesters in the same publications. Not only had the board of trustees clearly made a mistake, but the very grounds for their having any kind of oversight at the university had been thrown into doubt. If Cardinal Cushing were right, it seemed that the board of trustees had no business in making *any* interventions in the academic affairs of CUA.

The secular media also did not hesitate to connect the events at CUA to its own interpretation of the Second Vatican Council, judging that Curran represented the spirit of openness and change espoused by the Council while the conservative hierarchy and its decision to dismiss Curran embodied opposition to all that the Council had promoted. Thus Curran was described by the *Washington Post* as one "spurred by the spirit of freedom created in the Catholic Church by the reforms of the Second Vatican Council".[40] The bishops, on the other hand, almost all of whom had attended the Council and voted for the changes called for in its decrees, were said to be "backsliding now 'that they've gone back to their chancery offices and protectorates'".[41] If, in the past, the bishops' total authority in hiring and firing had been accepted by obedient lay faculty, such was no longer the case, and this development should be considered "Exhibit A in the continuing impact of the Second Vatican Council", said the *Post*. The "most compelling teaching" of Vatican II, according to the *Post*, is that the Church is the entire People of God; thus, authority in the Church can no longer be restricted to the pope and bishops, but rather "all [people] have an

---

[38] The board of trustees had already been aware, before its decision to dismiss Curran, of the faculty votes in favor of promoting him, as evidenced by McDonald's letters to Krol and Hannan in the spring of 1967, box 34a, ACK.

[39] Editorial, *Evening Star*, April 21, 1967, 10.

[40] Gerald Grant, "Fight for Academic Freedom Still Wide Open at Catholic U.", *Washington Post*, April 23, 1967, 1.

[41] Comment of an unidentified "high churchman", in Gerald Grant and William R. MacKaye, "Bishops Voted to Fire Curran with 1 Dissent", *Washington Post*, April 21, 1967, 1.

advisory role in the governance of the Church." Furthermore, the *Post* asserted, the Council had declared that bishops were not necessarily theologians—in fact, the conciliar decrees had been written not by the bishops but by theological experts, the *periti*.[42] The bishops had clearly stepped beyond the bounds of their competence in an attempt to restrain the new spirit of freedom that Vatican II had unleashed in the Church embodied by the youthful Father Curran. Given the theological, academic, and social climate of the late 1960s, such an attempt had, not surprisingly, proven entirely futile, in the judgment of the media.

Thus, the main points made by the secular press regarding what had transpired at Catholic University were these:

1. The real reason for Curran's dismissal was that he supported a change in the Church's teaching on birth control.

2. Curran was a youthful, easygoing, balanced, and respectable scholar.

3. The controlling board of trustees had acted unreasonably and incompetently in its decision to dismiss Curran and was divided within itself.

4. Curran and his liberal teaching embodied the new freedom and openness called for by the Second Vatican Council, while the old, conservative bishop-trustees opposed the Council's reforms.

The decision to reinstate the young priest-professor was interpreted as an absolute and unquestionable victory for freedom, justice, and personal liberty.

---

[42] William R. MacKaye, "Impact of Vatican II is Seen in Walkout", *Washington Post*, April 22, 1967, 1.

The Influence of the AAUP
on Catholic Higher Education

The implications of the Curran controversy did not extend merely to the internal life of CUA or simply to Catholic institutions of higher education. They also extended to the question of how effectively Catholics would be able to win respect within both the academic community and the wider social fabric of late-1960s America. The outcome of events at Catholic University was to have a profound and lasting effect on the future identity of American Catholics, and the CUA faculty knew it. This awareness explains much of the persistence and tenacity with which Curran's supporters defended him against the board of trustees; they were convinced that the future development of their vision of academic freedom at all Catholic institutions of higher education in the United States would hinge on the outcome of the Curran controversy.

The involvement of schools at CUA in a controversy that mainly concerned the School of Theology was an indication of widespread concern over the repercussions of the Curran affair in the greater American academic community. This concern was first explicitly mentioned in the resolution passed by the School of Philosophy on April 19, 1967; it was included in other resolutions and was finally inserted as an amendment to the resolution of the entire faculty assembly on April 20 by Dr. Kirby Neill, professor of English and member of the AAUP National Committee on Academic Freedom in Church-Related Schools. This amendment declared that the treatment of Curran by the board of trustees was a total embarrassment, not only for CUA as it sought accreditation as a competent American university, but also for all Catholic educators throughout the United States. Its wording was emphatic: "Whereas this directive puts this University outside of the American academic community and raises grave questions for the continuation of Catholic Higher Education in America, in the minds and hearts of Catholic Teachers and Students over the entire country".[1]

The amendment's reference to "the American academic community" referred in large measure to the accepted principles of academic freedom enunciated by the AAUP during the twentieth century, which were considered normative for any institution that wished to be taken seriously within American academia. The organization had first given formal expression to its principles in 1915, revised those norms in 1940, and then further amended them throughout the 1960s, bringing an immense amount of pressure on Catholic and other religious institutions of higher education to distance themselves from any formal oversight by ecclesiastical authority.[2] The language of the various AAUP statements came across at first glance as simple and self-evident: on behalf of university professors, the AAUP sought the right to pursue the truth, to do so in liberty, and to ensure that no individual's rights would be taken away in this regard. By effectively using rhetoric of freedom and rights, the AAUP norms defined academic freedom in a way that made the presence of any sort of higher ecclesiastical authority at a church-run university seem outdated, unnecessary, and flatly un-American.

Until the 1960s, Catholic education, including higher education, had been predicated on the existence of a previously arrived at synthesis of classical humanism, Thomistic philosophy, and the Catholic faith. The neoscholastic synthesis of faith and reason that prevailed at Catholic universities and seminaries in the first half of the twentieth century

---

[1] Assembly of Ordinary Professors, resolution, April 20, 1967, "Minute Book" folder, "Faculty Assembly 1965–1978" box, ACUA.

[2] The main relevant statements of the AAUP are: "General Declaration of Principles", *Bulletin of the American Association of University Professors* 1 (1915) and 40 (1954–1955); "Statement of Principles on Academic Freedom and Tenure", *Bulletin of the American Association of University Professors* 26 (1940); "Statement on Procedural Standards in Faculty Dismissal Proceedings", *Bulletin of the American Association of University Professors* 50 (1964); *Report of the Special Committee on Academic Freedom in Church-Related Colleges and Universities*, in *Bulletin of the American Association of University Professors* 53 (1967).

sought to impart to the student a contemplative appreciation for the wisdom and knowledge of the Catholic Tradition, a fountain from which the student could drink as a privileged recipient of the labors of all who had gone before him in the Western intellectual heritage. Beginning in the 1930s, however, a certain tension had arisen: American Catholic universities had attempted to combine the neoscholastic synthesis with an emphasis on research as was championed by top universities such as Harvard and Berkeley. The union of these two intellectual currents proved exceedingly difficult to manage. The modern ethos of critical scholarship, with its emphasis on the method of the empirical sciences, was inherently antithetical to the idea of the existence of a previously accepted corpus of unchanging truth.

This encounter of two drastically different models of learning created a genuine crisis for Catholic universities: the traditional neoscholastic synthesis no longer sufficed, yet there was no new system to integrate the overwhelming volume of knowledge gained by research with the supernatural truth that was known by faith. Some within Catholic academia responded to this tension by unequivocally rejecting the "cult of research" as incompatible with the Catholic intellectual tradition.[3] Such an extreme position seemed to leave little space for possible cooperation between Catholic intellectuals and scientific research. Other Catholic intellectuals had been to some extent protected from this conflict by what John Tracy Ellis and others lamented as the "ghetto mentality" prevalent in Catholic institutions of higher education in the first half of the twentieth century.[4] Yet the rapid postwar expansion of departments and programs at almost every Catholic institution of higher education meant that Catholic professors and administrators had found themselves thrust into the midst of a debate that had been evolving for quite some time in American higher education with a decidedly antireligious bent.

---

[3] Cf. George Bull, "The Function of the Catholic Graduate School", *Thought* 13 (1938): 364–80.

[4] John Tracy Ellis, "American Catholics and the Intellectual Life", *Thought* 30 (1955): 351–88.

The Roots and Development of the AAUP

The development of the AAUP's stated principles of academic freedom had its roots in the historical context of higher education in Germany, where many American intellectuals had studied in the late nineteenth and early twentieth century. The conception of *Lehrfreiheit* ("freedom to teach") as it developed in the German universities in that era took form in a milieu that clearly regarded the Church as the enemy of scientific knowledge. Such a conception of academic freedom was the fruit of positivistic scientism and intellectualism, which opposed dogmatic faith not only on the intellectual level but also on the moral and socio-ethical level. Such dogmatic antidogmatism had the practical consequence of changing the entire purpose of higher education as Western civilization had known it since the time of its foundations, as one turn-of-the-century German thinker put it:

> It is no longer, as formerly, the function of the university teacher to hand down a body of truth established by authorities, but to search after scientific knowledge by investigation, and to teach his hearers to do the same. . . . For the academic teacher and his hearers there can be no prescribed and no proscribed thoughts. There is only one rule for instruction: to justify the truth of one's teaching by reason and the facts.[5]

The influence of such antidogmatic ideology within German higher education came to the United States and drove the redefinition of what constituted the essence of a university. Research took on the nature of a religion for those who saw it as the key to discovering not only truth in the empirical sciences but also truth about transcendent existence. In 1957 two professors of history at Columbia University who were influential members of the AAUP published the landmark work *The Development of Academic Freedom in the United States*, which declared: "Academic freedom has come to signify the brotherhood of man in science that is akin in inspiration to the brotherhood of man in God. . . .

---

[5] Friedrich Paulsen, *The German Universities and University Study*, trans. Frank Thilly and William W. Elwang (New York: C. Scribner's Sons, 1906), 228–31, in James John Annarelli, *Academic Freedom and Catholic Education* (New York: Greenwood Press, 1987), 3.

[It is] the symbol and guardian [of science], equated not only with free intellectual activity, but an ethic of human relations and an ideal of personal fulfillment."[6]

The AAUP's guiding philosophy sought to minimize if not eliminate any interference of religious authority in the academic endeavor. Arthur Lovejoy, another early organizer of the AAUP, made this objective clear in his 1930 definition of academic freedom for the *Encyclopedia of the Social Sciences*:

> Academic freedom is the freedom of the teacher or research worker in higher institutions of learning to investigate and discuss the problems of his science and to express his conclusions, whether through publication or in the instruction of students, without interference from political or ecclesiastical authority, or from the administrative officials of the institution in which he is employed, unless his methods are found by qualified bodies of his own profession to be clearly incompetent or contrary to professional ethics.[7]

The vision of academic freedom espoused by Lovejoy's definition was expressed concretely in the AAUP's Statement of Principles first issued in 1915 and revised in 1940. These statements established norms for the relation of individual faculty members to the governing board of a university, especially in the case of a religious institution. The 1915 statement acknowledged the tradition by which religious organizations had the right to establish a college as "an instrument of propaganda in the interests of the religious faith professed by the church or denomination creating it". The AAUP, however, expressed its serious reservations about such religiously motivated institutions: "[They] do not, at least as regards one particular subject, accept the principles of

---

[6] Quoted in Philip Gleason, *Contending with Modernity: Catholic Higher Education in the Twentieth Century* (New York: Oxford University Press, 1995), 15. Richard Hofstadter (1916–1970) and Walter P. Metzger (1922–) coauthored *The Development of Academic Freedom in the United States* (1957).

[7] Quoted in Annarelli, *Academic Freedom and Catholic Education*, 4. Arthur Lovejoy (1873–1962) was professor of philosophy at Johns Hopkins University, founder of the *Journal of the History of Ideas*, first chairman of the Maryland chapter of the American Civil Liberties Union, founder of the American Association of University Professors, and a strong proponent of the right of faculty members to teach unencumbered by ideological restrictions. His most noted work is *The Great Chain of Being* (1936).

freedom of inquiry, of opinion, and of teaching."[8] In the judgment of the AAUP, these schools were concerned with the promotion of private religious opinion rather than unfettered truth and as such could not be said to be free. The AAUP was confident, however, that these schools were gradually losing their religious identity:

> Such institutions are rare, however, and are becoming ever more rare. We still have, indeed, colleges under denominational auspices; but very few of them impose upon their trustees responsibility for the spread of specific doctrines. They are more and more coming to occupy, with respect to the freedom enjoyed by the members of their teaching bodies, the position of untrammeled institutions of learning, and are differentiated only by the natural influence of their respective historic antecedents and traditions.

Any school not distancing itself from the doctrinal teaching of its founding religious body ought to be asked whether it had "a right to be regarded seriously as a member of the family of institutions of higher learning". Religious doctrine was the enemy of freedom and thus of truth. Adherence to dogma constituted the narrow promotion of private propaganda rather than openness to the universal common good, in the judgment of the AAUP.

Because institutions of higher education were generally supported by public contributions (through funding from local and federal governments), the AAUP asserted that university trustees had no right to think of themselves as being analogous to private employers, with the right to impose "their personal opinions upon the teaching of the institution"; still less could they employ "the power of dismissal to gratify their private antipathies or resentments". The 1915 statement declared that professors likewise had a duty to the public that came *first* before any other obligation: "The responsibility of the university teacher is primarily to the public itself, and to the judgment of his own profession." This duty to the public meant that there could be no constraint on the professor's academic work: "It is obvious that here again the scholar must be absolutely free not only to pursue his investigations

---

[8] "General Declaration of Principles", *Bulletin of the American Association of University Professors* 1 (1915): 21; and 40 (1954–1955): 90–112.

but to declare the results of his researches, no matter where they may lead him or to what extent they may come into conflict with accepted opinion."

Such absolute freedom necessitated the enforcement of the principle whereby professors could be judged only by their faculty peers, individuals with open minds. Professors were never to be judged by a board of trustees, arbitrarily imposing its predetermined opinions on an institution. Such freedom from outside judgment would enable the professor to pursue his vocation, which was primarily one of discarding anything old: "It is a primary duty of a teacher to make a student take an honest account of his stock of ideas, throw out the dead matter, place revised price marks on what is left, and try to fill his empty shelves with new goods."[9] The "dead matter" to be thrown out was religious doctrine that had once been taught as truth but had become impractical and irrelevant in the twentieth century. True academic freedom was incompatible with the existence of objective articles of faith and objective moral norms.

By 1940, when it issued a revised "Statement of Principles on Academic Freedom and Tenure", the AAUP had become even bolder in its rejection of the legitimacy of any and all religious oversight at institutions of higher education.[10] The 1940 statement exerted an enormous influence on Catholic universities during the crucial post-World War II years of institutional expansion and Catholic cultural assimilation. Again proclaiming a commitment to the "free search for truth", the statement delineated certain rights to which all professors were entitled: freedom of research and publication, freedom of discussion in the classroom, and freedom from censorship by the institution. The professor had a corresponding duty to exercise restraint and discretion by not giving the impression that he represented the institution when he publicly expressed his opinions. Of particular importance for Catholic institutions was the proviso regarding institutions that held a stated religious orientation: "Limitations of academic freedom because

---

[9] William T. Foster, as quoted in *General Report of the Committee on Academic Freedom and Academic Tenure, Bulletin of the American Association of University Professors* 1 (1915): 36.

[10] "Statement of Principles on Academic Freedom and Tenure", *Bulletin of the American Association of University Professors* (1940):1, 49–51.

of religious or other aims of the institution should be clearly stated in writing at the time of the appointment." This requirement acknowledged the right of the sponsoring religious body to establish boundaries that were not to be violated by teachers, boundaries essential to the defining religious commitment of the institution. The teacher likewise had a duty to avoid discussing "controversial matter which has no relation to his subject". This condition indicated, however, that if the matter of controversy were within his field of teaching expertise, then the professor had the right to enter into the controversy with his students.

Regarding tenure, the 1940 AAUP statement declared that its purpose was to guarantee teachers freedom in teaching and research as well as a measure of financial stability. After a probationary period not to exceed seven years, teachers were to be granted continuous tenure, after which time their service could be terminated "only for adequate cause". During the probationary period, new teachers were to enjoy the same right of academic freedom as any other professor. If termination was to be sought, the matter was to be investigated by both a faculty committee and the governing board of the institution. The teacher under investigation was to be informed in writing of the charges against him and to have the opportunity to defend himself before all those who were judging him. Testimony during the hearing was to include that of teachers and other scholars. The 1940 statement here spelled out the basic requirements of due process, mandating a fair hearing in which a professor would be judged by his academic peers and not by any supervisory authority or governing board.

Perhaps the most significant line of the 1940 statement defined the purpose of the university as being for "the common good and not to further the interest of either the individual teacher or the institution as a whole". In defining a dichotomy between "the common good" and "the interest of the institution as a whole", the AAUP laid the foundation for the entire controversy over the meaning of academic freedom at Catholic universities. When those entrusted with the responsibility of governing a Catholic institution of higher learning attempted to intervene in the academic affairs of the university in the interest of the school's religious mission, they were opposed by those who claimed to be acting to further the common good, as distinct from the supposedly narrower good of the Church or the good of the denomination. This impasse proved impossible to resolve without one side or the other compromising its principles. As events at CUA unfolded, it was the board of trustees more than the School of Theology that showed itself willing to accept compromise in its position, and the result was that, to a large extent, the creed of the AAUP rather than that of the Catholic Church became the guiding philosophy of America's premier pontifical university.

Until the 1960s, the 1940 statement's permission for a religious limitation on academic freedom had enabled Catholic universities in the United States to accept the presence of chapters of the AAUP on their campuses. CUA had been able to preserve its Catholic identity by declaring that, unlike other institutions of higher learning, it had a professed mission of "indoctrinating" students in the Catholic faith. The statement "Freedom of Teaching and Research" issued as an appendix to the 1956 *Handbook of the College of Arts and Sciences* explained the university's twofold commitment to both faith and learning, to being both American and Catholic:

> Catholic University differs in the following respects from many institutions of learning in America:
>
> a) It proclaims that it does indoctrinate, in the sense that it positively teaches a system of values and tries to impart to its students certain definite principles of life and action.
>
> b) Because it is not only American but Catholic Christian, it recognizes a somewhat larger number of absolutes than are recognized by an institution not under Catholic auspices. For instance, it adheres to the Apostles' Creed as absolute truth and to the teaching of the Catholic Church as an unerring guide in matters of faith and morals.[11]

Such an expressly doctrinal statement, affirming the "unerring" nature of the teaching of the Catholic Church in faith and morals, was for decades accepted—if begrudgingly so—as non-controversial within the American educational community. But the ideological terrain of academia shifted rapidly and dramatically during the 1960s.

---

[11] In John F. Hunt and Terrence R. Connelly, *The Responsibility of Dissent: The Church and Academic Freedom* (New York: Sheed and Ward, 1969), 108.

First, in 1962 the AAUP issued the statement "Faculty Participation in College and University Government".[12] It declared that governing boards of universities were to acknowledge the faculty as "essential participants" in the formation of educational policy. It was the faculty who held the primary responsibility for determining educational policy, while the governing board was to intervene adversely to the will of the faculty "only in exceptional circumstances and for reasons that are communicated to the faculty".

Then in 1966, the AAUP's "Statement on Professional Ethics" affirmed the responsibilities incumbent upon the individual professor in exchange for his right of academic freedom.[13] As a citizen, the professor had a duty to promote free inquiry and "to further promote public understanding of academic freedom". Respect, honesty, and a commitment to seeking the truth were affirmed as essential to the vocation of the professor. The language of these norms was balanced and reasonable, seemingly conscious of the duty that the intellectual held toward both the academic community and the civil community at large.

However, a quotation from the 1964 report of a special committee of the AAUP indicated that the antireligious nature of the AAUP's guiding philosophy remained as strong as ever:

> In light of the historic commitment of the academic community to academic freedom, and the dangers inherent in restrictions on that freedom, even when these are believed to be essential to the accomplishment of basic institutional aims, the Committee urges that religious privilege not be employed to provide a sanctuary in which to avoid the full responsibilities of institutions of higher education.[14]

Such an antagonistic position toward both religion and the existence of objective truth was bluntly declared in 1966 at Notre Dame by David Fellman, president of the AAUP and professor of political science at

---

[12] "Faculty Participation in College and University Government: Statement of Principles Approved by the Council, October 26, 1962", *Bulletin of the American Association of University Professors* 48 (1962): 321–23.

[13] American Association of University Professors, "Statement on Professional Ethics", *Bulletin of the American Association of University Professors* 52 (1966): 57–58.

[14] *Report of the Special Committee on Academic Freedom in Church-Related Colleges and Universities*, 369.

the University of Wisconsin.[15] Speaking at one of the most prominent American institutions of Catholic higher education, Fellman praised the academic freedom and political freedom that were part and parcel of the American experience and gave a succinct definition of what this freedom of debate and discussion meant in terms of first principles: "No one's particular truth . . . can be regarded as such a final truth that it is never, thereafter, subject to critical treatment by others." The great American tradition of political freedom, Fellman asserted, refused to hold any absolute principles: "Its only final truth is the conviction that there are no such things." Fellman expressed "grave apprehensions" concerning power and authority, invoking John Stuart Mill's declaration that "all silencing of discussion is an assumption of infallibility" while asserting that "no one, not even the most powerful public official, is infallible." Fellman defined freedom as "the right to disagree" and further declared that "the method of freedom is not designed to achieve a body of final, correct answers."

Fellman passionately defended his definition of academic freedom, basing his arguments on the various statements of the AAUP and especially the 1940 "Statement of Principles". He affirmed the various goods of academic freedom in teaching and research, the right of students to object and to debate within reason, and the right to due process in any and all disciplinary proceedings. Fellman was emphatic that the community of scholars was not to see its right to independent judgment hampered by any governing board in the performance of its duties. Invoking the AAUP norms, Fellman spoke of the academic community's duty to "shock": "The scholar is necessarily a disturbing person . . . professionally committed to raising questions about accepted ideas and institutions." The purpose of education was likewise one of "shock": "The aim of science is to discover new truth", Fellman declared, "but

---

[15] David Fellman, "Academic Freedom and the American Political Ethos", in Edward Manier and John W. Houck, eds., *Academic Freedom and the Catholic University* (Notre Dame, Ind.: Fides Publishers, 1967), 60–79. David Fellman (1907–2003) was professor at the University of Nebraska from 1934 to 1947 and then at the University of Wisconsin from 1947 to 1978 and a member of the AAUP for sixty-one years. He served on its Committee A from 1957 to 1971, was chairman of that committee from 1959 to 1964, and was president of the AAUP from 1964 to 1966. He continued as a member of the governing board of the AAUP Legal Defense Fund into the 1990s.

every new truth means the disappearance of old error and frequently involves a shock to existing opinion." The very purpose of the university, in Fellman's view, was to administer this "shock" to modern society and even, if need be, to those who governed the institution.

Such was the prevailing philosophy of the president of the AAUP on the eve of the Curran affair at CUA. If at one time such a definition of freedom as inherently antidogmatic could have been dismissed as merely the opinion of a fringe group of intellectual radicals, by the mid-1960s the denial of objective truth was becoming one of the central tenets of American culture and especially higher education. Evidence of this wider cultural mentality had been clearly seen in the 1957 opinion of the United States Supreme Court in its decision *Sweezy vs. New Hampshire*, which declared its commitment to the elimination of the "straitjacket" of absolute truth that would "imperil the future of our nation":

> No field of education is so thoroughly comprehended by man that new discoveries cannot yet be made. Particularly is that true in the social sciences, where few, if any, principles are accepted as absolutes. Scholarship cannot flourish in an atmosphere of suspicion and distrust. Teachers and students must always remain free to inquire, to study, and to evaluate, to gain new maturity and understanding; otherwise our civilization will stagnate and die.[16]

In its language and tenor *Sweezy* read exactly like one of the many declarations of the AAUP. Another notable example of the mindset of the time regarding the meaning of freedom was a 1968 statement by Harold Howe II, commissioner of education in the Lyndon B. Johnson administration:

> The university community must be free to state its findings and express its judgments. To the extent that it finds established belief to be specious, it must be free to proclaim that finding. To the extent that it finds an unconventional practice potentially beneficial, it must

---

[16] *Sweezy v. New Hampshire*, 354 U.S. 234, 250, in *Bulletin of the American Association of University Professors*, 53 no. 3 (September 1967): 306. *Sweezy* was a First Amendment case with regard to due process of the law. The petitioner had delivered a lecture at the University of New Hampshire in 1954 and had been accused of holding Communist sympathies. The petitioner refused to answer any questions about his personal beliefs or opinions. The case was decided on June 17, 1957.

be free to discard convention. And the university must guard the university community's right to do these things.[17]

The vocation of university professors was declared specifically to be to challenge belief and discard dogma. The very definition of freedom now excluded any submission to the authority of a creed, set of doctrines, or juridical authority extrinsic to the academic community. By the late 1960s the American academic community became passionately convinced that the very future of civilization hinged on the elimination of religious restrictions at institutions of higher education. In undertaking this necessary elimination mandated by the AAUP, colleges and universities had to be prepared, Fellman declared, to withstand "the storms of moral indignation from the larger community". This indignation could be taken as a certain indicator that progress toward greater freedom was moving along nicely. Anyone who failed to act with courage and conviction at such a critical moment of history by remaining attached to outmoded ideas of perennial truth was clearly and even self-evidently a threat to the public good.

Such was the creed of the AAUP in 1967, and it found in the halls of American academia many faithful adherents who were ready to sacrifice all other principles in professing it. The one unchanging certainty of the AAUP creed was that everything must change. And in making that principle of absolute change the *alpha* and *omega* of its tenets, academic freedom as defined by the AAUP arrogated to itself the status not just of a guiding principle of education but of an ideological worldview. It was a worldview decidedly incompatible with a profession of faith in the objective content of Christian revelation as taught by the Tradition of the Catholic Church.

The CUA administration had generally shown coolness toward the presence of the AAUP on campus during the first half of the twentieth century. Roy J. Deferrari, professor of classics at CUA from 1918 to 1960, noted in his memoirs that the various bishop-rectors during his tenure were less than enthusiastic toward the presence of a chapter of the AAUP at CUA.[18] Deferrari, the first CUA faculty member to join

---

[17] Harold Howe II, commencement speech at Adelphi University, June 9, 1968, in Hunt and Connelly, *The Responsibility of Dissent*, 53.

[18] Deferrari (1890–1969) was something of an institution at CUA, serving as a member of the Department of Greek and Latin (1918–1960), director of summer sessions

the association, believed that the presence of an AAUP chapter would help facilitate communication at CUA so that the administration could be more aware of faculty concerns. Indeed, according to Deferrari the main concern of the CUA chapter meetings until 1960 was to complain about faculty salaries. The 1960s, however, witnessed the explicit invocation at CUA of the principles of the AAUP as a key source of the opposition on campus to the authority of the bishop-rector and the board of trustees.[19] The vision articulated in the 1915 "Statement of Principles", explicitly declaring the AAUP's desire that ecclesiastically governed institutions such as CUA cease to exist, were repeatedly invoked and were in large measure successful in obtaining their stated objective of the elimination of religious authority in the practical life of the university.

The rapid ideological developments of the 1960s ridiculed attempts on the part of Catholic universities to walk a middle road between being Catholic and being American. If a certain blending of the two identities had been tolerated in the past, such a double identity was now in fact impossible. By 1969 John Hunt and Terrence Connelly, the attorneys of Cravath, Swaine, and Moore who defended the dissenting professors at CUA pro bono, openly declared that universities would have to make a definitive choice between being American and being Catholic.[20] Charles Curran's own definition of academic freedom showed very clearly his own acceptance of the bedrock "American" principles of the AAUP: "The university as such must be a free and autonomous center of study with no external constraints limiting either its autonomy or its freedom."[21] He firmly maintained that only by embracing such a definition of academic freedom could a Catholic university be *both* Catholic *and* American. It was this conviction that impelled him to undertake dissent against the Magisterium's in-

---

(1930–1960), dean of the Graduate School of Arts and Sciences (1930–1937), and secretary-general of the university (1937–1960).

[19] Roy J. Deferrari, *Memoirs of the Catholic University of America: 1918–1960* (Boston: St. Paul Editions, 1962), 311.

[20] Hunt and Connelly, *The Responsibility of Dissent*, 108. John F. Hunt, brother of Father Robert Hunt of the CUA School of Theology, studied law at Columbia. Connelly had been an undergraduate at CUA and studied law at New York University.

[21] Charles E. Curran, "Academic Freedom: The Catholic University and Catholic Theology", *Furrow* 30 (December 1979): 740.

volvement in CUA's internal life. Curran summarily dismissed the idea that religious institutions could maintain a doctrinal standard for certain professors as "an understanding of academic freedom which is opposed to and destructive of the accepted understanding in the American academe". The "destructive" nature of requiring a profession of faith, according to Curran, was that it asserted the legitimacy of "a specific doctrinal test of a religious nature" and also simplistically maintained that one of the purposes of teaching was "to solidify and deepen the faith of the student". Curran also disagreed strongly with the idea that if students lost their Catholic faith while at a Catholic college, this might somehow reflect unfavorably on their professors.[22]

In the assessment made by Curran and his confreres, such outdated ways of thinking were declared to be in error *because* the "accepted understanding" rejected them. In their view, while the preconciliar Catholic ghetto mentality had once submitted to the clerically driven agenda of blindly teaching the static dogmas of the traditional Catholic faith, such narrowness had now happily yielded to the enlightened moment of the late 1960s, which was witnessing the universal replacement of such a restricted agenda with an open and broad-minded embrace of freedom. Any Catholic university that was serious about being fully American (and thus fully a university) was, in the view of the AAUP, wisely throwing off the repressive shackles of the Magisterium that impeded it from having the freedom to pursue the truth, as well as the narrow-minded sense of being "simply a pastoral arm of the Church".[23] According to the ideology of academic freedom, the moment had come for the Catholic university to relinquish its attachment to the *particular* good of being governed by the (closed and narrow-minded) Catholic hierarchy for the sake of the *common* good of the entire (free and open) secular American society.

It was this definitive choice that lay at the heart of the conflict at CUA. While an earlier acceptance of a certain balance between the two had been tolerated by the AAUP, by 1967 this coexistence was no longer an option in the eyes of those in power in the world of higher education. The supposedly American principles of the AAUP

---

[22] Ibid., 743.

[23] *1971 Report of the North American Region of the International Federation of Catholic Universities*, quoted in Curran, "Academic Freedom: The Catholic University and Catholic Theology".

at Catholic University declared outright war on any attempt by the CUA board of trustees to use its authority to protect the university's Catholic identity. The Magisterium of the Catholic Church as embodied in the American bishops was declared by the AAUP to be illegitimate when it sought to exercise oversight of Catholic education.

In the turbulent atmosphere of the late 1960s, it was extremely difficult, if not impossible, for a university to attempt to be faithful both to the Catholic profession of faith and to the tenets of academic freedom as defined by the AAUP. The attempt to straddle these two guiding philosophies was in essence an attempt to say "We accept the Creed" and "We reject the Creed" in the same breath. The fact that so many Catholic institutions attempted this impossible harmonization in the years following Vatican II indicates that confusion reigned among Catholic educators about either the nature of the Catholic faith commitment or the nature of the guiding philosophy of the AAUP. The fact that those years witnessed a plethora of meetings and statements by persons and groups on all sides of the debate attempting to reconcile "Catholic identity" with "academic freedom" as defined by the AAUP is a striking indicator of just how deep and widespread that confusion was among Catholic clergy, religious, and educators.

The "Land O' Lakes Statement"

The ideology of the AAUP came into full flower in Catholic higher education with the "Land O' Lakes Statement on the Nature of the Contemporary Catholic University".[24] The statement made explicit and open what had for some time been developing in a more or less quiet way at various Catholic universities that were generally independent of each other.

The statement was written in July 1967 by twenty-six representatives of American institutions of Catholic higher education, including two bishops and two high-ranking superiors of the Holy Cross Fathers and the Society of Jesus, who gathered in Land O' Lakes, Wisconsin.[25]

---

[24] See appendix B. See also Neil G. McCluskey, ed., *The Catholic University: A Modern Appraisal* (Notre Dame: University of Notre Dame Press, 1970), 336–41.

[25] A list of the entire body that gathered at Land O' Lakes is included in appendix B.

This self-selected group consisted of the leading advocates of unrestricted academic freedom in American Catholic higher education.[26] Five presidents of major Catholic universities—Notre Dame, Boston College, Georgetown, Fordham, and St. Louis University—attended the meeting. Catholic University did not officially participate in the conference but sent Reverend F. Raymond Fowerbaugh, assistant to the president, as an observer. Together this group of highly influential Catholic educators produced a statement informing the American bishops that their interference in the life of their universities was no longer welcome. In fact, they declared, the oversight of the bishops was an embarrassment to these schools that were striving to enter the American mainstream and seeking acceptance by their peers in secular higher education. The statement was reported by the press as a "declaration of independence"[27] by Catholic universities, and indeed it marked a watershed in the history of the relations of these institutions with the hierarchy of the Church. In the words of Philip Gleason, Land O' Lakes marked a symbolic turning point: "The church's future path might remain unclear, but her 'cold war with modernity' was definitely over."[28]

Focusing on the "rapidly evolving" identity of the Catholic university, the "Land O' Lakes Statement" called for each university to be "a university in the full modern sense of the word". The distinguishing quality of the modern university was simply defined as "academic excellence". The condition for such academic excellence was simple:

> To perform its teaching and research functions effectively the Catholic university must have a true autonomy and academic freedom in the face of authority of whatever kind, lay or clerical, external to the academic community itself. To say this is simply to assert that institutional autonomy and academic freedom are essential conditions of life and growth and indeed of survival for Catholic universities as for all universities.

The statement declared that what distinguished a Catholic university from other universities was an atmosphere in which "Catholicism is

---

[26] Gleason, *Contending with Modernity*, 317.

[27] Neil G. McCluskey, "This Is How It Happened", in McCluskey, *The Catholic University: A Modern Appraisal*, 7.

[28] Gleason, *Contending with Modernity*, 317.

perceptibly present and effectively operative." The key to this "operative presence" was the existence of a department of theology. This presence was "essential to the integrity of a university", and the academic competence of that department was thus doubly important. It was the task of the theological faculty to "engage directly in exploring the depths of Christian tradition" so as to arrive at "the best possible understanding of religion and revelation". The statement called for a constant dialogue between theology and the other academic disciplines; this conversation was to be a unique characteristic of the Catholic university and would enable it to engage modern culture with a distinct contribution. Furthermore, the Catholic university had the duty of continually making a critical evaluation of "all aspects and activities of the Church and should objectively evaluate them". If this critical role had been almost nonexistent in the recent past, the writers of the statement hoped to herald the dawning of a new age when such continual evaluation and counsel would enrich the entire Church. Finally, with regard to undergraduate education, the statement reprobated any practice of censorship, because "the intellectual campus of a Catholic university has no boundaries and no barriers." Only in the absence of intellectual boundaries could the student arrive at that self-fulfillment that was the goal of the education given by a Catholic university.

Freedom from external interference, intellectual engagement, dialogue with the modern world and all of academia, critical evaluation of the Church, and the absence of all boundaries to intellectual inquiry: this was the ambitious scheme advanced by the "Land O' Lakes Statement". If such an undertaking seemed monumental, this only added to the enthusiasm of the educators who signed the statement. What was being called for was an overhaul of the entire structure of Catholic higher education, both administratively and philosophically. While acknowledging that a great deal of experimentation would be necessary in order to enter the uncharted waters of academic freedom, Land O' Lakes unhesitatingly affirmed that "changes of this kind are essential for the future of the Catholic university." It concluded by expressing the admirable hope that "the Catholic university of the future will be a true modern university but specifically Catholic in profound and creative ways for the service of society and the people of God."

The Marriage of the AAUP and
Postconciliar Theology

The signers of the "Land O' Lakes Statement" understood that they were calling for a revolution in Catholic higher education that would consciously seek a rupture with all that had preceded it. Their viewpoint was one that saw a vast divide, an all but total separation, between the Church of the post-Reformation era and the Church of the post-Vatican II era. The former was seen as one that, since the Enlightenment, had choked off freedom within higher education and, along with freedom, the ability to discover the truth; the latter was seen as an open institution that was ready to grant autonomy to professors and hence would fully empower the Catholic university to pursue the truth. Whereas the "former Church" had relied on obedience and juridical authority to enforce control, the signers of the statement hoped that the "renewed Church" would jettison control altogether. In the minds of the signers, the apologetic ghetto of Trent had been entirely replaced by the ecumenical openness of Vatican II. Any dissent from this viewpoint was mocked as being an outmoded and archaic way of thinking from the "pre-Vatican II Church", which was an entirely different entity from the Church of 1965 and beyond. This interpretation of Vatican II as having severed the postconciliar Church from all that preceded it (aptly named by Pope Benedict XVI the "hermeneutic of discontinuity") played a prominent role in the thinking and action of the key figures in Catholic higher education during the turbulent years of the late 1960s.[29]

The tension caused by the hermeneutic of discontinuity was in evidence at the September 1968 meeting of the International Federation of Catholic Universities (IFCU) in Kinshasa, Congo. At this meeting, over one hundred delegates from some fifty Catholic institutions met to discuss the nature and role of the contemporary Catholic university. The Land O' Lakes Conference had been held the year before, as had three other conferences in Europe, South America, and Africa, as a

---

[29] See Pope Benedict XVI's address to the Roman Curia, December 22, 2005, http://www.vatican.va/holy_father/benedict_xvi/speeches/2005/december/documents/hf_ben_xvi_spe_20051222_roman-curia_en.html.

preparation for this plenary meeting of the IFCU. Neil McCluskey, S.J., who served as dean of education at the University of Notre Dame and was one of the signers of the "Land O' Lakes Statement", described an atmosphere of intense polarization in no uncertain terms: "The group was hopelessly split." He related with evident disdain the way in which the meeting unfolded: "Speaker followed speaker to warn (frequently in Latin) against 'false' autonomy or 'absolute' autonomy and to defend the need of the Catholic university to depend on the magisterium of the church." McCluskey described listening with disbelief as many speakers simplistically maintained that Catholic higher education required a juridical role for the hierarchical Magisterium: "The traditionalists would not allow even the possibility that an institution could be constituted Catholic without juridical relationship to Church authority."[30]

McCluskey noted the great uneasiness among the American delegates to the IFCU over the use of the phrase "institutional commitment" in the description of a Catholic university. The Americans argued against it, he said, for if such a commitment "were translated in action to be a kind of uncritical obedience by the entire university toward every level of ecclesiastical authority" that would result in something other than a university. The idea of the hierarchy of the Church holding practical authority over Catholic universities was for McCluskey and his peers decidedly something to be discarded along with the preconciliar past.

With similar disdain, at the 1968 meeting of the Catholic Theological Society of America, Robert Hunt of the CUA School of Theology spoke vehemently in opposition to the intrusion of the Magisterium into the internal affairs of theology and proposed in its stead another authoritative source by which Catholic universities could regulate them-

---

[30] McCluskey, "This Is How It Happened", in McCluskey, *The Catholic University: A Modern Appraisal*, 1–28. Neil McCluskey (1920–2008) entered the Society of Jesus in 1938. From 1966 to 1971 he was professor of education at Notre Dame. He held a Ph.D. in social history from Columbia University and was very involved in the movement for the renewal of Catholic higher education in the postconciliar years. He served as the secretary at the 1967 Land O' Lakes Conference and was the chairman of the committee that drafted the final statement of the IFCU conference in Kinshasa, Congo, in September 1968: "The Catholic University in the Modern World" or "The Kinshasa Statement". McCluskey left the Society of Jesus and was laicized in 1975.

selves: the statements of the AAUP.[31] Hunt called for the application of the principles of academic freedom accepted in other disciplines to be applied, without qualification, to the teaching of theology:

> In a word, I see no cogent reason in theory why the Catholic theologian and the student of Catholic theology cannot live by the canons of "academic freedom" as developed, operative and normative in the United States today, largely as formulated by the various statements of the AAUP. I see one all-embracing reason why they must live by these canons: otherwise, we are incapable of good Catholic theology and only good theology serves the Church and all mankind!

In his project of helping all mankind, Hunt invoked the threefold academic freedom that the AAUP's 1940 and 1965 statements had championed: freedom for faculty to teach "the truth as they see it", freedom for students to be taught by "unconstrained teachers", and freedom for students to take "reasoned exception" to the views of their teachers. In addition, argued Hunt, both teachers and students should be guided by "all the other specifications appearing in the continuing AAUP dossier".

What role, then, would the Magisterium play in the teaching of theology? Hunt defined it clearly:

> The teachings of the Sacred Magisterium, in the conventionally received understanding of the term, are part of the total data which the Catholic theologian must integrate into his work. He must be aware of them, evaluate them, and give them their proper weight and place in his work. If he does not, the problem is professional qualification and competency and is duly provided for in the standard working norms accepted in the American academe.

The Magisterium was understood by Hunt to be one voice within the sphere of theological inquiry, a voice certainly to be respected and given due consideration, but ultimately one that had no greater or lesser authoritative weight than any of the other numerous voices contributing to the greater body of theological knowledge. It could not claim to have any kind of uniquely authoritative position in the sphere of

---

[31] Robert E. Hunt, "Panel Discussion," *CTSA Proceedings* 23 (1968): 245–67.

theology, said Hunt, for even if a theologian's position was directly contrary to its teaching, he ought to be disciplined by the judgment of his peers rather than by any judgment of the Magisterium. Lest there still remain any confusion about this relationship between the hierarchical Magisterium and theology, Hunt concluded his remarks by laying down this absolute principle: "The Sacred Magisterium, which serves a function different from that of theologians, can never, under any circumstances, directly enter or pre-empt the Catholic theological academe. The Sacred Magisterium as such and *per se* is simply incompetent in theology as such and *per se*." With striking clarity Hunt's remarks reveal the full extent of the hopes of the American Catholic educators and theologians who rallied behind the cry of academic freedom: the more the hierarchical Magisterium could be relegated to the irrelevant sidelines—or even if it could be removed altogether from the theological enterprise—the more Catholic higher education could place itself at the relevant center of contemporary culture and progressive thought.

Here then was the essence of the renewed Catholic university, according to the "Land O'Lakes Statement": it would be "a community of scholars in which Catholicism is perceptibly present and effectively operative", but under no circumstances would that "operative Catholicism" involve what McCluskey described with aplomb as a "juridical relationship to church authority". It would be a university that enjoyed, according to Hunt, the total absence of any intervention by the Magisterium "under any circumstances". In the words of University of Notre Dame President Theodore Hesburgh, the Catholic university would be a *university* first and foremost, meaning that it would "follow the established university rules of freedom and autonomy" and thus have "a combination of many strong, free, and autonomous faculties". These faculties were called to excellence and competence for "God's honor and glory". In addition to this excellence as a university, what made the institution distinctively Catholic was the presence of a "strong, vital, and creative theological faculty", which would be the greatest strength of the Catholic university. And, Hesburgh emphatically declared, this strength, vitality, and excellence *could not be attained* if the Magisterium held any kind of actual, effective authority in the life of the university: "It [the task of theology] is not something that can be accomplished in the face of arbitrary controls from outside the university's professional community of researchers and scholars."[32]

According to McCluskey, Hunt, Hesburgh, and Curran's ascendant generation of postconciliar theologians, the greatest obstacle to the renewal of the Catholic university and indeed of the Catholic Church was the hierarchical Magisterium. The more the Magisterium could be removed from the university, the more theology could get on with the task of what postconciliar theologians called "creative self-realization".

Because the board of trustees at Catholic University was composed entirely of bishops, the movement for academic freedom championed by the AAUP and the movement by postconciliar theologians to redefine the Magisterium coincided perfectly in the late 1960s at CUA. The language of academic freedom and scholarly inquiry could be used in the service of promoting the new postconciliar hermeneutic of the Magisterium of the People of God. In fact, this redefinition of both academic freedom and the Magisterium is exactly what the professors of the CUA School of Theology would succeed in doing, in a masterful and extremely effective way, in the aftermath of the April 1967 controversy surrounding Father Charles Curran. The academic year 1967 to 1968 would witness the ascendance of these theologians into a position of unparalleled influence in the postconciliar development of Catholic education and theology in the United States.

---

[32] Theodore M. Hesburgh, preface to McCluskey, *The Catholic University: A Modern Appraisal*, x.

II

THE SCHOOL OF THEOLOGY
TAKES CONTROL OF CUA

4

After the Strike: The Embers Smolder

As the dust settled from the strike at the end of April 1967, the various parties involved had much to reflect on. The specific details of the way the strike had played out had left many unanswered questions. For example, what might have happened had the bishops held a formal hearing in which Curran was given the chance to defend himself and to make his own case for his position? What might have happened had the timing of the announcement of the board's decision been slightly delayed and issued after the end of the academic year, when students and a good number of the faculty would not have been present on the CUA campus and thus would have been unable to produce the drama and energy created by the strike? What would have happened if the bishops had held their ground a bit longer and insisted that their decision to dismiss Curran was final? Any of these contingencies could have made for a quite different outcome.

In his memoirs, Charles Curran has attributed the success of the 1967 strike to the combination of a number of essential conditions: the faculty had serious grievances with the university administration (especially with Bishop McDonald's interference in academic affairs), the student body desired to play a greater role in the life of the university, and the Second Vatican Council had called for a renewal of Catholic life. Curran has also noted the brilliant execution of the strike in its various details: it was well organized, it united faculty and students from across the entire university, and it was conducted in a peaceful, respectful, and exemplary fashion by courteous, well-dressed students who kept a "positive" and "upbeat" spirit throughout the week. Such a positive spirit was embodied, according to Curran, in the message

on a sign seen frequently during the strike: "Even my mother sup-
ports Father Curran."[1] Curran became an icon of the great hope of
the generation coming of age within the Church in the late 1960s that
Catholic education was finally undergoing a long-overdue change for
the better. As such, the roots of the widespread sympathy for Curran's
cause extended far deeper than those of the frustration over the immediate situation at Catholic University.

From the very first day of the controversy, Charles Curran had stated
clearly that the issue went far beyond him personally and involved
"both Catholic theology in America and Catholic university education". His main objection to the way in which he had been dismissed
was that there had been no specified charges, nor had he been given
a chance to defend himself. He in no way denied "the direction and
guidance of the Church by the bishops", but he had felt compelled to
act because "the competency and authority of the faculty of the School
of Theology and the competency and authority of the academic senate of the Catholic University" had not been respected. It was only
the "harassment" he had received from the board of trustees that had
led him reluctantly and regretfully to bring the matter into the public
forum. Curran's protest was thus, in his eyes, a matter of demanding
justice not only for himself but for the entire academic community; indeed he maintained that *not* protesting would have been an even greater
act of injustice.[2]

In making its corporate decision to strike in support of Curran, there
had been complete solidarity between the priest-professor and his faculty peers in focusing solely on the question of academic freedom.
The April 19, 1967, resolution of the School of Theology initiating
the faculty strike had focused on the threat posed by Curran's dismissal
to the stability of the university's entire academic community. As the
strike had progressed, the members of the School of Theology as well
as other CUA faculty had continued to emphasize that the Curran
controversy could not be adequately resolved without addressing the
deeper problem of which it was only a symptom: the near-total breakdown of communication within the institutional structures of Catholic University. The resolution of the immediate problem on Monday,

---

[1] Charles Curran, *Loyal Dissent: Memoir of a Catholic Theologian* (Washington: Georgetown University Press, 2006), 38–39.
[2] Statement of Father Curran, April 18, 1967, box 14, folder 1, AMK.

April 24, 1967, had thus included not only Chancellor O'Boyle's announcement that Curran was being reinstated but also the promise of a meeting of the board of trustees with the entire faculty of the School of Theology and with the rest of the CUA academic community. O'Boyle had also announced that a new board of trustees Committee on Survey and Objectives would be established with Dr. Carroll A. Hochwalt as chairman.[3] This twofold promise of dialogue and change was seen at the time as an encouraging sign by many of the university faculty.

The convergence of all of these various factors in the strike had not only achieved a total victory for Curran over the authority of the CUA board of trustees but had also created a largely new situation for Catholic theologians throughout the United States. These theologians had learned that the authority of the American bishops was neither as monolithic nor as absolute as it had once seemed and that through perseverance and passionate dedication they could obtain the freedom to teach "without constraint" that the AAUP had declared essential to the future of religiously affiliated schools. From the standpoint of organization and public relations, the strike had been flawlessly executed. It had achieved exactly the response and effect it had intended, and a door had been opened through which the theology faculty could take control of CUA and its mission.

The Report of the School of Sacred Theology

One month after the faculty strike, on May 20, 1967, the theology faculty submitted its *Report of the School of Sacred Theology* to the board of trustees, claiming for themselves the voice that they had demanded in assessing the strengths and weaknesses of the university.[4] The theologians' argument, consistent with all that had been said during the April strike, was that the academic integrity of Catholic University

---

[3] Statement of Archbishop O'Boyle, April 24, 1967, "School of Sacred Theology Minutes" box, "School of Sacred Theology Minutes, 1967–1968" folder, ACUA. Carroll Hochwalt (1899–1988), a former vice president of Monsanto Corporation, was a new member of the board of trustees. His vigorous work on the Committee on Survey and Objectives led to his election as the first chairman of the reorganized board of trustees in 1968. See C. Joseph Nuesse, *The Catholic University of America: A Centennial History* (Washington, D.C.: 1990), 421, 422, 432.

[4] *Report of the School of Sacred Theology*, box 1, AMK.

had been compromised by the arbitrary action of the board in removing Curran from his professorship. Their stated motive in making their grievances known to the board was purely and simply the greater good of Catholic theology, the institutional good of the university, and the academic reputation of Catholic education within the greater American academic community. The report expressed hope that there would be a new spirit of communication and dialogue between the faculty and the board of trustees and suggested various goals and objectives for CUA's immediate future. These essentially called for the elimination of the excessively clerical structure of authority at Catholic University and a consequent embrace of greater freedom and openness as commonly defined by the greater American academic community. The report unequivocally called for as little involvement of the board in the operation of the university as possible. Particularly in theological matters, any disputes were to be investigated and judged by the members of the School of Theology themselves, with the possible involvement of the Catholic Theological Society of America (CTSA) if absolutely necessary, while any potential intervention by the bishops in overseeing the School of Theology was envisioned as being so rare as to hardly merit mention. In the mind of the theology faculty, the authority of the Magisterium was a detriment to the life of Catholic University.

The report quoted an address given by Pope Paul VI to theologians in 1966 emphasizing the unique role of theology in the renewed postconciliar Church. The Holy Father had noted that theologians hold a "midway position between the faith of the Church and the Church's Magisterium", a role that called them to answer "questions which arise when [the Catholic] faith is compared with actual life". Theologians were to "interpret the general mental outlook of our age and the experiences of men in order to understand and resolve their questions in the light of salvation history".[5] The report then connected these words of Paul VI to a statement issued by the CTSA in December 1966 about the right and even the duty of theologians to dissent from theological opinions taught by the Magisterium:

> We call attention to a possible danger of confusion between doctrines of faith and matters of theology. The latter holds an exalted but al-

---

[5] Paul VI, from *Libentissimo Sane Animo*, October 2, 1966, in *Report of the School of Sacred Theology*, 1.

ways ancillary position in the Church. Theological opinions do not of themselves call for the assent of faith. To hold theological views contrary even to more common theological opinions does not of itself put a theologian in conflict with the doctrinal teachings of the Church.

The invocation of this position of the CTSA, presented in light of Pope Paul's words, manifested a distinct agenda on the part of the CUA School of Theology: certain "theological opinions" of the Magisterium were not in touch with "actual life", the "experiences of men", and "the general outlook of our age", and so it was the right and even the duty of theologians to hold and teach views contrary to these "opinions". The teaching of the Catholic Church, particularly her moral teaching, was somehow incompatible with "actual life" and needed to be "mediated" (translation: adapted, changed, loosened up) by a generation of new, young theologians who were implicitly wiser and more pastorally sensitive than the bishops who guarded the deposit of faith.

Such dissent was lauded by the May 20, 1967, report as an example of the "humble and courageous freedom of expression" that paragraph 62 of *Gaudium et Spes* had called for on the part of all of the Christian faithful "about those matters in which they enjoy competence".[6] The report thus asserted—in the name of Vatican II—the competence of theologians over and above that of bishops, who were presumably too out of touch with the exigencies of "actual life" to be able to teach Christian faith and morals adequately and effectively. By disagreeing with the bishops and the Magisterium, the School of Theology asserted, theologians were in fact serving the truth: "We are at your service, but precisely for this reason we lay claim to your understanding support, so that we may pursue our increasing task free of unfounded suspicions. Unless the loyalty of the theologian to the Church is presupposed, fruitful theological endeavor will be hindered." Indeed, the theologians argued that it was their very loyalty to the Church that impelled them to speak out at this critical juncture on behalf of freedom, openness, and dialogue against the restricting bonds of clerical authority.

The School of Theology then called for new procedural norms that would govern the relationship between it and the bishops. These norms

---

[6] *Report of the School of Sacred Theology*, 2.

followed upon the above definition of "service to the Church by loyal dissent" by proposing a balance of five essential "values" to be fostered by the procedures of the university:

1) The rights and duties of the bishops in their divinely given offices.

2) The good of the entire Catholic community in the United States of America.

3) The rights and duties of the Catholic theological faculties in the United States of America.

4) The rights and duties of the intellectual community in Catholic higher education.

5) The individual human rights and duties of all concerned.

These norms listed the prerogative of the bishops first, but in fact they equated the authority of bishops with that of theologians and of the "entire Catholic community". The bishops' teaching was described as one value among many that had to be considered in discussing and formulating the Church's teaching. While the report acknowledged that the balance between the views of bishops and those of theologians was always a delicate matter, it also asserted that the status of Catholic University as a pontifical university created such a unique situation vis-à-vis the authority of the Church that it required unique procedural norms for the teaching of theology.

A set of procedural norms was proposed by the theologians, to be used "in the event of conflict (real or apparent) between any member (or members) of the School of Sacred Theology of The Catholic University of America and any member (or members) of the American Episcopate." All communication was to be mediated via the new theological commission of the National Conference of Catholic Bishops (NCCB). This commission would inform the dean of the School of Theology of any concern, and the matter would first be investigated internally by the faculty. The faculty would then make a report, take any necessary action, and inform the commission of how the matter had been resolved. The theologians hoped that such a procedure would be able to resolve most cases: "It is anticipated that normally this procedure would suffice to clarify and to resolve the theological problems that have arisen."

Such self-management of the School of Theology was expected to suffice in the vast majority of cases. It would be only in an "exceptional and unlikely case" that any further recourse would be necessary. In such a rare case, the commission was to ask the CTSA to appoint an ad hoc committee of scholars to investigate the matter further. This committee (of professional theologians) would then report its findings to the commission. It could hardly be imagined that the recommendations of professional theologians would not be acceptable to the commission, but in that "altogether extraordinary event", the matter would then be referred to the entire NCCB for investigation. In this situation, further described as "most unusual", the theologian would have the right to call witnesses in his defense. It was recommended that other fields of possible conflict would likewise be best resolved in a similar fashion through the mediation of professional associations such as the CTSA, the College Theological Society, the Catholic Biblical Association, or the Canon Law Society of America.

The potential role of the American bishops in overseeing the doctrinal integrity of the CUA School of Theology was clearly defined by its own professors in May 1967: they were to intervene as infrequently as possible. Indeed, it would be unusual and most extraordinary that a theologian would ever be investigated by the bishops. Instead, the monitoring of any controversy was to be accomplished through the mediation of various societies of experts with competence in these matters, which by implication the bishops did not possess. The maintenance of doctrinal integrity within the School of Theology would ideally be an entirely autonomous endeavor.

The *Report of the School of Sacred Theology* was presented by the professors at a joint meeting between representatives of the board of trustees and the ad hoc Committee on University Government, which had been formed by the university faculty. At this meeting the faculty representatives expressed hope that a new spirit of collaboration would mark the previously strained relationship between the trustees, the administration, and the faculty of CUA.[7] The report proposed that the

---

[7] "A Statement to a Joint Meeting of Representatives of the Board of Trustees and of

faculty strike had been a symptom of much larger problems—namely, the absence of communication and consultation between the university administration and the faculty, the arbitrary and overcentralized nature of the university's authority structure, and the absence of a long-range plan for the university's future. The combined effect of all these situations was a "deterioration of confidence within the University", a loss of prestige within the American academic community (especially the Association of American Universities), and an urgent risk that the impending decennial accreditation visit of the Middle States Association in the fall of 1967 would result in an "adverse report" for CUA.

The theologians also boldly proposed the remedy for CUA's troubles: the clerical structure of authority that governed the university must be eliminated or at the very least minimized. Their report made several demands regarding the restructuring (essentially the de-clericalizing) of the CUA administration: that five faculty members be named to the board of trustees, that one of these be admitted to the board's Executive Committee, that the academic senate's structure be revised to make it more representative of the entire university, that the requirement that the rector and vice-rector be priests be eliminated, that a new interim rector be named immediately, and that the board choose the new rector from a list of candidates put forward by the university faculty. These proposals had been made, the report noted, by the Committee on University Government, which had been appointed by the "virtually unanimous action" of over four hundred faculty members, united in their "pervasive conviction that the normal mechanisms of university government have broken down". In the aftermath of the Curran controversy and the university strike, there could be no more business as usual at CUA. In order to serve basic justice, implement the vision of Vatican II, and salvage the national reputation of CUA among American universities, the faculty was demanding a complete overhaul of the administrative structure of the university.

---

an Ad Hoc Committee on University Government of the Catholic University of America", 1, "Faculty Assembly 1965–1978" box, "Faculty Assembly 1966–1967" folder, ACUA.

The Position of Dean Kevane and
the School of Education

The remarkable and unprecedented show of support for Father Curran during the April 1967 strike, although it presented itself as a unanimous and spontaneous movement in the name of freedom and justice, was in reality not without opposition. Despite the deafening cry defending Curran as a victim of injustice at the hands of the board of trustees, a minority position supporting the board's action sought to make its small voice heard, agreeing wholeheartedly with Curran's supporters that the issues at stake in his dismissal were far greater and more far-reaching than simply the immediate situation. As the protesters outside the CUA library rallied around the cause of academic freedom, another group likewise sought to express their opinion about the Curran controversy and its implications for the fate of Catholic higher education throughout the United States. This exercise of freedom brought about a serious conflict within the Catholic University community for much of the 1967–1968 academic year and ultimately led to the expulsion of one of its members. This lesser-known controversy, directly related to and consequent upon what is now known as the Curran affair, began when Monsignor Eugene Kevane, dean of the CUA School of Education, asked some difficult questions about the implications of Father Curran's case. In so doing, he effectively sacrificed his academic career for the sake of what he believed were the higher principles of truth and fidelity to the Magisterium of the Catholic Church.

In 1967 Eugene Kevane[8] was completing his third year as dean and his ninth year as a member of the CUA faculty. The fifty-four-year-old

---

[8] Kevane's (1913–1996) published works include *Augustine the Educator: A Study in the Fundamentals of Christian Formation* (Westminster, Md.: Newman, 1964), *The Lord of History: Christocentrism and the Philosophy of History* (Boston: Daughters of St. Paul, 1980), and *Teaching the Catholic Faith Today* (Boston: Daughters of St. Paul, 1982). In 1969, after leaving Catholic University, Kevane founded the Notre Dame Pontifical Catechetical Institute and committed his priestly ministry to the development of catechetics. He authored the *Faith and Life* catechetical series in widespread use throughout the United States. See Margaret M. Fitzgerald, "Rev. Msgr. Michael Eugene Kevane—In Memoriam", *Hebrew Catholic* 64 (Winter 1997), 11–15, http://www.hebrewcatholic.net/msgr-eugene-kevane/.

priest had been ordained for the Diocese of Sioux City, Iowa, in 1937 and, after serving as a chaplain in the United States Army Air Forces during the Second World War, had devoted his priesthood to Catholic education. During his tenure as dean, Kevane worked to establish a prominent faculty for the CUA School of Education and to update the school's curriculum to incorporate classes addressing new developments in the field of education such as educational technology, international and comparative studies, and programs for exceptional children. Meticulously organized and unswervingly loyal to his sense of duty to the Church, Kevane had marked his life by service and scholarship. He understood his role at Catholic University as having both the privilege and honor of directly assisting the American bishops in their mission by teaching educators how to teach the content of the Catholic faith to the next generation. Kevane was greatly disturbed by the position staked out by Curran in his clash with the board of trustees, and he believed that the principle of academic freedom invoked by the School of Theology in Curran's defense also gave him the right to voice his disagreement with Curran's position. Kevane may thus also be described as a dissenter, in that he dared to disagree with the dissenting theologians at the moment of their greatest popularity. How that dissent was received by the champions of academic freedom raises provocative questions about the true nature of the openness and tolerance expressly avowed by Charles Curran's supporters as their guiding principles.

When the controversy over Father Curran's dismissal first erupted in April 1967, the School of Education passed a resolution[9] with a notably different tone from those of the schools that declared themselves to be in solidarity with the School of Theology. In a statement issued on April 20, 1967, the School of Education announced that it would "refrain from passing judgment on the Father Curran case" until the theological commission of the Bishops' Conference reviewed it. The school professed its loyalty to the Holy See and to the United States Conference of Catholic Bishops, "especially in the area of the teaching of Sacred Doctrine on all levels of education". If professors are not in union with the "doctrine and government" of the Church, the School of Education declared, they "are no longer within the Catholic Church". These professors refused to join the faculty strike due

---

[9] "Statement of the School of Education", April 20, 1967, box 12, AMK.

to their "obligation in conscience" to honor the just rights of their students. "The embodiment of knowledge and wisdom on religious matters is not to be found in the group of scholars and specialists in the Sacred Sciences," they wrote, "but rather in the Successors of the Apostles, in whom as a body the charism of religious truth dwells." This statement was sent by Kevane to the various other schools of the university and was introduced by a cover letter stating that "the stand of the School of Education on this point reflects the position of true Catholic educators."[10]

The School of Education believed that the real issue at stake in the Curran controversy was the authority of the Magisterium. The education professors perceived the walkout orchestrated by the School of Theology to be a direct challenge to the doctrinal and ecclesial authority of the American bishops, not only at CUA but also within the entire Catholic Church in the United States. By refusing to join the protest, the School of Education stood in support of the juridical authority of the bishops over Catholic higher education.

The reaction on the CUA campus against the School of Education's statement was intense. The School of Theology was justifying its admittedly radical action by invoking the principles of academic freedom and basic human rights. When the School of Education refused to cooperate, the School of Theology accused it of being opposed to both of these goods. So strong was the outcry against the School of Education that on Sunday, April 23, Kevane met with four of his fellow professors to write a "clarifying statement",[11] which began by noting the completely abnormal situation that had arisen at Catholic University. There was so much confusion on campus, it said, that "reasonable discussion of the problem has become impossible, and the conduct of normal functions of the University has ceased, *de facto*, to exist." The statement reiterated the School of Education's allegiance to the doctrine and authority of the Catholic Church, yet it also attempted to be conciliatory by affirming a certain limited agreement with the School of Theology on the question of academic freedom. It declared the School of Education's "sympathy and solidarity with the majority of the members of the Faculty body of the University in their legitimate

---

[10] Kevane to the other schools of CUA, April 20, 1967, box 12, AMK.
[11] "Clarifying Statement of the School of Education", April 23, 1967, box 12, AMK.

position concerning the protection of academic freedom and of human rights wherever applicable to the present case". The School of Education also declared that it would temporarily suspend classes, "hoping for the restoration of normal conditions for effective teaching at the earliest possible moment". It expressed its grave concern for the students, who had the right to receive credit for the courses that had been suspended and to take the comprehensive examinations that had been postponed. The clarification was thus a practical concession to the fact that the entire university had been brought to a standstill, as well as a declaration of limited agreement with the stated reasons for the walkout of students and faculty.

Kevane explained the position of the School of Education in a *National Catholic Register* interview published soon after the Curran walkout.[12] The central question regarding the Curran controversy, he said, was what role the Magisterium was to have in the teaching of theology. This role had not been "abrogated by Vatican II"; it remained essential because "the purity and integrity of our faith depends upon the sacredness of our teaching authority vested in the Holy See and the Bishops." Kevane explained that the role of the Magisterium in the theology department of Catholic universities was not a threat to the American value of academic freedom in secular disciplines. "We stand foursquare for academic freedom for lay professors in the natural sciences and disciplines", he said. "We are not sure the priest-professor's academic freedom [in the sacred sciences] is to be defined in exactly the same way." Furthermore, those who were redefining academic freedom in a way that put it at odds with the legitimate authority of the Magisterium of the Church formed a grave threat to CUA's identity. Their attack on the Church's legitimate authority, said Kevane, was carefully considered and not simply a spontaneous outburst against injustice. Kevane spoke of an "organized effort to despoil our university of its Pontifical character, namely, its statutory bond with the Holy See and the U.S. Bishops' Conference. . . . You even get the feeling they seem to want to sever these connections, . . . to sever this bond that makes us what we are." By their open refusal to obey the authority of the bishops in the case of Curran, Kevane maintained, the Catholic University faculty (and the students who followed them) had directly

---

[12] "Double-Edged Issue: Freedom and Authority", *National Catholic Register*, May 7, 1967, 1.

attacked the very source of Catholic University's greatness. The consequences of this attack, said Kevane, would surely be disastrous for the future of the university, of Catholic education in the United States, and indeed of the entire Catholic Church in America.

The School of Theology soon responded with a vehement defense against its "public calumniation" by the School of Education.[13] At its faculty meeting on May 17, 1967, Dean Schmitz led the passage of a resolution "Concerning Issues Raised by the School of Education", which specifically responded to its two resolutions as well as Kevane's interview in the *Register*. The School of Theology affirmed the value of "responsible dissent" and the right to disagree within a university community yet declared that "right reason demands a reply when an entire school of a university has been publicly calumniated."

The theology professors disagreed vehemently with the account of events that had been given by the School of Education. The Curran walkout was not marked by "confusion" and a lack of "reasonable discussion"; rather the CUA faculty had given almost unanimous consent to cease functioning until Curran was rehired. The School of Education had caused a great amount of trouble by "injecting" the question of the authority of the Magisterium into the matter, said the theology professors. The issue was exclusively an academic and administrative matter; it was not doctrinal or theological, nor did it involve the teaching authority of the Church. Finally, the School of Theology took offense at the way the School of Education had professed its loyalty to the Magisterium in its resolutions, implying that the School of Theology had been disloyal:

> We resent and repudiate the implication relative to the School of Theology when the School of Education saw fit on this occasion to reaffirm its own loyalty to the Holy See and the American Hierarchy. . . . Their statement . . . [implies] serious deficiencies on the part of the School of Theology. . . . In context these statements are nothing short of libelous.

The theology professors explained that their role as theologians implied neither submission nor obedience to the bishops (such an understanding of ecclesiastical authority was decidedly preconciliar) but was

---

[13] "Concerning Issues Raised by the School of Education," resolution of the School of Theology, May 17, 1967, box 12, AMK.

rather a relationship of mutual collaboration in which the theologians could assert their views on at least an equal footing with those of the Magisterium. By claiming that the hierarchical Magisterium held "the charism of religious truth" within the Church, the School of Education had, in the opinion of the School of Theology, denied the teaching of Vatican II:

> We marvel at those members of the School of Education who "hold firmly to the fact that the embodiment of knowledge and wisdom on religious matters is not to be found in the group of scholars and specialists in the Sacred Sciences, but rather in the Successors of the Apostles in whom as a body the charism of religious truth dwells" (Statement of April 20, 1967). This is in open contradiction not only to the doctrinal teaching of the Second Vatican Council but to the clear statement of Pope Paul VI to an assembly of theologians on October 2, 1966: "Divine truth is preserved in the whole Christian community by the Holy Spirit."

The May 17, 1967, statement of the School of Theology was a perfect expression of postconciliar theology, with its call for a "pluridimensional Magisterium", in which statements of the Church's hierarchy were to be subject to the approval of contemporary theologians.[14] Unity with the Magisterium in no way implied obedience to the hierarchy. Theologians had a right and a duty to dialogue with the Magisterium in pursuit of the truth and if need be even to dissent from the Magisterium, as an expression of loyalty, so as to make the bishops more open to and aware of the working of the Holy Spirit within the Church. The School of Education, on the other hand, maintained that union with the Magisterium did in fact imply obedience in matters relating to theology.

Kevane responded promptly on May 19 with a letter to Dean Schmitz in which he attempted to explain that the position his school had taken had not been intended as a judgment against the School of Theology.[15] He expressed his regret that such an "unfortunate" interpretation had been made. The only intention of the School of Education, according to Kevane, had been to bring clarity to their "position as Catholic educators regarding a problem which the news media were pub-

---

[14] See Richard A. McCormick, "The Teaching of the Magisterium and the Theologians", *CTSA Proceedings* 24 (1969): 245.

[15] Kevane to Schmitz, May 19, 1967, box 13, AMK.

licizing as involving doctrinal as well as academic questions". Here Kevane referred to the numerous news accounts that stated Curran had been dismissed because he held doctrinally unorthodox views in moral theology. The secular media had presented the CUA strike as a protest against the teaching authority of the Church. Thus, the School of Education had merely wished to clarify its principles: "The School of Education did not introduce the doctrinal issue, but merely made reference to it in a declaration of principle that had no direct nor personal implications on the position adopted by the School of Theology in the case of Father Curran." Kevane also stated that the School of Education recognized it was not competent in theological matters and had no desire to enter into "theological polemics" of any kind. Rather, the faculty had simply "exercised the right of free expression of [their] own views" as educators and as free men. It was their heartfelt wish that, for the good of Catholic University and the entire Church, a spirit of mutual understanding and cooperation would prevail among all the faculty of the university. Kevane expressed his willingness to discuss the matter personally with Schmitz if he so desired. The tone of his letter was apologetic for any misunderstanding and hopeful that in the future there would be collaboration and dialogue within the CUA academic community.

Despite Kevane's hopefulness, there was to be no future collaboration between the Schools of Theology and Education during his tenure as dean. Just as the majority opinion within the School of Theology and within the greater university community had overwhelmingly supported Curran, so now it overwhelmingly turned against Kevane. As the academic year 1966–1967 came to a close, a movement against Kevane took shape that would culminate in his dismissal as dean in the spring of 1968.

Kevane was well aware of the smoldering resentments on campus in the aftermath of the faculty strike. In a handwritten note to Archbishop Krol on May 17, 1967, Kevane stated that if CUA gave the appearance of having returned to tranquility, this was only the result of a silence generated by fear: "There are members of the School of Theology who will never speak their minds in public, out of a fear or 'terror' that has taken over here."[16] They would talk freely, said Kevane, only if there were "the privacy of a canonical visitation". Kevane enclosed a sampling

---

[16] Kevane to Krol, May 17, 1967, box 34a, ACK.

of the many notes of support, admiration, and gratitude he had received from various educators around the country for the position he had taken in the Curran controversy.[17]

Krol replied to Kevane with a short letter in which he indicated that he was well aware that matters were far from settled at CUA:

> The final chapter on the disturbance has not, in my judgment, yet been written; albeit this is a chapter that may well be written by the people who had been contributing their nickels, dimes, quarters and dollars annually for the support of the University. I hope I am wrong —and yet I have had evidences [*sic*] this will be the reaction of some people.[18]

Krol was prescient in his understanding that the events at CUA would not only continue to cause tumult in the Church in the United States but also cause outrage among the American laity. These lay faithful expected, rightly or wrongly, that the professors of Catholic University, whose salaries they paid by their generous donations, would teach the faith in union with the Magisterium, whose authority they recognized as definitive in matters of faith and morals. The School of Theology dismissed this expectation as containing a simplistic or preconciliar understanding of the authority of the Magisterium. No less than the School of Education, the School of Theology was intent on seeing the practical implementation of a proper understanding of the authority of the Magisterium in the academic life of CUA.

At the end of April 1967, Charles Curran could be said to have won round one in his contest with the American bishops. All who were involved understood that the struggle was far from over, and both sides still hoped that their interpretation would prevail as time progressed. During the following academic year, 1967–1968, CUA would see two significant developments: the advancement of Curran's interpretation of the practical authority of the Magisterium and the ascendancy of the AAUP's definition of academic freedom contained in the "Land O'Lakes Statement". These trends would culminate in the "Statement of Dissent" from *Humanae Vitae* on July 30, 1968. Before that, however, they would result in the dismissal of Monsignor Kevane as the dean of the School of Education. The story now turns to a pivotal debate that occurred at CUA during the 1967–1968 academic year.

---

[17] Ibid.
[18] Krol to Kevane, June 3, 1967, box 34a, ACK.

5

Institutional Developments
at CUA: 1967–1968

In the months following the Curran controversy, Catholic University underwent significant structural and administrative changes that would contribute in no small part to the further development of the culture of dissent initiated by Curran and his supporters.[1] At the April 1967 board meeting (the same meeting at which the board decided not to renew Curran's contract), the trustees created a new Survey and Objectives Committee to evaluate the administrative structure of the university and to assess its immediate and long-term goals in the rapidly changing environment of American higher education. This committee was chaired by board member Carroll A. Hochwalt and included four archbishops, five laymen, and three faculty representatives.[2] Hochwalt believed that Catholic higher education was in need of "overhauling and renewal". At his direction, the committee hired the academic consulting firm Heald, Hobson, and Associates to recommend improvements to CUA's administration. Meanwhile, in the fall of 1967, the Middle States Association of Colleges and Secondary Schools (MSA) made its decennial accrediting visitation to CUA. The confluence of the work of these advising bodies led to significant and rapid changes

---

[1] For a basic summary and chronology of this process see C. Joseph Nuesse, *The Catholic University of America: A Centennial History* (Washington, D.C.: 1990), 420–32.

[2] Archbishops Krol, O'Boyle, Hannan, and Cody served on this committee, as well as laymen John Clarke of Chicago, Leo A. Daly of Omaha, Daniel J. Donohue of Los Angeles, and Stephen Jackson and Charles P. Maloney of Washington. The faculty representatives were Deans James P. O'Connor, Donald E. Marlowe, and Reverend Frederick R. McManus. See Nuesse, *The Catholic University of America: A Centennial History*, 421.

to the administrative structure of CUA during the year following the Curran strike.

The Working Paper on Objectives

As part of the accreditation process, the Survey and Objectives Committee was charged with formulating the objectives of CUA. On November 1, 1967, Dean James P. O'Connor sent to all the deans of the various schools a copy of the *Tentative Working Paper on the Objectives of the Catholic University of America*.[3] O'Connor's cover letter explained that the draft had been prepared by a faculty committee led by Dean Donald E. Marlowe and was the result of widespread consultation.[4] Comments had been solicited from each school of the university and from over forty faculty members. The paper identified five major areas of concern: academic freedom, graduate studies, theological studies, American academic life, and service. The introduction of the paper provides a key to understanding how the faculty understood themselves and the role of a university at what all agreed was a critical moment in the history of CUA:

> A university is a community of scholars, both masters and novices, set apart to discover, preserve, and impart truth in all its forms. Essentially it is a free and autonomous center for study. In practice it is also an agency serving the needs of human society. It must possess in sufficient abundance the means and the personnel necessary to achieve these ends.
>
> A Catholic university has a further trust to give its proper intellectual and academic witness to the heritage of Christian faith and humanism. Therefore it welcomes the collaboration of all men and scholars of good will who, through this process of study and reflection, contribute to that heritage.
>
> A Catholic university in our nation must be a worthy member of the American academic community. Its stature will be judged by the standards and procedures accepted and honored in American institutions. Hence, it must achieve and cherish its rightful place within the academic world.

---

[3] CUA Committee on Survey and Objectives, *A Tentative Working Paper on the Objectives of the Catholic University of America*, box 1, AMK.

[4] O'Connor to CUA faculty, November 1, 1967, box 13, AMK.

An institution designated as THE CATHOLIC UNIVERSITY OF AMERICA has particular responsibilities to serve, within its province, as an American and as a Catholic university with both national and international concerns. It must respond to the needs and aspirations of the people who gave it birth, sustain it, and in it place their hopes.

The three terms *university*, *Catholic*, and *American* spelled out in the introduction all had a role to play in determining the university's objectives, and each was presented as being somewhat in tension with the others.

The paper carefully defined certain terms and goals. *Academic freedom* meant that scholars would be free to search for the truth "in an atmosphere where freedom is fostered and where the only constraint upon truth is truth itself". CUA's focus on *graduate studies* meant that the university must strive to achieve a certain "intellectual respectability" within the American academic community so that it could form true intellectual leaders. The *advancement of theological studies* was an area of special concern to the university because of its religious affiliation, and its desire was to become a true national center of such theological study. In describing how Catholic University was to make a contribution to *American academic life*, the paper set the goal that CUA "should occupy a place in the American academic community comparable to that held by some half dozen excellent, medium-sized, privately endowed, graduate-oriented institutions". This ambitious goal was declared to be attainable due to the "stronger potential base of support" that CUA enjoyed in comparison with other Catholic universities in the United States. Finally, CUA would provide a *service* to the Church and to the nation by its high-quality research and its collaboration with the international academic community, the federal government in Washington, and the urban community of Washington, D.C.

Bearing in mind the freshness of the Curran controversy, the *Tentative Working Paper* is noteworthy more for what it did not say than for what it did say: it made no mention whatsoever of the role of the Magisterium in the life of the university or of the juridical relationship between CUA and the American bishops other than the vague reference made to the university's "religious affiliation". Combined with its definition of academic freedom, the paper seemed to uphold and promote the principles of the AAUP. An unspecified reference to "Christian heritage" coupled with the constant repetition of the importance of being respected by the American academic community added to the impression that the writers of the paper were Curran supporters.

Kevane's Evaluation and Position

Two days after the *Tentative Working Paper* was distributed to the faculty, Kevane sent a memorandum to the academic senate recommending a series of revisions to the draft.[5] His assessment of the paper, sent on November 3, 1967, provides an excellent summary of Kevane's view of the nature of Catholic higher education and displays his keen understanding of what was really at stake in the debate over academic freedom then transpiring in American higher education.

Kevane saw the need for a more exact definition of a specifically Catholic university. It was all very well, he wrote, to define "a university in the natural order", but in the context of the prevailing ideological currents within the American academic community there was a danger that the words *university* and *Catholic* were seen as being in conflict, if not diametrically opposed to one another. Defining academic freedom as absolute autonomy created "the danger of precluding a proper openness for the quality denoted by the adjective 'Catholic' . . . so that the adjective 'Catholic' becomes merely nominal, and not a term describing the actual quality of excellence of a university that is Catholic." Thus, the working paper's opening statement that a university is "essentially . . . a free and autonomous center for study" struck Kevane as ambiguous, for this was the "ideological hallmark of the secularized university". The exact meaning of *freedom* at a pontifical university needed to be explained.

Kevane likewise saw potential for confusion in the idea that the university's purpose was a general role of serving the "needs of human society". Such service could be effective only if it kept its specific focus on serving "a particular, indeed theandric, society, defined in Vatican II in terms of 'The People of God' ". Only by accomplishing this particular mission could the more general mission be accomplished.

A specifically Catholic mission implied that CUA's personnel must

---

[5] Kevane to the academic senate, memorandum, November 3, 1967, box 4, AMK.

be properly qualified. How important, then, was the "good will" mentioned by the paper—namely, the good will of the faculty toward the specifically Catholic heritage espoused by the university. Those who did not have "a good will toward this heritage", on the other hand, could not teach students without compromising the mission of the university. In fact, if their presence was tolerated in the name of a merely secular idea of freedom, Catholic University "would actually lose its freedom to be itself". It was essential, Kevane argued, that CUA be completely and uncompromisingly Catholic in its identity. He objected to the ambiguity of the statement in the *Tentative Working Paper* calling for CUA to give "witness to the heritage of Christian faith and humanism". He argued that the word *Christian* should be replaced by the word *Catholic* in order "to avoid all obscurity and ambiguity, stating 'The Catholic Faith and Christian Humanism'".

Kevane also expressed concern about the desire that CUA be "a worthy member of the American academic community" whose "stature will be judged by the standards and procedures accepted and honored in American institutions." This "obscure phrasing", he said, made it possible to introduce a "secularized ideology . . . so that our Catholic University would actually lose its freedom to be itself". While it was certainly a legitimate aspiration to be "fully American" in the realm of research and the proper autonomy of each discipline, Kevane cautioned that it was imperative to be on guard against "unsound philosophies and ideologies that undermine even the American heritage". The American tradition of religious liberty recognized the right of a university to be committed to a particular religious identity as part of its exercise of freedom. To attempt to deny that identity in the name of an intolerant secularism was, said Kevane, inherently un-American.

Kevane also sought to amend the paper's definition of academic freedom. While the phrase "the only constraint upon truth is truth itself" had a catchy ring, he said, it raised serious questions: What is the relationship of revealed truth to the mission of a Catholic university? If a Catholic university refuses to uphold revealed truth as taught authoritatively by the Magisterium of the Church, could it still claim that it was freely choosing to be a Catholic university? If the hierarchical Magisterium is understood to be a constraint upon seeking the truth, is there not a fundamental misunderstanding of the Magisterium's role in the service of revealed truth? "Respect for and love of the Sacred

Magisterium, with obedience to the procedures that make it actually operative on the human scene," wrote Kevane, "do not put a constraint on truth, for the Magisterium is the living voice of Him who is 'Truth Itself.'" A Catholic university most perfectly exercises its freedom to seek the truth by perfect submission to the teaching of the Magisterium. Anything less, said Kevane, would imply a lack of faith in the teaching authority of the Church and hence in the Catholic faith that is the heart of the specific mission of a Catholic university.

Kevane's argument responded cleverly to those who were setting up freedom and authority in opposing corners of the academic ring. By arguing that a Catholic university could be free to accomplish its specific mission only by remaining faithful to the Magisterium, Kevane turned the argument back against those who wanted the oversight of the bishops removed from CUA in the name of academic freedom. By explicitly invoking Vatican II and its emphasis on the Church as the People of God, Kevane attempted to refute the argument of Charles Curran and his supporters that they were on the side of renewal while Kevane and his ilk were on the side of an outdated and restricting tradition.

The fundamental issue dividing Kevane and Curran and the determining factor in their respective approaches to the nature of academic freedom was the question of faith in the divinely guided nature of the Church's Magisterium. Kevane believed that the guidance of the bishops was the essential key to the university's mission to pursue the truth, while Curran believed that the guidance of the bishops had become a grave obstacle to this same mission. Both men acted accordingly.

Kevane reflected more deeply on the issues that he believed lay at the root of CUA's crisis of identity in letters he wrote in late August 1967 both to his diocesan ordinary, Bishop Joseph M. Mueller of Sioux City, and to Dr. Donald E. Marlowe of the academic senate.[6] His correspondence on this topic is significant not only because of the ideas contained therein but because they were specifically endorsed by CUA's chancellor, Archbishop Patrick O'Boyle of Washington. O'Boyle wrote to Bishop Mueller complimenting Kevane's insights as "especially good". Philosophically and theologically, wrote O'Boyle, they "came right to

---

[6] Kevane to Mueller, August 21, 1967; Kevane to Marlowe, August 21, 1967; box 4, "Objectives of CUA" folder, AMK.

the point and indicated what is needed in the reorganization of the University".[7] O'Boyle asked Bishop Mueller's permission to present Kevane's comments to the Survey and Objectives Committee.

In his correspondence with his bishop, Kevane expressed his conviction that the controversies afflicting CUA could be traced back to the restructuring of the university in the 1930s:

> The point I was making regarding the purpose of The Catholic University of America concerned the aberration from that purpose that set in about 1930, when an internal re-structuring took place upon the image and model of the secular university. It has left this University more "secularized" than, for instance, Johns Hopkins at Baltimore, and provides a standing open door to the contemporary philosophical currents that are in such contrast to the philosophical fundamentals urged upon us by the Magisterium. I believe that this longer background must needs be considered if any *sanatio in radice* for The Catholic University of America is to be effected at the present time, or if advantage is to be taken of the current opportunity to renew this University according to the mind of Vatican II and its authentic interpretation by the Holy See.

Kevane saw the Curran controversy not as an aberration but as the culmination of a long process of secularization that threatened not only CUA but the entire structure of Catholic education in the United States. This process began at CUA, according to Kevane, with the establishment in 1930 of the graduate School of Arts and Sciences, which eventually included "formally avowed atheists" among its ranks. The secularists on the faculty were, in his opinion, an organized group that had purposes alien to the Catholic faith—namely, "achieving 'secularization' of or exercising control over the University". Little by little, Catholic University had embraced a secular model of operation and self-understanding while paying lip service to a certain Catholic and religious identity. The result was inevitable: the secular element slowly but surely pushed aside the Catholic element, and the juridical oversight of the bishops was seen by many as an impediment to success.

Kevane also focused his critique on the 1937 statutes affirmation: "The aim of the Catholic University of America is to search out truth

---

[7] O'Boyle to Mueller, September 7, 1967, box 4, AMK.

scientifically."[8] Kevane noted that the ambiguity of that phrase had become "increasingly fateful for over forty years". On the continent of Europe and in Christian philosophical circles everywhere, he explained, the phrase implied that truth is sought "according to the distinctive methods of theological science, philosophical science, and the empirical sciences", which are different from each other. "In our English-speaking world of British Empiricism and American Pragmatism, however, a powerful pressure has been mounting for decades at The Catholic University of America to interpret this basic purpose in terms of philosophical Positivism, as if it meant 'exclusively by methods of research proper to the Empirical sciences.' "

Such exclusivity meant that theological methodology was being replaced by that of the empirical sciences. As a result, theology was not free to exercise itself according to its own proper methodology and was suffering the loss of its essential nature. "This involves a philosophical aberration," wrote Kevane, "a displacement of authentic pluralism in research methodology by a monolithic approach and mentality." The truth was better served, reasoned Kevane, by openness to diverse methodologies than by a narrow-minded insistence on the empirical method. In this openness lay the greatness of both the Catholic *and* the American traditions of education, and Kevane was convinced that such authentic pluralism was the key to CUA's living up to the full potential that its name implied.

Kevane maintained that the situation in which CUA found itself necessitated the implementation of intermediate practical objectives that would guard the university's freedom to be itself, that is, a pontifical Catholic university: "An institution within the People of God, participating in its post-conciliar renewal, according to the mind and documents of Vatican II authentically interpreted by the Holy See". According to *Lumen Gentium*, this conciliar renewal meant that "everything should proceed *sub ductu magisterii* [under the guidance of the Magisterium]."[9] This, said Kevane, was the unique mission of a pontifical university. It would be inherently false to think that such a university was "univocally like all other universities". It was indeed true to say that it was a university in the full sense of the word, dedicated

---

[8] *The Statutes of the Catholic University of America* (1937).
[9] See *Lumen Gentium*, nos. 12, 18–29.

to teaching the truth, seeking to understand rightly the meaning of academic freedom and tolerance for diverse opinions. Yet at the same time it existed and functioned "in the higher order of the Catholic Faith", which entailed a unique methodology in the study of theology and philosophy. Kevane was emphatic that this Catholic aspect of its identity in no way hindered its mission as a university but rather enhanced it immensely:

> A university is not less a university for being "Catholic" and "Pontifical," but more so, just as a Catholic journalist is not less good as a journalist because of his quality of being a Catholic person, but rather more so in his natural good represented by journalism. So too for a Catholic medical doctor or a Catholic businessman. And so likewise for a Pontifical Catholic University. Neither the adjective "Catholic" nor the adjective "Pontifical" derogates from or destroys the noun "University." The objectives that are being articulated at this time for The Catholic University of America ought, we believe, to be definite on this point, liberating the National Pontifical University from inhibiting philosophisms for its authentic role and mission for our country and for the People of God in the United States. In last analysis, it is by being free to fulfill the qualitative excellence denoted by those two adjectives that it will exemplify fully on the human scene the natural good denoted by the noun "university."[10]

The Catholic University of America needed to have the freedom to be fully itself. Having been set on a path of secularization in the 1930s, it had embraced, along with the entire American academic community, a very narrow and exclusive definition of scientific inquiry. A broader and more pluralistic view of such inquiry understood the indispensable role of the Magisterium within the specific methodology of the theological sciences. It was Kevane's great hope that his academic peers both within CUA and without would have the open-mindedness to accept his broad and pluralistic argument. He was to find few open minds among his colleagues at CUA.

---

[10] Kevane to Marlowe, August 21, 1967, box 4, AMK.

The Evaluation of CUA by the
Middle States Association

During the same fall semester of 1967, the Middle States Association made its official decennial accreditation visitation to CUA. The evaluating team of five educators, including two administrators from Catholic institutions, submitted a formal evaluation report in October based on the findings of their visit.[11] The repeatedly emphasized message of this report was that Catholic University needed to set for itself new and clearly articulated objectives in accord with a secular model of academic freedom. A redefinition of itself was absolutely necessary in order for CUA to be accepted within the wider American academic community, an imperative made all the more urgent by the atmosphere of change and flux that had enveloped both society in general and higher education in particular. The tone of the document was one of unapologetic bias against the perceived rigidity and outdated authority of the Magisterium, while enthusiastically favoring a dynamic of "freedom", "realism", and "courageous change". It would be difficult to imagine a more clearly stated position of opposition to the involvement of the hierarchical Magisterium in higher education than that espoused by the MSA evaluation report.

From the very beginning of its report, the MSA team noted that the prevailing spirit in American higher education was one of change. This meant that if CUA were to be accepted by its peers as fully American, its administration would need to recognize that it "is an institution caught up in the compelling necessity for change and redirection". At the same time, the university was "not yet certain of the purposes which must control that change and realigning of direction". While the anger of the faculty and students who had demonstrated in support of Father Curran the previous April had given way to a new spirit of hope that new "objectives will restore pride and confidence to themselves

---

[11] *The CUA Evaluation Report for the Commission on Institutions of Higher Education of the Middle States Association of Colleges and Secondary Schools* (hereafter cited as MSA evaluation report), archives of Cardinal Lawrence Shehan, Files re CUA reorganization; Curran Case, c. 1966–1974, unprocessed, AAB. The members of the MSA evaluation team included two Catholic educators: Laurence J. McGinley, S.J., president of Fordham University from 1949 to 1963 and Norbert Hruby, president of Aquinas College in Grand Rapids, Michigan from 1969 to 1986.

and to their institution", the university needed to act quickly to define those objectives:

> During this year, a new set of objectives for the University must be thought out, understood, disseminated, accepted, permanent leadership must be obtained, a new governing structure must be established. Time and timing in these circumstances are of critical importance. Much must be done quickly, in the right order, and successfully if Catholic University is to be restored to the place it wishes to hold among the universities of America.

The MSA team was hopeful because the professors and students seemed open to such rapid change:

> The ferment at Catholic University at the present time is generally healthy. Hope has replaced frustration, self-criticism has been substituted for the complacency and self-deception that concealed rather than considered problems and weaknesses, cooperation has replaced distrust. Yet, changed attitudes cannot assist Catholic University until they can result in constructive action predicated upon widely accepted, clearly understood objectives.

The report identified four major obstacles to CUA's being an exemplary institution, structural problems within the university administration that were obstacles to the "new dynamics of change" that were sweeping American higher education.

First, the oversight of a Roman congregation hindered the freedom that was essential to the nature of a university. Catholic University's structure of authority was described as the product of two opposing dynamisms, "one European with the objectives and structures of the great Roman seminaries; the other American involving personnel and objectives in the tradition of a modern university". This analysis explained the tension at CUA as European-American, the result of different academic models and traditions of higher education. The so-called European model (meaning a model in which the authority of the Magisterium held a functional role within the life of the university) had to be discarded:

> It is clear that Catholic University cannot continue to walk down both paths any longer, and that in finding its own proper role it must

have the sympathetic understanding and freedom to act which it needs from the pertinent Roman congregation.

Academic freedom, said the MSA report, was not compatible with any real, practical oversight by the authority of the Church. There could be only one or the other, academic freedom *or* ecclesiastical oversight, and the presence of either one by definition excluded the other. According to the report's recommendations, the moment had come for CUA to make a decisive choice for academic freedom to the absolute exclusion of the juridical authority of the Holy See.

The second identified problem was related to the first: the role of the board of trustees, predominantly composed of the bishops of the United States, in the governance of the university. These bishops served interests that were at odds with the freedom needed by the university to carry out its fundamental academic mission:

> The board of trustees is predominantly the magisterium of the Church in America, a body which has always tended to be conservative in nature. Responsive to their own mission, the individual members composing this ruling hierarchy have been, and perhaps still are, characterized by individual views which accord higher priority to their own regional concerns and consequent subordination of the University's interest to them. Their responsibilities, of necessity, produce a preoccupation with parochial elementary and secondary education, and their absentee trusteeship prevents the development of appropriate concern until there is trouble of critical proportion.

Thus there were three strikes against the hierarchy's involvement in the mission of the university: they were inherently "conservative", their first concern was being local bishops rather than educators, and they were preoccupied with parochial education. Each of these problems was effectively described in the same either-or terms as in the conflict between freedom and authority: the bishops' spiritual concern of shepherding the Church was said to be inherently at odds with the university's academic concern of achieving scholarly competence and excellence.

CUA was effectively being told to choose between two mutually exclusive purposes: serving the spiritual mission of the Church or serving the academic mission of an American university. The MSA team clearly saw the presence of bishops on the board of trustees as hindering in every way the freedom of the university to be dedicated completely to its academic mission. A university could not, by definition, be governed by an authoritative Magisterium. Any idea of preserving a static and outdated orthodoxy was declared to be inherently opposed to the all-surpassing value of academic freedom.

The third problem identified by the MSA was the requirement that the rector of Catholic University be a priest, if not a bishop. The evaluation declared that a priest-rector could not effectively lead the academic community because his first loyalties were elsewhere: "His orientation has been more to the Magisterium of the Church and his board of trustees, in short his own constituency of bishops, than to the academic community over which he presides." This apparent conflict of interest led to the same dichotomies present in the first two issues: academic freedom was inhibited, the university's mission became ambiguous, and the resulting tension created at CUA "an internal pervasive mood of self-criticism which often amounts to corrosive self-disdain and disparagement". This self-criticism, according to the evaluation report, was due not merely to the particular qualities of the present rector or his administration but to the simple fact that the rector was a member of the clergy. Any priest- or bishop-rector would, by the very fact of being a clergyman, create a spirit of self-disdain at the university. To overcome these difficulties, a lay rector for CUA was essential.

Finally, the MSA report identified what it believed was the most grievous problem present in the institutional structure of the university: it had been committed to stability, while the present moment in the cultural and academic world was defined by change on every level. The report painted a picture of an irresistible tide of change that the administration of CUA had futilely and foolishly attempted to resist:

> Those who still yearn for vanished national moods of stability and harmony are no longer in leadership positions in the American academic community. It is a day of faith in flux and of a commitment to change. Ferment will be a normal condition for some time to come. An appetite for a new look is now a professional requirement. Planning

which takes account of tomorrow's needs rather than today's necessities becomes imperative in a day of rapid change.

Here was the MSA team's most revelatory statement yet, calling for faith and commitment from the leadership of CUA—not to the Catholic faith but to the flux and change that were the essence of the sixties. Authority and structure were out, while self-determination and upheaval for its own sake were in. The idea of a rector or a governing board of trustees who were members of a clerical body endowed with spiritual authority was so diametrically opposed to "tomorrow's needs" that even *having* such a structure of authority was seen as laughably outdated. "Unilateral authoritarian decisions are no longer possible in the academic community", the MSA declared (unilaterally). "They are replaced by procedures and relationships which stress community and action by consensus." A trustee, president, or rector now had a "collegial" role of a leader among equals; he was emphatically not one who possessed any kind of independent authority of governance. CUA's outdated structure exemplified what the MSA report called the "unenlightened authority and remote centralized bureaucracy" that had instigated the revolt in the greater world of higher education by militant students and faculty seeking "self-determination and representative participation". Here the MSA even invoked the Second Vatican Council, which had authoritatively called for the "increased laicization and democratization of the Church", although the report noted this had not yet happened in the constricted atmosphere of Catholic University. If this process of democratization was inevitable in the life of the wider Church, it was above all imperative that it take place within an institution of Catholic higher education.

The MSA concluded its assessment with a sweeping condemnation of CUA's outdated authority structure:

> Does the Catholic University of America understand the dictum that an institution of higher learning is incurably democratic and must operate in an atmosphere of freedom where decisions are made and policies established not through a superordination or subordination of persons and groups? The evidence is that the Catholic University of America has still largely to achieve that understanding.

With these scathing words, the MSA evaluation declared that CUA could retain its identity as "Catholic" only if that identity was redefined to eliminate *any* practical oversight by the Magisterium. Because American higher education was "incurably democratic," there was no place whatsoever within its operational structure for any hierarchical authority that claimed the power to define a priori truth, thereby taking away the academic freedom of university professors.

Moreover, the unstoppable movement toward democracy in higher education required that the title *pontifical* be eliminated from the university's name:

> What is the real meaning, value, validity and importance of being pontifical in today's America? It is an albatross around the University's neck. It is clear that Catholic University cannot continue to walk down both paths any longer, . . . it must have . . . [the] freedom to act which it needs from the pertinent Roman congregation.

In the view of the MSA, *American* and *Catholic* were two descriptors that could not admit of the other's presence in higher education, unless the meaning of *Catholic* was so modified as to mean "Catholic without the oversight of the Magisterium". In effect, the MSA was calling for the formulation of a new "American Catholic" identity for CUA and other Catholic universities, in which the word *Catholic* indicated the presence of a vaguely defined spirit or tradition but certainly did not imply the allegiance to the teaching of the Magisterium that the term *Catholic* had always implied. At this critical moment in the history of higher education, the Middle States Association was giving an ultimatum to CUA (and by implication to other schools like it): either become "American Catholic" and survive or remain "Roman Catholic" and fade away into irrelevancy. The driving force behind this absolutist either-or demand for rapid change was, of course, the ideology of academic freedom of the AAUP. This ideology was to make great inroads at CUA during the academic year 1967–1968, perhaps most significantly in the case of the dismissal of Eugene Kevane from his deanship of the School of Education. Kevane's removal was necessary in order to lay the foundation for continuing developments at CUA: dissent from the principles of the AAUP had to be removed.

6

The Campaign to Remove Dean Kevane

Acting Rector Whalen
Seeks to Replace Kevane

As the fall semester of 1967 got under way, the CUA board of trustees named Father John P. Whalen to a one-year term as acting rector of the university. Whalen, a priest of the Diocese of Albany, replaced Bishop McDonald, who had served as rector since 1957 and whose removal and replacement had been called for from all sides in the aftermath of the Curran strike. Whalen had been a theology professor since 1961 and was also the founder and head of Corpus Instrumentorum, an independent academic publishing house that was producing Father Curran's latest book on moral theology. Whalen's evident sympathy for his colleagues in the School of Theology would play a significant role in developments at CUA during his months at the helm.

On the day of his appointment, the thirty-nine-year-old Whalen held a news conference in which he described himself to the local and national media as a member of the "radical center" and a believer in "creative tension" in the Church.[1] He declared that he had entirely supported the five-day strike the previous April, describing the boycott as "in a sense creative" and affirming that those involved "were expressing very valid feelings". He said he hoped to bring "a sense of urgency and excitement" to his new position, a sense "of being overworked and being happy that we are working too hard". He called for the faculty to be less restricted: "If it is not free, I am not doing my job very well." And he confessed to being "worried about the pressures" that the hierarchy would put on him in his position as acting rector. Whalen's words show clear parallels between his thinking and that of

---

[1] "Catholic U. Strike Backed By Rector," *New York Times*, September 30, 1967.

the Middle States Association evaluation team regarding academic freedom and the role of the hierarchy in the life of Catholic University.
Given Whalen's clear connections to and sympathy for Curran and the
"American Catholic" dissenting tendency within CUA, Dean Kevane
must surely have realized that Whalen's interpretation of recent events
was diametrically opposed to that of the School of Education.

Within a very short time after Whalen's appointment, a movement
was afoot to remove Kevane from his position as dean. Those who
claimed to be "in the know" asserted that Whalen, who as acting rector held authority to name deans, would not under any circumstances
reappoint Kevane to his position.[2] When the education faculty met
for a confidence vote on the deanship in early October 1967, some of
the lay education professors indicated that they had been pressured by
faculty members in other departments to vote against Kevane. Despite
such pressure, Kevane won the vote of confidence from the School of
Education's faculty, receiving ten votes to Reverend Thomas J. Taylor's
nine. This vote would ordinarily simply be ratified by the rector.[3]

During the first week of November 1967, Kevane wrote to two bishops on the CUA board of trustees, Cardinals Krol and Cody,[4] and described a powerful group of priests and lay professors within the CUA
academic community who were doing everything in their power to
prevent his reappointment as dean, despite the fact that he had been
re-elected to his position by his own school's faculty.[5] He wrote to
the cardinals: "They may not be successful in their efforts, and there

---

[2] Letter to the Editor by Marguerite Follett, Ph.D. (member of School of Education),
National Catholic Register, December 24, 1967, AMK.

[3] Charles Curran has noted that the faculty vote at Catholic University was and is
"very, very important" due to the unique structure of CUA, whereby more importance
is given to the faculty than at almost any other American university. The reason is that
CUA is constituted along the German model of having "Ordinary Professors" who hold
"Ordinary power." As an example of this unique weight of faculty authority, Curran
noted that if the Rector/President went against the decision of the Academic senate, the
Academic senate held the right to appeal directly to the board of trustees (Personal Interview with Curran, April 15, 2009). Curran's observation sheds light on how significant and extraordinary Acting Rector Whalen's persistent campaign to dismiss Kevane
from the Deanship, thereby overturning the faculty vote of the School of Education,
truly was.

[4] Krol, Cody, and O'Boyle had all been made cardinals by Pope Paul VI at the con-
sistory of June 26, 1967.

[5] Kevane to Krol, November 6, 1967, box 12, AMK.

may be no problem on that score; on the other hand, they are bringing heavy pressure to bear on the acting rector, and may have their way." He described an environment that made it almost impossible for him to function in his position, so great was the persecution being brought against him:

> I have been almost "alone" here for some time and have to do everything in the face of an ongoing campaign of harassment and obstructionism. Realistically, I have to wonder whether I can continue to function academically in this atmosphere and under these conditions. The Catholic University of America no longer enjoys peace and freedom for academic research and educational planning in the context of the stated and published mind of the Church.

He asked the cardinals for their advice and prayers, noting that "some of the larger issues of our time are involved." He had good reason to ask for prayers, as the harassment he had been experiencing since the events of the previous April was about to intensify and come to its culmination within a few short weeks.

On November 10, 1967, the *Tower* published the agenda for the acting rector's first meeting with the board of trustees.[6] Father Whalen would be briefing the board about the MSA evaluation and also seeking the board's approval of various administrative appointments, including approval for Father Taylor to replace Monsignor Kevane as the acting dean of the School of Education. "In view of the present weakness of the school [of Education]," wrote Whalen, "it is recommended that a committee be appointed to search for an extern to be appointed as dean effective September 1, 1968."

When the trustees met on November 12, Whalen asked them to approve the replacement of Kevane.[7] The board noted that Kevane had received a majority of both the consultative vote (10-9 over Taylor) and the deliberative vote (2-1 over Taylor) of the education faculty. Whalen questioned the validity of the votes, however, due to the fact that several of the faculty members were writing their dissertations under Kevane and thus "may have felt obligated to him". Whalen enumerated a list of reasons why he felt the replacement of Kevane was

---

[6] Tom Brannan, "Report Will Brief Board of Trustees", *Tower*, November 10, 1967, 1.

[7] The account of the meeting is taken from the minutes of the CUA board of trustees, November 12, 1967, section 8, 2, box 32c, ACK.

desirable: the MSA evaluation had raised serious questions about the School of Education, Whalen had received much correspondence about the school since he had become acting rector, Kevane did not seem to have "sufficient control of the school", and academic standards in the School of Education were suffering and had been questioned by a statement of the Graduate Council on October 19, 1967. Whalen further asserted that Kevane, who held degrees in philosophy and religion, was not recognized as a scholar in the field of education.

Judge Stephen Jackson, lay member of the board, asked Whalen whether any provision had been made to give Kevane a hearing, a step that, considering the outcry just seven months earlier over Curran's dismissal without a hearing, would seem to have been quite important in any process of removing a sitting dean. Whalen responded that he did not think any hearing was necessary since Kevane would retain his position as a full-time faculty member.

Cardinal Krol then intervened in defense of Kevane, stating that he had serious questions regarding Whalen's recommendation. Krol noted that Kevane had been proposed by a majority of his own faculty, that the School of Education was a large school of the university, and that furthermore the conditions seemed to be very similar to those of the previous spring, when Curran's dismissal had resulted in a serious disturbance. Archbishop Hallinan agreed with Krol, stating that as the one who had voted against Curran's dismissal the previous spring for lack of any hearing, he saw a definite parallel in the present attempt to remove Kevane. Cardinal O'Boyle suggested that a small committee be created to investigate the matter.

Father Robert Trisco,[8] academic vice-rector, spoke up in support of Whalen's effort to remove Kevane. Trisco felt confident there was no danger of any repercussions such as had happened with Curran, since it was generally known that Whalen was going to make this recommen-

---

[8] Trisco, longtime professor of Church history in the CUA School of Theology and religious studies, was aware of hostility against Kevane but said that he himself did not share those feelings. To him the question of Kevane's replacement was a strictly procedural and administrative matter. In his position as academic vice-rector, Trisco found Kevane difficult to work with. He described Kevane as a "stubborn and inept administrator" and suggested that Kevane attempted to cover up his administrative shortcomings by defending the Magisterium (written comments submitted to the author, November 2009).

dation to the board of trustees. In fact, said Trisco, if Kevane's removal were not approved by the board, it could be "construed as a lack of confidence" of the board in the new rector. In the name of unity, then, Trisco urged the board to approve Kevane's dismissal without further delay.

Trisco's argument was not very convincing to the bishops, who continued to defend Kevane. Archbishop Dearden asked whether anyone had taken the time to help Kevane to correct any of his faults and to improve his administration of the School of Education. Archbishop Hannan contributed the observation that during his time as the auxiliary bishop of Washington he had always found Kevane both "docile and cooperative".

Again the faculty attempted to push through Kevane's dismissal. Dr. C. Joseph Nuesse, executive vice president of the university, pointed out that Kevane would not be losing his position on the faculty; he would merely be removed from the deanship. Like Trisco, Nuesse said he felt confident there would be no "explosive reaction" against his "not being reappointed".

In the end, however, the board of trustees refused to act without giving Kevane the chance to defend himself. Judge Jackson reiterated that it was imperative that the dean have the opportunity to appear and state his case. The board thus authorized O'Boyle as chancellor to create a committee that would consult with Whalen and Kevane about the most advisable action to be taken with regard to the School of Education. This committee, whose members were still to be named, was further empowered to act in the name of the trustees without any further authorization from the board. It was to act as quickly as possible. Kevane would in the meantime continue to serve as dean of the School of Education, but with the title of acting dean. The campaign to oust Kevane, which the *National Catholic Reporter* described later in November as "simply vindictive", had met a temporary glitch, but it would not be long before it came to a successful conclusion.[9]

---

[9] "Bid to Oust Strike Foe Tests New CUA Rector", *National Catholic Reporter*, November 22, 1967.

Defense of Kevane from
within the School of Education

The publication of Whalen's inflammatory words in the *Tower* about "the present weakness in the school" brought about a swift response from the School of Education in defense of its reputation and academic integrity. At the regular meeting of the CUA academic senate on November 16, 1967, six days after Whalen's report was published, Dr. Jose A. Baquero, professor of the School of Education, read a statement he and Kevane had signed that voiced the objection of the School of Education to the assertions made in the *Tower* that the school suffered from weakness.[10] Their statement declared their moral obligation to defend the reputation of their school, faculty, and students from such a destructive accusation and declared their readiness to be scrutinized by "competent, objective, and unbiased scholars". This objection was placed in the minutes, but there was never any official response from the academic senate to the School of Education, and the objection essentially did very little to stem the tide of accusations against Kevane's competency as dean.

In addition to this formal protest by the School of Education, there were also various individuals within the department who attempted to defend Kevane's reputation. On November 13, 1967, Father John P. O'Malley, O.S.A., a student in the School of Education, wrote to Cardinal Krol asking for his help so that the school would not lose Kevane. He enclosed for Krol's consideration a letter that a group of education students had written to Whalen declaring their unequivocal support for Kevane: "We affirm, without exception, that Monsignor Kevane is the finest teacher we have ever encountered in our educational experience. His classes are rich in content, in scholarship, and in presentation."[11]

These superlative words in support of Kevane are difficult to reconcile with Whalen's assertion that Kevane did not seem to have sufficient control of the School of Education. Even were Kevane not an

---

[10] Minutes of the CUA academic senate (hereafter cited as Minutes, academic senate), November 16, 1967, 298, academic senate records, box 2, "Academic Senate Minutes 1963–1968" folder, ACUA.

[11] O'Malley to Krol, November 13, 1967, box 34c, folder 33, ACK.

outstanding teacher, O'Malley wondered why there was such a move afoot to stifle him, especially since in the Curran controversy the previous spring there had been such outraged cries for academic freedom to prevail. As O'Malley and the School of Education were about to learn, the CUA professors who had rallied behind academic freedom in defending Curran were not so keen on that freedom when a fellow professor disagreed with their position. Academic freedom, it seemed, was limited to those who would use that freedom to dissent from the authority of the Magisterium. It apparently did not include the freedom to defend the Magisterium and question the dissenters.

Another strong statement defending Kevane was written on December 12, 1967, by Sister Mary Verone, S.N.D., director of the elementary education program in the School of Education. Verone, who had taught at CUA since 1939, wrote to both Cardinal Krol and Auxiliary Bishop Clarence E. Elwell[12] of Cleveland, both of whom she had known during her time working in education in Cleveland. She begged their help in preventing the removal of Kevane from the deanship. Krol found Verone's letter so illustrative that he forwarded it to Cardinals O'Boyle and Shehan and to Archbishops Hannan and Hallinan.[13] Verone's letters to Krol and Elwell, written separately but containing similar content, describe a vicious attack against Kevane. They offer a unique perspective on the true nature of the campaign against him within the academic community of Catholic University:

> Our Dean, Monsignor Kevane, is literally enduring a persecution and a martyrdom. There exists in our School of Education a clique of ambitious priests who are positively intolerable. The lay men, with the exception of one or so, are with Monsignor. The conduct of this obnoxious clique has been scandalous and shocking to the lay faculty, some of whom are not even Catholic. This situation is very serious, most disheartening and regrettable.[14]

By Verone's account, a group of "five or six priests" among the faculty of the School of Education had employed disruptive tactics against

---

[12] Clarence Elwell was the vicar general of the Diocese of Cleveland and served as Episcopal Vicar for Education. He described Sister Mary Verone favorably in his December 15, 1967, cover letter to Krol, endorsing her as "both a good mind and an exemplary religious" (box 34c, folder 33, ACK).

[13] Krol's personal notes, box 34c, folder 33, ACK.

[14] Verone to Elwell, December 12, 1967, box 34c, folder 33, ACK.

Kevane's authority at a recent faculty meeting, preventing the approval of graduate students' dissertation topics in an effort to make those students disgruntled against their dean. Verone further explained the circumstances surrounding the faculty vote on Kevane's deanship: "Faculty members were threatened if they would vote for Monsignor." She described the consultative vote in which she had participated: Kevane received ten votes, Taylor nine, and Father John Ashton[15] one. She had also witnessed the deliberative vote of the three full professors, who voted 2–1 in favor of Kevane over Taylor. The group of professors opposed to Kevane, however, could not and would not accept his twofold endorsement by the faculty, said Verone. She described how, before the election, Father Ashton told a lay faculty member, whom he was trying to persuade to vote against Kevane, "No matter how it turns out, the new rector will not appoint Monsignor Kevane." Evidently the priests aligned against Kevane had received personal assurance from Whalen that Kevane was finished as dean.

Verone's letters made clear to the bishops that the situation in the School of Education was only one part of a much bigger problem at Catholic University. Beyond the immediate controversy over Kevane, the entire mission of CUA to teach the Catholic faith in its integrity and fullness was under attack. Verone lamented the widespread confusion and unapologetic dissent that was becoming a hallmark of the catechesis offered by the priests and religious who were graduates of CUA. She maintained that dwindling contributions to CUA were a sign that faithful Catholics were outraged by the "identity crisis" it was undergoing.

In the midst of this difficult situation, Verone expressed how she was all the more grateful for Kevane's steady presence in leadership and his fidelity to the faith of the Church, and she told the bishops how much his students admired his teaching. The movement against Kevane by some of the faculty was the result of ambition and hatred of authority, she said, and it was placing a tremendous pressure and strain on him. Describing Kevane as "a man of Truth", Verone encouraged the bishops to act swiftly in his defense: "I sincerely hope that the committee assigned at the November Bishops' meeting will unearth this insidious

---

[15] John Ashton was a priest of the Diocese of Youngstown, Ohio, and professor of the School of Education.

undercurrent formed by this clique of five or six priests. The air must be cleared." Without the support of the cardinals and bishops, Verone said, the School of Education would "collapse". Her final assessment of the matter to the bishops was unflinching: "The devil has a hand in stirring up this unrest. . . . The whole thing is evil and unhealthy. They want to break him."[16]

Undoubtedly some would find Verone's rhetoric excessive. Yet this religious sister and experienced educator was keenly aware that the Catholic identity of CUA was hanging in the balance. The great irony of the situation was that those who had so vigorously campaigned in defense of academic freedom in the case of Curran were now equally vigorous in their determination to silence without a hearing the voice that had dared to oppose them.

Verone hoped that the bishops entrusted with guiding and oversee-ing CUA would by their courageous and united action put a stop to the campaign to oust her dean. Unfortunately for her and for Kevane, the board of trustees in the winter of 1967–1968 had neither the acu-ity nor the strength to defend the one voice that had defended their position during the faculty strike. The board placed Kevane's fate into the hands of the special committee, which in the end would punt it back to Whalen.

Whalen's Letter Attacking Kevane

The special committee to decide Kevane's fate met for the first time on December 16, 1967, at the Mayflower Hotel.[17] At this initial meeting it reviewed documentation in the case and asked Whalen to write a letter stating his case for seeking the removal of Kevane from the dean-ship. Whalen responded on December 22, 1967, with an exhaustive at-tack on Kevane's competence as dean, which included a list of twenty-eight allegations.[18] The first nine allegations were about the School of

---

[16] Verone to Krol, December 12, 1967, box 34c, folder 33, ACK.

[17] The special committee to investigate the School of Education was appointed on November 20, 1967, by Cardinal O'Boyle. It was chaired by Cardinal Shehan and in-cluded O'Boyle, Archbishop McDonough of Louisville, and Bishop Russell of Virginia, as well as lay board members Judge Stephen Jackson, Andrew Maloney, Lewis Guarnieri, and John McShain.

[18] Whalen to Shehan, December 22, 1967, box 1, AMK.

Education: for example, it was not properly accredited, it employed graduate students as teachers, its faculty was divided, it had inadequate admission requirements and "unclear aims", and it did not comply with the requests of the higher administration of the university. The final nineteen allegations were focused more directly on the person of Dean Kevane, accusing him of being an "unqualified", "unscholarly", and "vindictive" man, who had "no reputation as an educator either on the campus or off it". Kevane reacted violently to criticism, was incompetent in his direction of dissertations, lacked leadership ability, and refused to consult faculty in decision making. He did not communicate with students, nor did he collaborate with the other schools of the university. He refused to cooperate with the National Catholic Educational Association (NCEA).[19] He had engaged in questionable financial practices.[20] And, finally, Monsignor Kevane was "alleged to be dictatorial".

To this litany of allegations Whalen added his own remarks, which he began by stating, "I think I should say there are no 'charges' against Monsignor Kevane." Rather, wrote Whalen, he merely was expressing his "deep concern" that Kevane had "not been an effective administrator". This incapacity for administration had created a situation in which "no one presently in the school can do anything for it", and thus Kevane needed to be replaced at once by "an extremely well-qualified and strong extern". Whalen advised the board of trustees to take "immediate action", and as far as he was concerned, the sooner the better.

Kevane's Defense before the Special Committee

Kevane responded to Whalen's attack on January 18, 1968, with a twenty-one-page, typed response to Cardinal Shehan and the special committee.[21] Kevane's highly detailed response had one ongoing re-

---

[19] During the CUA strike the National Catholic Educational Association had been outspoken in its criticism of the American bishops and unabashed in its sympathy for Curran.

[20] Kevane had involved CUA in an educational venture in Guayaquil, Ecuador, through Professor Jose Baquero of the School of Education. The administration of this venture was problematic and had brought Kevane into conflict with the administration of CUA.

[21] Kevane to the special committee, January 18, 1968, box 1, AMK.

frain: the issue was not the allegations or even himself; the issue was the very essence of the mission of the Catholic University as pontifical and Catholic, and, because of the unique position of influence held by the university, the issue was "the future of the Church in this country". Kevane had led the School of Education in maintaining "the specific position of the Catholic Faith regarding the Magisterium during the Father Curran incident in April, 1967." Kevane was emphatic that the present campaign to remove him from his deanship was directly related to that course of action. He explained how he had been expecting such a campaign to oust him ever since his refusal to support the Curran strike:

> Even before that sad affair concluded, it was being heard, on and off the Campus, that the Dean of the School of Education would be dealt with in due time. A few days after those demonstrations were over, Rt. Rev. Msgr. E. Robert Arthur, of the Archdiocese of Washington, telephoned me to ask whether I was aware that an effort apparently was to be made to "get" me because of my stand in opposition to the demonstrations and to the boycott of classes by teachers and students. He had heard a prominent member of the USCC [United States Catholic Conference] staff say that those on the University faculty who were fostering the boycott would find a way to "get" me. It has been widely expected, therefore, that some such attack as this present one would be made against me and the School of Education. This is the punishment, it has been decided, which fits our crime.

Kevane's crime, of course, was that he had striven to maintain the principle that instructors in the ecclesiastical disciplines could proceed in their work only "by virtue of a mandate from the Successors of the Apostles", in other words, subject to the authority of the bishops.

Kevane asserted that Whalen was disingenuous in failing to make any connection between the present allegations against the School of Education and the position it had taken regarding the Curran affair. In fact, Whalen's letter appeared to Kevane to be "a studied effort to ignore the widely known connection and place the entire matter in the realm of 'school administration'". The possibility that Whalen was ignorant of this connection was, according to Kevane, "absolutely inadmissible". Rather it was obvious to Kevane that an organized campaign was under way, which, if not directly connected to Whalen, was using him to achieve its goal of ousting Kevane. He expressed "astonishment" that these allegations were brought to the board of trustees "without affording me any opportunity to comment on [them]". Given the fact that Whalen had assumed the position of acting rector only a few weeks earlier, Kevane found himself forced to conclude that Whalen was either "simply unequal to his task" or else "a conscious partner in the campaign".

Kevane responded to Whalen's long list of allegations with the simple answer that absolutely no evidence was given for them, nor was the existence of any evidence alluded to. As such, the allegations were "a series of gratuitous assertions". The allegations were repetitious, which Kevane said was "merely a device to make the charges appear to have substance". The allegations obscured matters, Kevane said, by focusing on him personally and served to distract the board of trustees from the "real issues", which were "the Magisterium of the Catholic Church; the nature and function of Catholic education; the pontifical character and Catholic quality of The Catholic University of America".

Kevane then embarked on a meticulous defense of himself against each individual charge. With regard to the first nine asserting the unprofessional character of the School of Education, Kevane maintained that the school operated in a manner consistent with the way it had been run when it was still a department of the Graduate School of Arts and Sciences. The alleged "division" in the school had existed only since the Curran incident the previous April, and it had been created by a vocal minority with which Whalen sympathized. Kevane gave a detailed account of the various projects that he had overseen as dean while at the same time expressing frustration that the vagueness of the accusations prevented him from being able to respond. More than once in his long response he made a statement along these lines: "I deny this allegation and stand ready for the instances to be cited, and to provide an explanation."

Turning to the allegations dealing with his person, Kevane grouped them all "under one heading, which might well be termed 'character assassination at the University level'". He continued, "These are points that are precisely designed to destroy a person, to nullify his ability to continue working in the context of a contemporary university." He noted the difficulty of defending himself by his own testimony against such personal charges and referred questioning to the faculty of the School of Education. As evidence of his scholarship, he invoked his scholarly work published in European journals, his contract with the series Ancient Christian Writers to publish a two-volume work on Saint Augustine, and his numerous published articles. He stated explicitly that the only instance in which he could recall ever having been "uncooperative" with other schools of the university was during the Curran strike. The position of the School of Education at that time had been in fact an exercise of academic freedom, said Kevane, for which the school had been punished severely.

With regard to the NCEA, Kevane defended his record of cooperation with it while at the same time noting that "the NCEA and I are at opposite ends as to who should control Catholic education in the United States: should it be the Bishops? or the NCEA?" His position on this question had put him fundamentally at odds with the NCEA: "The School of Education has been representing the position of the Bishops, defending their interests, and teaching that teachers should teach, not control." Any opposition to him from the NCEA could be explained, said Kevane, by his position on this critical issue.

Kevane told the board that they should not imagine that Whalen was taking an impartial role in reporting the allegations to them. Rather, Whalen was leading the attack:

> He *is* accusing me, and he cannot avoid his responsibility for doing so. He became a co-accuser when, without allowing me to be heard, he accepted as true the charges of those who presented them. If Father Whalen is not one of my accusers, he has been an unjust judge. In all honesty, I shall find it difficult to believe him or to trust him ever again.

Whalen's sympathies with those who opposed the School of Education were clear, argued Dean Kevane. Furthermore, the accusations against him had had a "killing effect" on both him and the entire School of Education. They were the latest attack in "a continuous harassment of the School of Education and its Faculty".

As part of his defense, Kevane made a statement about academic freedom that may be read as a manifesto of his thought in this regard:

> We stand for academic freedom, and at the same time we want to understand it rightly when it relates to the religious teaching carried out in the name and by the mandate of the Church. I personally do not

try to impose my views on anyone, nor my opinions regarding people, but I certainly claim the right to dissent with the same academic freedom and the same freedom of conscience that others claim for themselves. Furthermore, I do not subscribe to the view that there cannot be deep differences of opinion in a university Faculty and strong expressions of these differences. But no one has the right to be discourteous, much less unjust, in the matter.

Kevane then offered the bishops a poignant glimpse of the interior suffering he had undergone as a result of the campaign against him and his department. He prefaced these remarks by saying that he made them "frankly and in great anguish". His description of what these events had done to him personally and of how he understood their broader significance was unambiguous:

> The ordeal suffered in these past weeks and even months is too great a price to pay for the Deanship of any school. If I were to consult only my own convenience, probably I would have done nothing more than deny to the Trustees the charges that have been made against me. However, there are things more precious than my convenience. I have endured all this psychological warfare since last April and I am making this fight because I prize the valid rights of the Magisterium of the Church. To me the issue is larger than we who are involved as persons, larger than our School of Education; the issue is the doctrinal authority of the Bishops, and I think the careful and significant wording of the settlement of the strike last April bears me out. Indeed, I must say that the issue is the very question whether the Church is to continue her school in the United States at all.

Kevane implored the trustees to understand that he was being persecuted for defending *their* position: "This fight . . . is nothing else than the fight which was begun against you, the Trustees of the Catholic University of America, last April. . . . We are fighting your fight." He concluded his letter with a dire prediction of what the consequences would be if the forces arrayed against him realized their true goals:

> For if the plan succeeds to capture this official National Catholic University of the American Hierarchy, there will be incalculable future results. The seeds of religious doubt, doctrinal confusion, and outright crisis in Faith will be sown over the entire United States through the very schools and colleges operated by and in the name

of the Church. And nothing could destroy these organs of the Catholic teaching program more assuredly than such an attempt to undermine from within the confidence of the American Catholic parents in the doctrinal purity and integrity of those same grade schools, high schools, and colleges.

The battle may not be lost if the force that opposes us has its way again. But if it does have its way, that organized force will be so much the more strongly entrenched and arrogantly self-assured, and I shall tremble for the future of this University. And since this University was established to be the keystone of the vast and successful teaching program whereby the Catholic Church has been giving her Sacred Doctrine to raise up the People of God in the United States, I shall tremble for the future of the Church in this country.

Kevane's prophetic words were a remarkably accurate description of what would in fact take place in the years following the coup at Catholic University.

The Endgame against Kevane

On January 20, 1968, Kevane testified on his own behalf before the special committee and gave detailed answers, with documentation, to all the charges that had been brought against him by Whalen. After three hours of discussion the committee decided to investigate the matter further. It met again on February 4, 1968, and again questioned separately both Kevane and Whalen, informing Whalen that it would issue its final report on the matter within ten days.[22]

In the meantime, as the committee was finalizing its conclusions, the CUA academic senate attempted to take the matter into its own hands. It called a special meeting on January 23, 1968, at which Dean Marlowe introduced a motion authorizing the rector to remove Kevane from his position as dean immediately, without waiting for the decision of the special committee.[23] The case for such a decision was presented quite simply: the statutes of the university empowered the

---

[22] *Report of the Special Committee*, February 12, 1968, box 34c, folder 22, ACK; Minutes, academic senate, February 8, 1968.

[23] The account of this meeting is taken from the minutes of the CUA academic senate, January 23, 1968, "Academic Senate" box 2, "Academic Senate Vol. 12" folder, ACUA.

rector to choose a dean, the special committee had not arrived at a decision in the matter, and in the judgment of the academic senate, the situation in the School of Education "urgently" required "an immediate change in leadership". Marlowe's motion invoked article 25 of the university statutes, which stated that in grave and urgent matters, the rector had the power to act on his own authority after consulting with the academic senate.

While there was some discussion regarding the gravity and urgency of the situation, there was little objection to the motion itself. The only two objections came from Kevane, who disagreed that the situation was urgent, and from professor Jose Baquero of the School of Education, who declared that he would vote on the matter only under protest, "as he felt the matter now rested in the hands of higher authority". In the end Marlowe's motion was approved by a secret ballot, sixteen to two, with two abstentions. Marlowe moved that all present would agree not to discuss the matter publicly until Whalen decided what action to take, and on this there was tacit agreement. All that Kevane could now do was await his impending fate at the hands of Whalen, who was finally about to achieve the victory he had unsuccessfully tried to push through the board.

Thus, the proposed dismissal of Kevane as dean was overwhelmingly approved by a body of faculty that had neither given him a hearing nor even allowed for the completion of the investigation called for by the board. The vehement insistence on following AAUP norms and ensuring that the accused party's rights be upheld and defended, all of which had been invoked to no end in Curran's case, was nowhere to be seen in Kevane's case. Meanwhile the statutes of the university, which had been criticized to the point of ridicule in the aftermath of the Curran affair, were suddenly invoked to justify what was, to all appearances, an arbitrary and even subversive action by the academic senate. This action of the senate, perhaps more than any other, was indicative of the true nature of the movement for academic freedom at CUA in the late 1960s.

On February 12, 1968, some three weeks after the academic senate had called for Kevane's dismissal, the special committee issued its final report on the School of Education. The report, signed by Cardinal Shehan as chairman and all the committee members, found that there was insufficient evidence to conclude that Kevane had been either inadequate or incompetent in his administration of the School of Education. Notwithstanding this decision, the committee left the final decision about Kevane's fate as dean in the hands of Whalen, whose prerogative it was to name deans of the university.[24]

On the following day, February 13, Whalen wrote to the board of trustees to inform them that he had received the committee's report and that accordingly he was acting immediately to replace Kevane with Reverend Aubert J. Clark, O.F.M.Conv., a former member of the School of Education, as acting dean of the school. Whalen also formed a committee to begin the search for a permanent dean.[25]

The official CUA press release on February 14, 1968, announced the new acting dean and stated that a national search would be undertaken for a permanent one "of national stature to strengthen the school from top to bottom".[26] It noted that "the entire School of Education faculty will have a voice in the final choice." It continued, "CUA deans and department heads are appointed by the Rector to two year terms, after a consultative vote by the faculty concerned." What the press release failed to mention, however, was that the results of the consultative vote of the faculty in the fall of 1967 had been ignored and overturned by Whalen. It noted that Kevane would stay on as a member of the education faculty, giving the impression that everyone involved was quite happy with the new developments in the School of Education.

Eugene Kevane had lost his long, hard-fought battle. However, there were no protests, no student walkouts, and certainly no press conferences orchestrated by the dismissed dean. Kevane's only comment on the matter was a letter he wrote to Cardinal Krol on February 26, 1968, to express his *gratitude* to the board of trustees. He felt that his professional reputation had been saved by the hearing and the report of the special committee.[27] Cardinal Krol replied with words of praise for Kevane and also a certain displeasure with the outcome of the situation:

---

[24] *Report of the Special Committee.*

[25] Whalen to the board of trustees, February 13, 1968, box 34c, folder 22, ACK.

[26] The Catholic University of America, "Catholic University Names Fr. Aubert Clark Acting Dean of School of Education, Announces National Search for Leading Educator to Head the School Permanently", press release, February 14, 1968, "Press Releases (1961–1968)" folder, ACUA.

[27] Kevane to Krol, February 26, 1968, box 34c, folder 22, ACK.

Your letter of February 26, expressing your debt of gratitude to the board of trustees reflects only the high caliber of your own priestly character.

I have, since action was taken, heard expression of surprise and disappointment. I have heard satisfaction expressed with the findings of the committee, and dissatisfaction that the action did not correspond to the findings.[28]

Could such private assurance of sympathy on the part of some bishops have brought any real measure of consolation to Kevane? He had risked his reputation and his career to defend the role of the bishops in the governance of CUA, and in many ways he had lost. But there is no further evidence of Kevane's reaction to his fate.

What of the School of Education? What was the mood inside that department? In a letter to Cardinal Krol on April 9, 1968, Sister Mary Verone described an "unsettled state of confusion":

Monsignor Kevane was found competent and adequate so the rector replaced him. It just does not make sense. Father Clark was brought in as acting dean on February 14. When the rector was asked if this was sanctioned by the trustees, he said, "No, but it will be in April." He seemed mighty sure about it. Since then, Father Clark has brought in Father Taylor as assistant. He really takes over completely when Father Clark is not in. This Father Taylor was very definitely refused the position [by the faculty vote] last November. As I see it we have three deans at the moment. This is the confusion that helps to tear down and to prevent the good that should be done.

Verone also noted that the confusion within the School of Education was discouraging some religious orders from sending more sisters to CUA. She expressed the hope that Krol would be able to take steps to rectify the situation at the next meeting of the board of trustees:

We are looking to the Bishops for support in the April meeting. We need their help if we want to retain the Pontifical character of the University. That is what some here do not want. This has been said publicly from the stage. They do not want the Bishops running this University. Once the strength of the Bishops is removed, they will

---

[28] Krol to Kevane, March 7, 1968, box 34c, folder 22, ACK.

secularize it. That seems inevitable. We are more concerned than we can say.[29]

Krol wrote Verone a brief reply on April 16, thanking her and stating that he appreciated the information.[30] However, her hope that relief would come to the School of Education as a result of the upcoming meeting of the board of trustees was not to be realized. At its April 21 meeting, the CUA board of trustees received the report of the special committee,[31] which explained how, despite finding insufficient evidence of any incompetence on the part of Kevane, the committee had recognized the rector's authority to choose a new dean. Krol asked whether there was any evidence of a crisis in the School of Education. Cardinal Shehan replied that he would not say it was a crisis but that there was "evidence of great tension". He noted that it had been evident to the committee that Kevane had no support whatsoever from the other deans of CUA. Shehan also remarked that the decision to make the Department of Education into a separate school, which had been made by the board in 1964 at the recommendation of Bishop McDonald as rector, had been premature.

At this same meeting, board of trustees chairman Carroll Hochwalt indicated that Whalen's decision to replace Kevane had been strongly approved by Heald and Hobson of New York. This company was in the process of making a yearlong study of CUA under the guidance of Whalen, Brother Nivard Scheel, and Dr. C. Joseph Nuesse, in consultation with nine specialists from various other top American universities.[32] Hochwalt's remark offers further indication that the influence of

---

[29] Verone to Krol, April 9, 1968, box 34a, folder 22, ACK.

[30] Krol to Verone, April 16, 1968, box 34a, folder 22, ACK.

[31] The account of the meeting is taken from the minutes of the CUA board of trustees, April 1968, section 7, box 30c, ACK.

[32] The Heald-Hobson report was issued on September 20, 1968. In addressing the School of Education, it described a situation of "dysfunctional malaise" for which it faulted the "former Dean", noting that he "had lost the confidence of most of the faculty". The nine academic administrators who contributed to the Heald-Hobson report were Charles W. Cole, president emeritus of Amherst College, past vice president of the Rockefeller Foundation, and former United States ambassador to Chile; L. E. Grinter, dean of the Graduate School at the University of Florida; Charles O. Galvin, dean of the Law School at Southern Methodist University; John C. Hetherston, vice president for coordinate planning at the University of Pennsylvania; Alton A. Linford, dean of the School of Social Service at the University of Chicago; David E. Purpel, assistant dean

the American academic establishment definitely played a role, however small or secondary, in the campaign to oust Kevane from his deanship. Devotion to the American educational ideal of academic freedom could not and would not permit dissent within the ranks of academia against the prevailing AAUP orthodoxy.

The Situation at CUA in the Spring of 1968

By the end of the spring semester of 1968, one year after the faculty and student strike had demanded and successfully obtained Charles Curran's reinstatement, the movement for academic freedom at Catholic University led by the School of Theology had made considerable advances. It had solidified its position as being squarely in control of ongoing developments at CUA, and it had used its power to oust the lone dissenting dean who had opposed it during the April 1967 strike. It had successfully guided the formulation of the working paper on university objectives and ensured that this paper essentially endorsed a definition of academic freedom in conformity with the educational ideals of the AAUP. It was firmly guiding the writing of the Heald-Hobson report and had the total sympathy of those on that committee who were in the position of making further recommendations for the development of the university. The emphatic recommendation of the MSA evaluation report that "much must be done quickly" to free CUA from the authoritative oversight of the Holy See and the board of trustees seemed to be progressing quite satisfactorily. Although there was still a priest in the position of acting rector, there was growing hope that a layman would be placed in that position as soon as possible. Catholic University was ever more fully embracing the "commitment to change" that the MSA report hoped would free it from the shackles of its pontifical status.

In the spring of 1968, after a year of upheaval and struggle at CUA, some observers may have thought (and some among the bishops may

---

of the Graduate School of Education at Harvard; Randall N. Saflund, CPA, former controller of the University of Rochester; William K. Selden, former executive director of the National Commission on Accrediting; and Randall M. Whaley, former chancellor of the University of Missouri at Kansas City and past vice president for graduate studies at Wayne State University.

have hoped) that the situation would calm down a bit, that perhaps some measure of relative stability would return to Caldwell Hall and Mullen Library. In fact, just the opposite was about to happen. The promulgation of *Humanae Vitae* by Pope Paul VI on July 29, 1968, threw Catholic University into a period of even more dramatic upheaval, bitter conflict, and international media attention. The events of the 1967–1968 academic year, which had really begun with the April 1967 strike, served as a necessary prelude to what followed during the 1968–1969 academic year. Having clearly established itself in control of CUA, the School of Theology had set the stage for an even more aggressive attack against the authority of the board of trustees, the American hierarchy, and even the pope himself. The story of how the professors of the Catholic University of America led an unprecedented movement of public and organized dissent against the teaching of *Humanae Vitae* soon became the next chapter in the ongoing subversion of the authority of the Magisterium by Catholic theologians.

III

THE TRIUMPH OF DISSENT

7

Cardinal O'Boyle Meets with the Dissenting Professors: August 20, 1968

The Statement of Dissent against *Humanae Vitae*

When Pope Paul VI issued his long-awaited encyclical *Humanae Vitae* on July 29, 1968, his condemnation of contraception as intrinsically evil and opposed to the good of marriage precipitated a crisis of authority of unprecedented proportions within the Catholic Church in the United States. An outspoken and organized movement of public dissent against the teaching of the Magisterium took shape across the country, centered at Catholic University, led by Father Charles Curran and many of his fellow professors in the CUA School of Sacred Theology. Their "Statement of Dissent", issued on July 30, 1968, began an open battle for control of CUA between the School of Theology and the board of trustees. That battle consumed the majority of the 1968–1969 academic year and ended in victory for the dissenting theologians when the board of trustees acknowledged that, because of the AAUP principles of academic freedom that the board had pledged to uphold after the 1967 faculty strike, it was in no position to determine the manner or content of theological teaching at CUA.[1]

The dissenting professors built on the foundation that had been laid during the 1967 faculty strike supporting Curran until they were virtually unassailable in their domination of the university. The opposition of the board of trustees (especially of Cardinals O'Boyle, Krol, and McIntyre) to the dissenters was time and again outmaneuvered and

---

[1] The detailed chronological account given here of the conflict at CUA surrounding the "Statement of Dissent" is largely drawn from the minutes of the CUA board of trustees meetings as well as the personal correspondence and records of John Cardinal Krol, who played a pivotal role throughout the proceedings.

outwitted by theologians who masterfully invoked the principles of the AAUP and the expectations of the American academic establishment to justify their direct and outspoken rejection of the teaching of the Church's Magisterium. The July 30, 1968, "Statement of Dissent"[2] was ultimately signed by over six hundred theologians throughout the United States. It declared that although the theologians acknowledged a "distinct role" for the hierarchical Magisterium within the Church, they also affirmed their own "special responsibility of evaluating and interpreting pronouncements of the magisterium in the light of the total theological data operative in each question or statement". Having thus introduced themselves as the ones who alone held the power to interpret the teaching of the Magisterium, the theologians then proposed to offer some "initial comments" on the just-issued encyclical as a way of responsibly caring for the good of the Church. "The Encyclical is not an infallible teaching", they said. They noted that many other historical pronouncements of the Magisterium had been subsequently shown to be "inadequate or even erroneous". While acknowledging various positive values expressed in the encyclical letter, the statement mainly objected to the very fact that the pope had attempted to make a definitive and authoritative statement in the postconciliar Church:

> We take exception to the ecclesiology implied and the methodology used by Paul VI in the writing and promulgation of the document: they are incompatible with the Church's authentic self-awareness as expressed in and suggested by the acts of the Second Vatican Council. The Encyclical consistently assumes that the Church is identical with the hierarchical office. . . . Furthermore, the Encyclical betrays a narrow and positivistic notion of papal authority.

The encyclical, declared the theologians, failed to take into account numerous elements that composed the "Magisterium of the People of God": the witness of married couples, the witness of other Christian bodies, the witness of men of good will, the witness of modern science; in short, the encyclical neglected "the life of the Church in its totality", just as the teaching it contained neglected the good of marital love in its totality by condemning specific individual contraceptive acts. The statement maintained that the encyclical presented an inadequate

---

[2] See appendix C for the full text of the "Statement of Dissent".

concept of natural law and placed an impersonal emphasis on sexual acts rather than focusing on married couples themselves. At the same time it displayed "an almost total disregard for the dignity of millions of human beings brought into the world without the slightest possibility of being fed and educated decently". In the judgment of the dissenting theologians, the encyclical directly downplayed the teaching of Vatican II, which had acknowledged the "historical and evolutionary character of humanity in its finite existence", and it showed no development over Pius XI's 1930 encyclical *Casti Connubii*, "whose conclusions have been called into question for grave and serious reasons".

In short, the encyclical letter of Paul VI was declared an incompetent and embarrassing document, one that the theologians could not and would not accept as the teaching of the Holy Spirit speaking through the Church. In fact, the theologians asserted that the papal Magisterium had become an obstacle to the working of the Holy Spirit and as such was threatening the sacred good of marriage. If the theologians did not alert the People of God that the pope's teaching was not infallible, they feared that countless Catholics would naïvely believe that the pope's teaching had to be accepted in faith, untold damage would be done to marital fidelity, and millions of people yet to be born in impoverished countries would have their dignity violated. For these reasons, in order to protect the Christian faithful from what they felt was the grave error and closed-mindedness of the pope, the dissenting theologians felt bound in conscience to speak out in dissent:

> It is common teaching in the Church that Catholics may dissent from authoritative, noninfallible teachings of the magisterium when sufficient reasons for so doing exist.
>
> Therefore, as Roman Catholic theologians, conscious of our duty and our limitations, we conclude that spouses may responsibly decide according to their conscience that artificial contraception in some circumstances is permissible and indeed necessary to preserve and foster the values and sacredness of marriage.
>
> It is our conviction also that true commitment to the mystery of Christ and the Church requires a candid statement of mind at this time by all Catholic theologians.

The theologians took exception to the ecclesiology and methodology of the pope, decrying his vision of papal authority as narrow and expressing dismay at his presumption in attempting to speak in a manner that they feared would be misconstrued as being definitive and infallible. The final words of the statement revealed the theologians' ecclesiology: *they* possessed the power to interpret pronouncements of the Magisterium, and their interpretation was both definitive and infallible. Their open and public act of dissent against the highest authority in the Church was the logical consequence of postconciliar theology: theologians had the task of protecting theology as a science from the intrusion of the pope and bishops, who were incompetent in theological matters. They were convinced that their action was courageous and even heroic, embodying a true openness to the Holy Spirit at a critical moment for the Church that would preserve the People of God from the narrow-mindedness of the Vicar of Christ.

The Chancellor Summons His Professors

Because the signers of the "Statement of Dissent" included a group of professors from both the CUA School of Theology and the Department of Religious Education, Cardinal O'Boyle as chancellor asked to meet with those faculty members who signed the statement in Caldwell Hall on August 20, 1968. The transcript of this meeting lays out the entrenched battle lines that came to define the American Church for more than a generation and gives a fascinating glimpse into the minute details of what must certainly be counted as one of the most significant days in the history of the Catholic Church in the United States.

The dissenting professors were convinced that their position was a necessary service to the Magisterium and the universal Church, while O'Boyle was just as convinced that their actions were subversive to his authority and that of the bishops on the CUA board of trustees. There was a not-so-subtle current of intellectual intimidation at play in the meeting: the theologians came prepared with their technical theological argument justifying dissent and the principles of academic freedom as defined by the AAUP, which they calmly and coolly presented on their behalf. O'Boyle, in contrast, gave the impression of being somewhat disorganized, a bit frustrated, and clearly inferior in his knowledge of theology, the statutes of the university, and the principles of the AAUP. The result was a long, drawn-out meeting in which the dissenters refused to give up an inch of their well-defined position and rejected O'Boyle's request for cooperation. The professors even refused O'Boyle's request to submit a simple written statement summarizing the theological justification of their position, on the grounds that it was much too subtle and complex to be contained in a brief statement. The immediate result of the meeting was a stalemate between the cardinal-chancellor and the professors, that is, between the Magisterium and the theologians. This stalemate was a strategic victory for the dissenters, who successfully defended their position without changing it even slightly and gave theological credibility to dissent by emerging from the meeting without any public reprimand from O'Boyle.

From the very beginning of the meeting, O'Boyle attempted to restrict the matter to addressing the faculty members of Catholic University who were signers of the "Statement of Dissent".[3] Thus, when Charles Curran made a motion that the names of all six hundred theologians who had joined in signing the statement be added to the minutes, O'Boyle objected that these names were irrelevant to the situation at CUA; in any event, he had grave doubts that the six hundred were all professional theologians. Curran, however, insisted the names be added, and Father Daniel Maguire[4] of the School of Religious Education concurred, saying that they were there to discuss "scientific theology" and that these other signers were "theologically significant". Maguire's contention was consistent with one of the key principles of postconciliar theology: theologians were the definitive and authoritative interpreters of the Magisterium and indeed actually composed the Magisterium. O'Boyle agreed to append the names of the six hundred signers to the official record but said he considered it "a very liberal concession".

The theologians calmly and eloquently testified to O'Boyle that they saw no reason why their statement should cause any difficulty whatsoever for Catholic University. They were simply acting "according to their competence" as theologians, said Father Robert Hunt, and also

---

[3] The entire account of the August 20, 1968, meeting is taken from the bound seventy-five-page transcript of the meeting, box 30a, ACK.

[4] Maguire had been one of Curran's chief supporters during the April 1967 strike.

"specifically according to the rules and regulations of the Academe which they are part of". Hunt referred directly to the source of the professors' justification for their dissent: the governing principles of the AAUP, by which they had exercised their right to academic freedom. In accord with the AAUP's policy of peer evaluation, the right to judge the competence of the dissenting professors' position lay entirely in the hands of their fellow theologians and professors; thus, the approval and support of the six hundred signers of the "Statement of Dissent" formed an essential part of their position.

But what of the hierarchy of the Church and the relation of the theologians to the Holy Father and the bishops? Curran was quick to assure O'Boyle that His Eminence could put his mind at rest: "There can be no doubt whatsoever about the orthodoxy and Catholic faith commitment of the people who have signed this particular statement. This statement involves no disrespect whatsoever for the Papal Office of the hierarchical magisterium of the Catholic Church." Curran and the dissenting professors were thus employing the same tactic that Krol had noted in his initial evaluation of Curran's writing in 1967: "By the time he finishes his essay, he is actually espousing or advocating something other than he avowed in the first part of his essay."[5] The "Statement of Dissent" began by acknowledging a "distinct role" for the Magisterium but then proceeded to dismantle that role piece by piece until there was nothing left of it but an opinion, and a narrow and even incompetent opinion at that, which not only could be but *should* be disregarded by reasonable Catholics.

Curran explained that, on such short notice and without any agenda for the meeting, he and his colleagues "were not prepared to give a total theological response". He did offer, however, to give a list of authors by which he could prove that dissent against the authoritative teaching of the pope was not only permissible but even necessary at times. He invoked numerous theological authorities who argued that in certain situations theologians could have an obligation to dissent. The dissenting theologians' position on *Humanae Vitae* was thus "in total conformity with orthodox Catholic teaching". Curran offered to read numerous citations to O'Boyle in Latin, but O'Boyle asked Curran to use English. Curran then said that he was "translating on sight" and contin-

---

[5] Krol's report to the CUA board of trustees, May 5, 1967, box 34a, ACK.

ued with his citations. By his overall tenor, Curran attempted to impress upon Cardinal O'Boyle the theologians' superior knowledge of theology and by implication their exclusive right to interpret the theological value and significance of the encyclical *Humanae Vitae*.[6] After running circles around the cardinal, Curran summarized his presentation with a reminder that the present informal, ad hoc meeting could not possibly bring any kind of theological closure to the matter:

> CURRAN. I think for the record we will say there is much other historical evidence that can be brought out, but that the time and inability to prepare for it do not permit us to do so now. And also definitely for the record, according to the agenda of this meeting, this meeting is in no sense to be construed as a hearing.
>
> O'BOYLE. Absolutely.
>
> CURRAN. And therefore if there are any future actions to be taken, this meeting in any sense cannot be considered as a hearing.
>
> O'BOYLE. That is right.

O'Boyle turned to Maguire, who assured the cardinal that the dissenting statement "would not be a problem for persons who are familiar with the history of Theology". Nor would it be problematic "for those who are keeping abreast of the very subtle debate on the nature of religious assent and the nature of dissent in the Church". The late medieval universities, Maguire explained, provided the same service

---

[6] Transcript of August 20, 1968, meeting of Cardinal O'Boyle and the CUA faculty members who had signed the "Statement of Dissent", 11–15, box 30a, ACK:

CURRAN. Our argument is based on solid Catholic teaching as found in the recognized manual authors of Theology. . . . The point I want to make is precisely this: There is not only a right to dissent, there is an obligation to dissent according to some accepted Catholic authors of Theology, and I will list them: Dieckmann, Lerch, Palmieri, Straub, Pesch, Harve, Vannoort. Also articles in the *New Catholic Encyclopedia*—

O'BOYLE. Excuse me, Father, are you prepared to cite those articles?

CURRAN. Yes . . . [*Gives citations.*] I would in particular cite the statement of Pesch, because precisely in this statement he says—do you want Latin or English?

O'BOYLE. You better use English. At least for me, and maybe there are others here.

CURRAN. I am translating on sight: "This so happens so that either the doctrine about which we are talking little by little is received by the whole church and thus is raised to the State of Infallibility, or little by little error is detected."

to the Church as that provided by the "Statement of Dissent", that is, protecting the Christian faithful from the misuse of papal authority. Maguire professed his sympathy and patience with those Catholics (perhaps including O'Boyle) who at the time were not fully aware of this understanding of the Magisterium and implied that they should be grateful for the work of dissenting theologians that was helping to keep reasonable Catholics who dissented from papal teaching within the Church. Invoking the work of Father Bernard Häring,[7] Maguire reasoned that

> very many Catholics who had formed their consciences over a long period of time with much study and prayer in a manner we support in this issue would have felt it necessary to leave the Church if we had not reinstated this abandoned tradition on responsible dissent and if we had not done this in a manner that would make it known to them immediately upon the public issuance of the encyclical.

Maguire thus put forth the blueprint for what Curran would later famously call "loyal dissent". The dissenting theologians had an *obligation* to dissent for the sake of the unity of the Church: far from their dissent's being a cause of scandal, it would have been a scandal for them to have *refrained* from dissenting. Their action was one of disinterested service to protect the Christian faithful from mistakenly believing that the teaching of *Humanae Vitae* was binding on their consciences.

A somewhat different perspective on the situation was given to O'Boyle by Father Carl Peter, a professor in the School of Theology who had *not* signed the "Statement of Dissent". Peter believed that while the professors had a right to dissent, the manner of the their dissent had hurt many Catholics: "I may be wrong, but I thought if they had taken more time, and exercised more care, with more precision, more Catholics would have been helped and fewer would have been hurt." He understood the position of the dissenting professors and in many ways agreed with it; however, his concern over the potential

---

[7] Bernard Häring, C.S.S.R. (1912–1998), German-born professor of moral theology at the Alfonsianum from 1950 to 1986. Häring was an influential *peritus* at Vatican II and served as secretary of the commission that drafted *Gaudium et Spes*. Charles Curran has stated that Häring had the most influence on his thought as a student in Rome. Häring's support for the "Statement of Dissent" in 1968 was a crucial factor in the dissent's successfully gaining theological legitimacy. See Charles E. Curran, *Loyal Dissent: Memoir of a Catholic Theologian* (Washington, D.C.: Georgetown University Press, 2006), 13–14.

damage to the Catholic faithful had led him to refrain from signing the statement.

Peter testified that his deepest concern was that the situation at Catholic University would damage the university *as a university*, and so he proposed a simple, practical solution. "My conclusion is this," he said, "we have got to live with it." In his mind, there was no reason why CUA could not accept the presence of the dissenting professors within the legitimate academic freedom that was the essence of its identity: "I believe if we can convince the people of this country that this is, one, a university in the best contemporary sense of this in America, and simultaneously Catholic, we will be doing a real service." In other words, CUA needed to be able to tolerate within its School of Theology teaching that differed from, even to the point of being at odds with, that of the Magisterium. "I think we can coexist", Peter said. "If we can convince our people that this is within the unity of the Catholic Faith, as it is, we can render a service to the universities, and the Catholicism of the country." Such "coexistence" would in fact be the long-term outcome of the *Humanae Vitae* controversy at CUA and other American Catholic universities: the rejection of the definitive teaching of the ordinary Magisterium came to be seen as a legitimate and even "normal" position for ordinary Catholics and for Catholic educators.

Also testifying was Father Berard Marthaler,[8] head of the CUA Department of Religious Education. Marthaler said that the "Statement of Dissent" actually clarified the true meaning of the encyclical, thereby correcting the false interpretation that had been given by the secular media. According to Marthaler, influential secular publications such as the *New York Times*, the *Washington Post*, and *Time* had simplistically interpreted *Humanae Vitae* to mean that Catholics could not practice birth control. "The headlines—'Pope Against Birth Control'—made the Pope, I think, look antiquarian, like he simply was not facing up to the realities of the times", he said. The secular newsmen erred, he explained, by thinking that the pope had binding authority over Catholic teaching. "They were not putting it in the broad context of

---

[8] Berard Marthaler, O.F.M.Conv. (1927–2014), was a professor of the CUA School of Theology from 1963 to 1997. He was the longtime editor of *The Living Light*, a national catechetical journal.

Catholic teaching," he said, "they were not reading against the whole tradition on Christian marriage, against what Vatican II did in regard to rights of conscience or anything else." The service rendered by the theologians was to offer a corrective hermeneutic of papal authority, one that realized that a papal encyclical was not in any way the final word on this or any other moral issue:

> We had to speak out, and had to show that there was another view within the church, that this had to be read against the whole context of what the Church was doing, and I think we have to make the people realize that it is in a university circle, in the academic world, we are in a position to help explain what Christian Doctrine is, and that we help to make them understand what the Magisterium is, that in a sense they can be truly loyal to it and not have their faith tested as they read the *New York Times*, or *Time* magazine, or whatever local tabloid they have to read.[9]

Here was the clearest statement yet of the "Magisteriology" of the dissenting theologians: the teaching of *Humanae Vitae* was *not* in fact morally binding, and it was the great task of theologians to help ordinary laypeople to understand this.

One by one, various other professors repeated to O'Boyle the main arguments of the dissenting position and assured him of their concern for the good of the Church. Father Russell Ruffino, professor of the School of Philosophy, even went so far as to declare that his dissent was the result of his personal affection for the pope:

> And beyond that I would say that the faith in Christ, the faith in the Holy Father, of all of us, I saw as not for a moment—and I hesitate even to say it, because it is so clear, so obvious, so real—not for a moment is it questionable, and I speak as one who lived seven years in the shadow of the cupola of St Peter's and felt a personal affection for the Holy Father.

Father Carl Peter also explained the significance of *Humanae Vitae* as he understood it: "When I have a papal encyclical I accept it as coming from the pope, and I pay much more attention to it than I do to other things that cross my desk."

---

[9] Transcript of August 20, 1968, meeting, 25.

Other professors of CUA presented O'Boyle with an academic rationale for dissent based in the tenets of the AAUP. Professor Kirby Neill of the English Department, a strong supporter of Curran during the April 1967 strike and a member of the AAUP National Committee on Academic Freedom in Church-Related Schools, declared that the dissenting professors were not speaking as members of the university staff or as faculty, but rather as individuals who were theologians, "and therefore the University as an institution really has nothing to do with what they said." Concurring with Neill was Mr. Jordan Kurland,[10] associate secretary with the Washington office of the AAUP: "It was a statement issued by a group over their own names, and not over the name of Catholic University. Obviously, the signatories all have identities, but I don't think there is any argument that they were speaking in an official university capacity." Agreeing with Kurland, Curran noted that the names of the dissenting professors had been grouped according to their respective schools merely for the purpose of identification and not in any official way, "as is usual in such statements". The position of the AAUP, as declared by its representatives, was that the "Statement of Dissent" was none of the chancellor's business whatsoever.

At this juncture, Father Whalen expressed his relief that the difficult situation at CUA seemed close to being resolved. O'Boyle had heard testimony from the dissenting professors, who had all made various protestations of loyalty to the Church and the Holy See, and the AAUP through its representatives had given its blessing to the action of the professors. Whalen declared that the good spirit at the meeting "rejoiced his heart". He expressed hope that the positive dialogue taking place could continue on a more frequent basis so that the theologians and bishops could be in continual conversation. He further expressed how much he was looking forward to stepping down soon from his post as acting rector.

Father Hunt concurred with Father Whalen's positive assessment of the meeting. Indeed, if there was any lingering concern about divisiveness, Hunt said, this must be attributed to certain members of the hierarchy who had spoken critically of the theology faculty: "One of the problems as I see it, just from being a citizen of this land and reading

---

[10] Jordan Kurland was the chairman of the AAUP's Committee A on Academic Freedom from 1965 to 2000.

newspapers, is that in some quarters this university is being implicitly or explicitly maligned, intentionally or unintentionally, by members of the hierarchy." Hunt expressed frustration with the fact that certain bishops had called the theologians irresponsible, an action that he said was itself irresponsible. In contrast with such criticism coming from some among the American episcopate, Dean Schmitz of the School of Theology noted with pride the acclaim he had received for CUA while he had recently been in Europe and the esteem in which it was held in places such as Bonn and Rome. He confidently asserted his pride in CUA for making "a real impact" on the international theological scene. "In this country we should have our own theology and it should be developed", Schmitz said. He took the opportunity to express to O'Boyle the fidelity of the CUA School of Theology to the Magisterium: "We would all like to reassure you we proclaim our loyalty to the Holy See." Schmitz's comments contain a perfect summary of the two mantras of the dissenting theologians: of course they were loyal to the Church and to the pope, and at the same time it was imperative for them to keep abreast of cutting edge developments in postconciliar theology. In Schmitz's view the bishops were understandably concerned about the former yet perhaps naïvely out of touch with the latter. If this naïveté had led to some "irresponsible" criticism on the part of the bishops, all would be generously forgiven by the theologians of CUA if they would simply be given the freedom to do their work. Such was the magnanimity that Schmitz felt his professors had displayed at this meeting in giving their patient explanation to O'Boyle.

One senses in the comments of Whalen, Hunt, and Schmitz a certain relief and optimism, indeed a sense of closure to the entire affair. Their remarks indicate a hope that the meeting would essentially be adjourned at this point, that O'Boyle would simply wrap things up and express a similar satisfaction with the detailed explanation that had been provided by the various professors. But such closure was in fact not what followed, not at all.

O'Boyle Requests a Written Explanation

Cardinal O'Boyle, who had remained silent for much of the morning's testimony, now offered his assessment of how matters stood between himself as chancellor and the professors under his authority: "I think the questions raised are so important and so complicated that it is very clear to me that I will have to take the matter under advisement." He explained that the purpose of the meeting, which he had initiated, was not to be a "showdown" but to enable him to understand fully the position of the dissenting professors. Having received a better understanding, he was now in a position to refer the matter to the entire CUA board of trustees for their consideration. To assist him and the board further in their evaluation, he asked if each professor would give a professional comment on the "Statement of Dissent", clarifying the precise theological grounds on which the statement stood.

O'Boyle requested clarification on two paragraphs in particular, those near the end of the statement, stating, "It is common teaching in the Church that Catholics may dissent" and "spouses may responsibly decide according to their conscience" to practice contraception in certain circumstances. O'Boyle asked the professors to send him, within a week, a simple explanation of the exact meaning of those two paragraphs.

Immediately, the good spirit that the theologians had sensed during the meeting, the spirit that had so encouraged Whalen, left the room. Maguire protested that he had a very busy week and would find it difficult to give "very good consideration" to such a written statement. O'Boyle replied by asking if a statement might be possible within ten days, but then Curran interjected with a clarification that the issue was not so much the time involved as that O'Boyle was not satisfied with what had already been stated during the first part of the meeting:

CURRAN. I was wondering how superfluous some of this is, in the light of what we have said today.

O'BOYLE. I think it would be fruitful, because some of you talked without notes, let's say that, and I think it would be fairer if each one of you expressed themselves in this way.

HUNT. What exactly do you mean? A rationale?

O'BOYLE. The reason for concurring with these two paragraphs, or for not concurring.

HUNT. That [a week or ten days] is hardly time for a serious, full, amply documented research paper if you want the reasons for concurring, because the reasons are enormous for some, quantitatively and qualitatively.

Another question I would have is if we are to give as theologians a rationale, or reckoning, and the reasons for concurring or non-concurring, or reservations, or the acceptance of these two paragraphs, to whom should they be addressed, in the sense of what purpose it would serve. The only persons that could evaluate this theological exposition would be a peer group, namely theologians, and if that is right, what purpose would you intend?

O'Boyle's request seemed simple enough from his point of view: a written summary of their position for the sake of helping the board of trustees to understand it. But in the minds of the professors, carefully formed by the principles of both postconciliar theology and the AAUP, the board held no competence whatsoever to evaluate their position —only their theological peers could do that. They believed that their theological position was none of the board's business.

O'Boyle was careful to repeat that he was not making any charges, but that he thought that the university statutes made provision for a panel of three bishops to meet with a faculty member if there was concern over his teaching. Consulting the statutes, O'Boyle was unable to locate this provision: "Well, I can't lay my hands upon it, but I know the other day I saw it." Father Curran replied immediately and politely with an exact knowledge of the statutes: "I don't think, Your Eminence, that Article 66 justifies that type of action." O'Boyle conceded that Curran might be right and came across as somewhat disorganized and uncertain of what exactly he was trying to accomplish. His weakness both theologically and procedurally continued to be exploited by the theologians throughout the course of the meeting and in subsequent interactions.

Father Marthaler proposed what was to become the favorite solution to almost every aspect of the *Humanae Vitae* controversy at CUA:

the matter should be referred to a committee. Marthaler said that the formation of committees seemed preferable to him, rather than asking individuals to answer in a "hurried" way. Although his suggestion was not implemented at this time, the stalling tactic of referring questions to investigation by committee was to become an effective part of the dissenting theologians' strategy in the coming months.

The dissenting theologians continued to evade O'Boyle's straightforward request that they provide him with an explanation of their position. They claimed that he had no right to ask for such an explanation, even as chancellor of the university. Curran stated that asking them for an explanation in and of itself violated academic freedom. O'Boyle repeatedly said that he was merely asking for a statement in an attempt to understand their position, and the professors more and more emphatically said it was *impossible* for them to explain the subtleties of their position in a statement. When O'Boyle again repeated that "what I am asking is a very simple request", Father Hunt replied:

> I think it is a very dangerous request . . . from the standpoint of a member of the academic community. It is dangerous, I think, when this is a relationship so clearly and beautifully established in this meeting between yourself as Chancellor, and ourselves as professors.

To Hunt's offer to send O'Boyle a bibliography on the subject, O'Boyle replied, "I have not the time, nor, I will admit it, the competency to go through it." O'Boyle's admission opened the door for Hunt to drive home his point even more firmly: if the cardinal lacked theological competency, then what was the point of the theologians' giving him individually written statements? One by one the other professors protested that their demanding schedules made a professional statement impossible. Father Farley would be away from his books due to travel in the coming weeks. Father Peter was going to "the Midwest", where there was "no adequate library", as was Father Marthaler. The only explanation Curran was willing to offer was his forthcoming book.

O'Boyle responded in obvious frustration: "Let's put it this way then. It seems if we are not going West, we are going South, or we are going somewhere." He offered to extend the timeframe to October if that would help the professors prepare their responses, but the professors remained uncooperative. A few of them said they would see if they might possibly come up with some sort of statement of their position.[11]

Once again O'Boyle attempted to cut to the heart of the matter. He asked Father Hunt to state simply what advice he would give as a pastor to a married man who asked him whether it was permissible to use contraception and what theological rationale he would use. Hunt replied that as a pastor he would encourage the man to follow his own "responsibly formed conclusions". As for the theological rationale, Hunt declared, "I don't think I would have to write a theological tract under those circumstances." O'Boyle tried to make his question even simpler: "I am no theologian," he said, "but I think you would have to go a little further and tell him how he would form these responsible conclusions."

Father Ruffino objected to O'Boyle's injection of a pastoral situation into a complex theological question:

> Your Eminence, I just want to say this. It is my understanding that [we] spoke out all as professional men, and that you are speaking to us professionally as Chancellor of the University. Therefore, while there is a pastoral dimension, as Father Hunt explained, the hypothetical case you presented to him was pastoral in another sense, and while it is eminently important that that question be answered because it is so practically important, it seems to me to be outside of the present discussion and the present purposes of our getting together; that we are talking professionally, scientifically, involved indeed with very important questions, but these questions, as everybody has indicated today, take a great deal of time to expound. I am saying this especially also as a philosopher, which is even yet one more step removed from the pastoral in the strict sense of the term, and I know myself it would take a long time to set down notions of natural law and so on, which I would want to explain. Just to set them down would take a great deal of time, would take almost a book to explain.

Ruffino's answer effectively communicated the near-total separation from pastoral implications with which the academics wanted to insulate their professional work.

---

[11] Fathers Peter, Rush, and Farley said that they would each attempt to create a statement, while Father Marthaler said he would work with others to prepare a joint statement of their position.

O'Boyle responded by once again cutting to the immediate and practical pastoral effect of the professors' statement: "I don't want to prolong this, but this statement from the theologians went all over the country. A great number of people were reading it, of course, and they say, 'Well, the theologians say in some circumstances it is permissible. *Finis*. Okay, so we are going to do it.'" People making this serious moral decision, O'Boyle said, needed more than the theologians' "Statement of Dissent" as the basis for forming their conscience. But Father Hunt again replied that no rationale could be given short of the book Father Curran had promised to publish shortly.

O'Boyle pressed the theologians further: Why, if the Holy Father had explained his position in only thirty-seven pages, could the theologians not give a succinct rationale for their response to the Holy Father's teaching? Perhaps, Father Hunt countered, His Eminence would like a commentary on the encyclical? Perhaps a colloquium could be held? The chancellor repeated his request to the end. The theologians, however, successfully evaded giving any direct written justification for their dissent.

Contentious Conclusion of the Meeting

Having exhausted the topic and exhausted each other, there remained one more formality for the record: Cardinal O'Boyle asked each professor individually whether he had in fact signed the "Statement of Dissent". Curran then gave the names of others connected with CUA who also had signed the statement. O'Boyle then proposed that a simple summary of the meeting be released to the press. His press release, however, met with protest. The statement said that the theologians "dissented from the encyclical", but, said Father Hunt, this was incorrect:

> Then the statement would not be fair, I think, to those who signed it.
> It would be saying some on the faculty were signers of the theological
> statement of dissent from the encyclical. That is not so. It was the
> dissent from some of the specific ethical teachings of the encyclical,
> not from the encyclical, because the statement acknowledged many
> of the valuable points contained in the encyclical.

In the end O'Boyle revised the statement to identify the professors as "signers of the theological statement of dissent from some aspects of the encyclical".

At long last the meeting was about to adjourn, but even its final minute was not to be without dispute. Father Hunt wished to know whether O'Boyle intended to hold a follow-up meeting with the board of trustees regarding the situation. O'Boyle responded vaguely, giving Hunt a taste of his own medicine: "Just as you explained when I was asking for that explanation of paragraph nine, I might well refer it, but when we would have a meeting I don't know."

The August 20, 1968, meeting between Cardinal O'Boyle and the dissenting theologians in many ways determined the course of the Catholic Church in the United States for more than a generation. From the beginning the theologians presented themselves as the ones in the driver's seat—educated, articulate, and precise in their knowledge of minute points of doctrine and procedure. O'Boyle, on the other hand, representing the American hierarchy, left the impression of having many holes in his knowledge of theology and of academic matters, of being generally frustrated with the theologians, and of naïvely hoping that a plea to the good will of the dissenters would somehow lead to a resolution of the dispute. The professors were emphatic that they could not be forced to give a statement of explanation of their position to the chancellor. O'Boyle's plea that they would give him a simple statement, essentially as a favor—a plea that the dissenters categorically rebuffed —served only to reinforce the impression of his incompetence.

The dissenting theologians emerged victorious from Caldwell Hall on August 20, 1968, confident that they were squarely in control of both the public spin on the controversy and the internal Church response to their actions. It was they and not the hierarchy who would set the tone of any further discussion or investigation regarding their position on *Humanae Vitae*.

Aftermath of the August 20, 1968, Meeting

The day after the meeting between O'Boyle and the professors, a front-page article in the *Washington Post* quoted Curran hailing the outcome of the meeting as a victory for the dissenting theologians. According to Curran, the meeting proved "that our dissent is not a rebellion, that our position is legitimate, and therefore acceptable".[12] Already

---

[12] The article by Kenneth Dole ran on the front page of the *Post* on August 21, 1968.

the masterful use of the media by the dissenting professors to garner sympathy for their cause had begun.

Curran's interpretation occasioned a sharp protest from his School of Theology colleague Father Carl Peter. Peter wrote a letter to the editor of the *Post* in which he strongly disagreed that O'Boyle had in any way given legitimacy to the dissenters' position: "Whatever the basis may have been for the proof referred to in Mr. Dole's article [in the *Post*], I did not see it in the attitude of Cardinal O'Boyle, who simply listened patiently to all of us."[13]

Peter's critique of his colleagues revealed that within the CUA School of Theology there was by no means unanimous agreement or support for the position taken by Curran and the eight other dissenting professors. In fact, there was much discomfort with it among at least some of the fifteen other professors in the School of Theology. On August 21, the day following the meeting with O'Boyle, Peter held a press conference in his native Omaha, Nebraska, at which he publicly disagreed with the position taken by Curran. While not denying the right of the theologians to dissent, Peter felt that they could have done so in a more prudent and less sensational manner:

> I think this is a time for calm discussion and study. The real thing I objected to was that the theologians who signed the statement opposing the Encyclical reacted too quickly. I believe that with just a little more care my colleagues could have avoided the impression that they were challenging the office of the Papacy. I was happy that our Bishops did not make any statement at all until after the statement of dissent from the theologians. To me this was a very good sign because the Encyclical is one of the most difficult to interpret that I have ever read.

Peter described his own position as one that offered a unique understanding of *Humanae Vitae*: the Pope had decided to enforce a ban on the practice of artificial birth control, which was a matter of ecclesiastical law, but this ban was not absolute in every situation and could be dispensed from in the case of serious medical reasons. Peter explained this position as being one of *interpretation* rather than of dissent:

---

[13] Father Carl J. Peter, letter to the editor, *Washington Post*, August 25, 1968, Archives of Father Carl J. Peter (hereafter cited as ACP), Boys' Town, Nebraska.

My interpretation is this. The encyclical prohibits the use of artificial means for contraceptive purposes. This is a law and binds Catholics in conscience. I do not think the ban is absolute in every case; like many other laws, there may be and I think there are excusing causes. That is my interpretation. It is not a dissent as I have said before. And I repeat, as an interpretation, it may be wrong. I do not think it is wrong. But if it is, I repeat this: I shall accept the correction.[14]

On August 28, 1968, Peter sent O'Boyle his own professional opinion regarding the "Statement of Dissent", in accord with the request the cardinal had made of the professors in attendance at the August 20 meeting in Caldwell Hall.[15] Peter asserted that his colleagues had not displayed adequate respect for the unique authority of the Holy Father, nor had they expressed their dissent in a respectful manner. There was unquestionably a right to dissent from noninfallible papal teaching, but the way in which his fellow professors had done so had caused more harm than good: "The right in question I consider defensible; the form and expression of dissent I could not accept." Peter stated his disagreement not only with the concluding paragraph of the "Statement of Dissent" (asserting that spouses could responsibly decide to contracept in some circumstances) but with "much" of the rest of the statement. He concluded his memo to O'Boyle by offering eighteen points summarizing his own personal interpretation of the encyclical, in which he declared his acceptance of its teaching and his doubt that its teaching was absolute:

> The ban on contraception is in my opinion real and binding in conscience. I do not consider it clearly absolute in every case. Nor do I think anyone ought to present it clearly as such. It needs . . . interpretation. . . . This is an interpretation and no dissent. If the interpretation is mistaken, I shall be found more anxious to learn than eager to defend my own opinion.

Peter's uneasiness with the position of his colleagues was shared by at least some of his fellow professors. On the same day that O'Boyle met with the dissenting professors, Eamon Kelly of the School of Theo-

---

[14] Press conference statement of Carl J. Peter, August 21, 1968, Omaha, Nebraska, ACP.

[15] Peter to O'Boyle, memorandum, August 28, 1968, ACP.

logy wrote Peter to express his own misgivings about the "Statement of Dissent" as well as the future of the school.[16] His letter revealed a deep frustration—from *within* the CUA School of Theology—with the movement of dissent led by Curran and with the numerous public statements being made to the media by the dissenting theologians regarding the Church's teaching authority and the person of Pope Paul VI. While Kelly had been in agreement with the April 1967 strike undertaken in the name of defending academic freedom, he now felt that the dissenters had pushed beyond the realm of what was appropriate and legitimate: "I suppose this is the hidden *agendum* that lay behind the . . . strike . . . , though I felt then that I could distinguish between two separable issues, and under the same circumstances would do the same again." His comments indicate an understanding that what was being undertaken by the dissenting theologians was in fact a redefinition of the authority of the Magisterium: they were rejecting the authority of both the Second Vatican Council and the pope and were setting up themselves in their place. It is apparent from Kelly's letter that within the CUA School of Theology in August 1968 there was not only division but also a clear understanding of the exact nature of what was being undertaken in the name of academic freedom: the issue was the Magisterium. There was hardly unanimous support for Curran as there had been sixteen months earlier during the faculty strike. Yet it is evident that Kelly felt that the portrayal of the situation in the media failed to make these nuances clear. "I too am sick of the all-inclusive tag 'The Catholic University theologians' and am prepared to say so publicly." He was deeply troubled at the thought of the effect of what was being said to the media by his fellow professors: "Such public statements . . . I regard as highly inflammatory, and the general (culmination of what we've seen develop these last few years) tone of 'well after all it's only another encyclical and of course not infallible teaching' upsets me immensely." Kelly was also frustrated that the media were presenting the story of what was transpiring at CUA as simply a repeat of the same dynamics of the 1967 strike: the portrayal of a closed-minded board of trustees, representing an authoritarian and repressive hierarchical Magisterium, in conflict with an open and respectful group of professors who wished simply to be allowed to exercise

---

[16] Kelly to Peter, August 20, 1968, ACP.

their work of teaching in freedom and peace. In this telling of the tale, it was the board of trustees and not the dissenting professors who were portrayed as acting unjustly. In many ways this "spin" described by Kelly has remained the commonly accepted interpretation of these events. Kelly's letter is a reminder that the situation at CUA in the fall of 1968 was extremely complex and contained many distinct personal positions and theological opinions.

8

The Board of Trustees Meeting:
September 5, 1968

The meeting of the CUA board of trustees that Cardinal O'Boyle had said was probable was indeed arranged as soon as possible and scheduled for September 5, 1968. This extraordinary meeting had only one purpose: to determine how the board would officially respond to the CUA professors who had affixed their names to the "Statement of Dissent" against *Humanae Vitae*. Six weeks had passed since the statement had first been issued, and the moment had arrived when the board of trustees had to make a definitive decision about what, if any, response it would make to the dissenting professors.

The Bishops Discuss Their Strategy

On the evening of September 4, 1968, the night before the meeting of the full board of trustees, the bishops on the board gathered in a suite at the Mayflower Hotel at O'Boyle's request for an informal meeting to discuss the pros and cons of the various options now before them.[1] O'Boyle distributed to the other bishops a five-page memorandum prepared by Germain Grisez, who served as his theological

---

[1] In attendance were Cardinals O'Boyle, Krol, McIntyre, and Shehan, as well as Bishops Baum, Casey, Hannan, McGucken, Shannon, Wright, and Zaleski. Two lawyers from CUA's legal counsel (Hamilton and Hamilton of Washington) were also present. The general description of this meeting comes from the author's interview with Germain Grisez on July 11, 2011, who was present at this meeting as theological adviser to Cardinal O'Boyle.

adviser throughout the controversies surrounding *Humanae Vitae*. This memorandum presented the bishops with five possible courses of action: to do nothing; to make a symbolic gesture, such as censuring the dissenting professors; to attempt to dismiss the dissenting professors; to close the ecclesiastical faculties of CUA; or to separate CUA from the Church and give it to the District of Columbia so that it could continue in existence as a secular university.[2] The memorandum acknowledged that doing nothing or merely giving a symbolic admonition to the dissenting professors was certainly an easier course of action but would undermine the authority of the bishops by showing that they were powerless to stop the rejection of papal teaching at their own university. It noted that article 66 of the statutes of CUA seemed to envision a trial of the dissenting professors before a panel of three bishops. Such a trial, however, would be time-consuming and costly, and, the memorandum stated, "the board of trustees probably would give in somewhere along the line." The dissenters would likely argue that article 66 did not apply in this situation because the teaching of *Humanae Vitae* was not infallible. The proposal to shut down immediately the ecclesiastical faculties had the advantage of being swift and effective in ending dissent at CUA, but the rest of the university would be gravely harmed and would likely suffer a loss of students, faculty, and prestige. Separating CUA from the Church would "merely formalize . . . what already is largely accomplished [in] fact" but would set a precedent that would quickly be followed by "all major Catholic institutions of higher education".

The bishops discussed the possibility of a strong action against the dissenting professors. However, they were advised by CUA's legal counsel to do nothing that might provoke legal action against the university. As described by Grisez, "these men were excellent lawyers, qualified and intelligent, and they were as convincing as they could be" that the board of trustees should avoid provoking a lawsuit at all costs.[3] The meeting ended late on the evening of September 4 without any definite decision about what would happen the next day.

---

[2] See appendix D. The memo is contained in the papers of Cardinal McIntyre, Mc 5493, AALA.

[3] Author's interview with Germain Grisez.

Tension and Frustration

On the morning of September 5, 1968, the CUA board of trustees convened at the Madison Hotel in Washington for what turned out to be a nine-hour meeting that would seal the fate of CUA.[4] From the outset the mood was one of tension and grave concern. As soon as the meeting was formally opened, Father Whalen challenged its legitimacy, because the bylaws of the board of trustees required that thirty-day notice be given before a special meeting of the board could be held. Cardinal Krol responded to Whalen by making a motion to waive the bylaws, which was quickly done by vote of the board.

Cardinal O'Boyle proceeded to read aloud the "Statement of Dissent" in its entirety. Whalen then related how he had organized a meeting in New York on August 18 between representatives of both the dissenting theologians and the American bishops. He had done so with the approval of Bishop Zaleski, chairman of the Doctrinal Committee of the NCCB, because, said Whalen, Zaleski thought "something positive ought to be done." Whalen related how he had hoped to keep the August 18 meeting on a "pastoral" level and thus to develop "a better understanding of the encyclical"; however, he had been unsuccessful: "It became a theological discussion [and] reached no agreement." All in all, the August 18 meeting had been for Whalen "a frustrating experience, though maybe it achieved something".

Zaleski described for the board of trustees his impression of the dissenting theologians:

> They were completely convinced of their position and that their dissent was in order and proper form. They felt the Pope was in error and that it was pastorally correct to advise married couples to use contraceptives under certain circumstances. They seemed to expect some softening of the papal attitude and showed no sign that they might back down or compromise.

Zaleski said there were tendencies in the theologians' position that went beyond the teaching of Vatican I and Vatican II, de-emphasizing the authority of the Holy Father and giving undue emphasis to the role of the consensus of the faithful in the development of doctrine.

---

[4] The account here is taken entirely from the minutes of the special meeting of the board of trustees, September 5, 1968, box 28d, ACK.

Bishop Wright of Pittsburgh,[5] who had also been present at the August 18 meeting, agreed with Zaleski's impression: the attitude of the dissenting theologians had been "definitely at variance with Vatican II". Yet Wright believed that the August 18 meeting had been a good idea. Both bishops thought that the discussion up to that point had been a good thing and that further discussion was desirable, since, as Zaleski said, "the theologians wanted to continue to talk."

O'Boyle's opinion of the situation was decidedly less optimistic. He described his August 20 meeting with the dissenting professors at Caldwell Hall as having left him "frustrated" because the theologians would not substantiate their position. O'Boyle noted that in spite of the press release that had been made public at the end of that meeting, the *Baltimore Sun*, the *Washington Post*, and the *Washington Star* had quoted Curran and Hunt saying that they felt "vindicated" by the meeting and that their "right of dissent" had been approved. O'Boyle believed their interpretation was erroneous and misleading.

Cardinal McIntyre Proposes Terminating the Contracts of the Dissenters

Cardinal McIntyre of Los Angeles then introduced a resolution offering the dissenting professors in no uncertain terms only two options —either they withdraw their support for the "Statement of Dissent", or they consider their contracts to be immediately terminated. The resolution declared that because the dissenting professors had formally declared themselves to be in opposition to the definitive teaching of the Magisterium, the board of trustees, in view of its responsibility for overseeing the purpose of the university, could draw only one conclusion. The "Statement of Dissent" "admits of no other interpretation than a violation and betrayal of the pledge contained in the oath of office and the Profession of Faith made by the professors as part of their contract with the University when they assumed and accepted

---

[5] John Wright (1909–1979) was Bishop of Pittsburgh from 1959 to 1969. In 1969 he became the prefect of the Congregation for the Clergy, at which time he was named a cardinal.

the responsibility of professorship". Because of this breach of contract, the resolution declared that the board of trustees could make no other conclusion but that the professors had terminated their contracts and thus resigned from their professorships. It concluded, "This resolution is hereby affirmed and promulgated by the board with sentiments of deep regret and prayerfulness."

McIntyre's bold initiative declared unambiguously what he perceived to be the essence of the situation at CUA: the dissenting professors were in "obvious conflict" not only with the encyclical *Humanae Vitae* but with the entire Tradition of the Church. By their own free choice and action, these professors had created "a contradiction . . . which admits of no other interpretation than a violation and betrayal". In McIntyre's view, this action of dissent in and of itself constituted a breach of contract, and so he believed that the board, recognizing that these professors had chosen to violate the terms of their hiring, must sadly conclude that they were no longer able to serve as professors of Catholic University. The language of the resolution was straightforward and manifested a certain simple logic: teachers of the Catholic faith needed to follow the teaching of the Catholic Church.

Archbishop Dwyer[6] of Portland made a motion to discuss the resolution. The minutes say only that "extended discussion followed", centering on two main points: on the one hand, the rights of the professors to academic freedom and the danger of CUA's being censured by the academic world if it failed to uphold these rights, and, on the other hand, the obligations of the university to the Holy See and the authoritative teaching of the Magisterium. At the end of the discussion, Zaleski proposed that the board of trustees hold a hearing at which the dissenting professors would express their views, while in the meantime the professors would pledge not to dissent publicly or to speak against the encyclical. McIntyre replied that he could not accept this proposal at all.

---

[6] Robert Dwyer (1908–1976) was bishop of Portland, Oregon, from 1966 to 1976. The *Washington Post*, in its coverage of the meeting, identified Dwyer "with the conservative wing of the American hierarchy" (September 6, 1968, A5).

Formulation of a Response to the Statement of Dissent

Attempting to bring some resolution to the tumultuous meeting, O'Boyle proposed that a small committee be appointed to formulate a statement on behalf of the entire board, consisting of Bishops Krol, Hannan, Shannon,[7] Wright, and Zaleski, as well as Mr. Laurence Hickey of the board of trustees. The meeting adjourned while this committee went to work.

At this critical and decisive moment, the board of trustees was in no small way influenced by the 1964 AAUP "Statement on Procedural Standards in Faculty Dismissal Proceedings".[8] This statement had been created as a supplement to the 1940 AAUP "Statement of Principles on Academic Freedom and Tenure", and it gave specific guidelines for the due process that should be followed in dismissal proceedings against faculty members. It stated that in an "effective college", a dismissal proceeding was to be "a rare exception". In the event of such a rare exception, the following procedures should be followed:

1. After a personal interview with the faculty member in question, the administration was to arrange for an elected faculty committee to investigate the matter and determine if a formal proceeding was necessary.

2. If such a proceeding was necessary, a *faculty committee* was to be entrusted with the task of investigating the professor in question by means of interviews and documentary evidence.

3. During such an investigation by the committee, the faculty member was not to be suspended, unless there was a threat of

---

[7] James P. Shannon (1921–2003) was auxiliary bishop of the Archdiocese of Saint Paul and Minneapolis from 1965 until 1968, when he resigned from the episcopacy because of his opposition to *Humanae Vitae*. Shannon served as head of the NCCB Commission on the Press and was known to have sympathies with the dissenting theologians, even, according to Curran, meeting privately with some of the theologians and helping them draft a statement defending their position (author's interview with Curran, April 15, 2009).

[8] American Association of University Professors, "Statement on Procedural Standards in Faculty Dismissal Proceedings," *Bulletin of the American Association of University Professors* 50 (1964), 69–71. A copy of this statement is contained in Krol's notes from the meeting of September 5, 1968, ACK.

immediate harm to himself or others caused by his continuance in teaching.

4. It was then expected that the governing board of the university would accept the decision of the faculty committee about the investigated faculty member's competence.

5. If there were any objection to the decision of the faculty committee, the governing board would return the matter to the committee, noting its objections.

6. Only after *reconsideration by the faculty committee* could the governing board overrule the decision of the committee.

7. Throughout the entire proceeding, no public statements about the matter were to be made by either the faculty member or the administration.

When the meeting reconvened, the committee had put together a draft statement that included nine essential points that the board of trustees wished to convey in response to the "Statement of Dissent". The list attempted to walk a tightrope between deference to the authority of the Magisterium on the one hand and the principles of the AAUP on the other:

1) to express fealty to the Holy Father

2) to show respect for academic freedom as understood in University circles

3) to relate Catholic University to the Catholic conscience

4) to subscribe to the right of due process

5) to sustain the Chancellor's concern for safeguarding Catholic doctrine

6) to defer to the hierarchy's Magisterium

7) to authorize the Acting Rector to initiate a formal inquiry in accord with due academic process

8) to relate matters of doctrine to the American hierarchy

9) to insure that University authority would not interfere with the academic work of the dissenters, who in turn would agree

to desist from criticism of *Humanae Vitae* and not teach contrary to the Magisterium[9]

These nine points attempted to enable both the bishops and the dissenting theologians to "have it all": they professed loyalty to the pope and a concern to safeguard Catholic doctrine while at the same time affirming the rights of the faculty to academic freedom (i.e., the right to dissent) and to due process (according to the AAUP's procedures) in any investigation of their teaching. The statement called for a faculty-run inquiry into the actions of the dissenting professors, following the blueprint of the AAUP norms in its entirety:

> The board directs the acting-Rector of the University to institute through due academic process an immediate inquiry as to whether the teachers at this University who signed the recent statement of dissent have violated by their declarations or actions with respect to the encyclical *Humanae Vitae* their responsibilities to the University under its existing statutes and specifically as teachers of theology and/or other sacred sciences.

The statement also called for silence on the part of the dissenting professors, who would remain in their positions for the duration of the inquiry:

> The board calls for no interruption of the proper academic function of any of these faculty members who agree to abstain for the period of the inquiry from any activities which would involve the name of The Catholic University and which are inconsistent with the pronouncements of the ordinary teaching authority established in the Church—above all, that of the Holy Father.[10]

Because this board of inquiry was to be entirely a *faculty* undertaking, this decision of the CUA board of trustees put the matter, at least for the time being, entirely out of the board's hands. Cardinal McIntyre's proposal to terminate the contracts of the dissenting professors was rejected on the grounds that it was too extreme and that it would bring censure upon CUA from the American academic community.

---

[9] Minutes, board of trustees, September 5, 1968, box 28d, ACK.

[10] The Catholic University of America, "Statement of the Board of Trustees," news release, September 13, 1968, "Press Releases (1967–1968)" folder, ACUA.

For McIntyre, concern to protect the teaching of the Magisterium came first. By contrast, the decision of the board of trustees to empower a faculty-led inquiry gave first place to concern for the principles of the AAUP. The official statement of the board of trustees following the meeting affirmed its concern for *both* the teaching of the Magisterium and the norms of academic freedom: "It is the intent of the board of trustees of the University by this action to protect its faculty from harm to their academic freedom and to protect the Catholic community from harm to the authentic teaching of the Church."[11] But in fact the board of trustees' decision to turn the matter over to a faculty inquiry made concern for academic freedom paramount, and it countenanced a certain respect for the Magisterium if and only if the Magisterium in no way restricted the academic freedom and "right to conscience" of the professors.

The professors agreed "not to teach contrary to the Magisterium", which meant in practice that they simply would not speak about *Humanae Vitae* and its teaching at all, which in turn meant that at Catholic University for the duration of the inquiry there would be no official teaching whatsoever about the most widely discussed and controversial theological issue of the day. The university that had been instituted by the American hierarchy to promote and defend the Catholic faith would be silent at what was arguably the greatest instance of cultural and academic opposition to the teaching of the Magisterium in the history of the Church in the United States.

At this decisive moment, still less than six weeks after *Humanae Vitae* had been released, the CUA board of trustees handed an undeniable victory to the dissenting professors. The proceedings of the "board of inquiry" would consume the entire 1968–1969 academic year at CUA. During that time, the CUA board of trustees, and by extension the American bishops, would have no role whatsoever in the investigation. The story line in which the bishops set their doctrinal authority aside and instead let the principles of academia dictate their response to a controversy was starting to become very familiar. And once again it was apparent that the bottom line—for both sides in the controversy— was what role the authority of the Magisterium would play in Catholic higher education.

---

[11] Ibid.

9

The Faculty Board of Inquiry: September 1968–April 1969

The Formulation of the Board of Inquiry

Father Whalen lost no time in implementing the decision of the board of trustees to create a faculty-run board of inquiry. Within a few days the acting rector personally interviewed each of the dissenting theologians and asked them to answer four questions:

1) For the record, did you sign the Statement of the Theologians bearing the date of July 30?

2) Do you at this time wish to withdraw your support from the Statement of the Theologians of July 30th?[1]

3) Are you willing to observe during the inquiry the conditions set down by the board of trustees in their September 5th resolution?

4) Are you willing to preserve silence about the acts of the elected faculty committee until the outcome of the inquiry has been reached?[2]

These four questions established in embryonic form at CUA the same conditions that would eventually come to be the enduring status quo between the Magisterium of the American bishops and dissenting theologians throughout the United States, which George Weigel has aptly

---

[1] This question was revised from its original formulation: "Do you intend to continue in your public opposition to the authentic teaching of the Magisterium as that opposition is set forth in your statement of July 30?" The reformulated question asked directly for the hoped-for response of a withdrawal of dissent.

[2] Whalen to O'Boyle, September 10, 1968, box 30a, ACK.

dubbed the "Truce of 1968".[3] The theologians were invited to with-draw their dissent, but, if they did not, their freedom to teach and to function as both professors and theologians was in no way restricted, so long as they agreed to remain silent about *Humanae Vitae* and the status of the faculty-run board of inquiry. It was presumed, of course, that the bishops would similarly remain silent about the entire matter for the duration of the inquiry. Given this state of affairs, it was in the theologians' interest that the proceedings of the board of inquiry would take as long as possible.

Shortly after completing his interview of twenty-one faculty members, Whalen wrote a "special communication" to the board of trustees, offering his assessment of the prevailing state of affairs at CUA.[4] He wrote that he could be objective about the situation because his commitment as rector was coming to an end, "thank God". He confessed how frightened he had been about the possibility of a disastrous ending to the matter: "I frankly feared there was enough division manifest and sufficient emotional content in the two positions for a schism to occur." Instead, he was now relieved to report that no serious damage would occur to the impressionable young minds sitting at the feet of the dissenting theologians: "I can tell you that I sincerely believe that no harm will come to the faith of your seminarians and students who are enrolled here." He also offered his assessment of the value of the dissenting professors for the university and indeed for the entire Church in America: "Universities are staffed by men of independent minds. This makes them to some degree unmanageable except by consensus of peers; but it also makes them perhaps the most valuable asset that our Church and our culture have at our disposal." One can imagine that the board of trustees was not too terribly impressed with Whalen's optimism.

Whalen initiated the inquiry process within the formal administrative structure of Catholic University. On September 12, 1968, he asked the academic senate to oversee the inquiry, and the senate agreed to proceed "in an atmosphere of reason, without resort to other forums".[5] The matter was to remain entirely an academic affair. The senate like-

---

[3] George Weigel, *The Courage to Be Catholic* (New York: Basic Books, 2002), 68–72.

[4] Whalen to the CUA board, "special communication", September 18, 1968, box 30a, ACK.

[5] Minutes, academic senate, September 12, 1968, "Academic Senate Records", box 2, "Academic Senate Minutes, Vol. 12" folder, ACUA.

wise affirmed its own responsibility to evaluate the "academic propriety" of the steps already taken by the board of trustees, thus asserting its particular competence in this entirely academic matter as a forum of professional academics.

Concerned that the proceedings could easily occupy an excessive amount of its time, the academic senate accordingly established a Standing Committee on Committees and Rules and recommended the creation of "two preliminary committees".[6] The first committee would be charged with assessing the "academic propriety" of the steps already taken by the board and monitoring observance of the stipulation that the professors make no public statement of dissent during the inquiry. The second was to look into procedures for the inquiry.[7] At this same meeting, the academic senate also adopted a resolution expressing "grave concern at the apparent inaction of the Trustees Committee on Selection of a Rector, and on the failure of the board to implement procedures recommended by the Senate on 14 December 1967". Clearly, faculty frustration with the administration of the university remained exceedingly high.

Meanwhile, coverage of the developing inquiry in the *Tower* noted that the Catholic University administration had high hopes that by its efficient handling of this difficult situation, CUA would "gain prestige by being involved in a landmark decision concerning academic freedom".[8] This increase in prestige could be equated with winning approval in the eyes of the AAUP, because while the AAUP had adopted a tentative statement on the rights of religion teachers and theologians in private institutions, it as yet had no final statement on the matter. The essential issue in the present inquiry was "whether a teacher in theology or the sacred sciences can search for truth with the same structure of academic inquiry as other disciplines".

The faculty board of inquiry was formally constituted by Committee B of the Catholic University academic senate on October 16, 1968. The procedural norms directed that five persons be elected to the board of inquiry by faculty representatives of the academic senate. The mission of the board of inquiry was to be in accord with the

---

[6] Beaumont, Tom. "Senate conceives special inquiry," *Tower*, September 27, 1968, ACUA.

[7] Minutes, academic senate, September 12, 1968.

[8] Beaumont, "Senate Conceives Special Inquiry", 1.

mandate given by the board of trustees at its September 5, 1968, meeting:

> The scope of the Inquiry shall be to determine whether the faculty members . . . who signed the recent statement of dissent have violated by their declarations or actions with respect to the encyclical *Humanae Vitae* their responsibilities to the University under its existing statutes and under their commitments as teachers of theology and/or other sacred sciences . . . and whether under accepted norms of academic freedom their actions have conformed with responsible academic procedures as well as with the spirit of this University.

The academic senate gave powers to the board of inquiry to receive evidence and testimony and to provide conclusions and recommendations for action to the rector and the board of trustees. It also laid down regulations regarding due process, the calling of witnesses, and the rights of parties being investigated by the inquiry—namely, the twenty-one dissenting faculty named by the board of trustees. The procedural norms outlined by the AAUP in its various statements on academic freedom and due process were meticulously followed. It was the clear intention of the CUA faculty that the highly publicized investigation undertaken by the board of inquiry would display to all of American academia that Catholic University was a place where the principles of the AAUP were highly esteemed.

The members of the board of inquiry were promptly elected by the CUA faculty.[9] Having received its mandate from the board of trustees and its procedural authority from the academic senate, the board of inquiry began its massive investigation as Catholic University and all of American Catholic academia awaited its findings.

---

[9] The board was chaired by Dean Marlowe. Its other members included E. Catherine Dunn, professor of English; Frederick R. McManus, dean of the School of Canon Law; Antanas Suziedelis, professor of psychology; and Eugene Van Antwerp, S.S., director of the Seminary Department of the NCEA. Dean Schmitz of the School of Theology served as an alternate. Acting Rector Brother Nivard Scheel was represented by Father Robert Trisco, professor of history and former academic vice-rector. Bishop James Shannon represented the board of trustees as an observer. Joseph P. Williman served as a faculty representative. Observers were also present from the AAUP and the American Association of Theological Schools. See C. Joseph Nuesse, *The Catholic University of America: A Centennial History* (Washington, D.C.: 1990), 403.

Awaiting the Report of the Board of Inquiry

The proceedings of the board of inquiry took up almost the entire 1968–1969 academic year. The tense situation at CUA was just one facet of widespread uproar and upheaval in the Catholic Church in the United States, as bishops throughout the country dealt with the aftermath of *Humanae Vitae* and its difficult reception among both priests and laity. In the Archdiocese of Washington itself, Cardinal O'Boyle faced open revolt from his clergy. On October 1, 1968, he announced disciplinary action against thirty-nine priests who dissented against the teaching of the encyclical.[10] In November 1968 the bishops of the United States issued a pastoral letter, *Human Life in Our Day*, which said that dissent against the Magisterium was a legitimate position for a Catholic scholar to hold if his reasoning had a solid foundation. This statement of the bishops was to be directly invoked by the report of the board of inquiry in justification of the dissenting professors. The response of the American bishops to dissent at this crucial moment was ambiguous at best.

Such ambiguity was perhaps more tolerable than the outright dictatorship of dissent that prevailed in many academic circles. At CUA the atmosphere was hardly conducive to dialogue and discussion for anyone who dared to disagree with the dissenting theologians. On January 17, 1969, Monsignor Kevane dropped Cardinal Krol a handwritten note in which he described a situation on campus marked by intimidation and fear: "The atmosphere on campus is beyond description. A priest who is loyal to the Church must live in silence. Priests dominate the dining room who are loud and angry against the Holy See and the Hierarchy in our country."[11] Academic freedom existed only for those who agreed with the dissenting theologians.

On December 23, 1968, Brother Nivard Scheel, C.F.X., who had succeeded Father Whalen as acting rector, wrote Dr. Marlowe, chairman of the board of inquiry, regarding the purpose of the special board.[12] Scheel's letter explained that the board of trustees felt itself

---

[10] See Morris J. MacGregor, *Steadfast in the Faith. The Life of Patrick Cardinal O'Boyle* (Washington, D.C.: Catholic University of America Press, 2006), 341–68.

[11] Kevane to Krol, January 17, 1969, box 34c, folder 33, ACK.

[12] Scheel to Marlowe, December 23, 1968, in Hunt and Connelly, *The Responsibility*

to be accountable to "several responsible publics" and thus was concerned to resolve "the question of how theological dissent can be expressed in the public forum with due respect for the teaching of the Holy Father and for the standards of free speculative inquiry accepted by responsible academic persons". The board of inquiry had been constituted by the board of trustees, wrote Scheel, to assist it in determining whether the *mode* of the dissent from *Humanae Vitae* was consonant with the norms for theological dissent "which are endorsed by custom and practice among professional academic persons". Scheel's letter emphasized that the board of inquiry was to make no accusations against the faculty, nor was it to attempt to enter into matters of theological competence which were the distinct prerogative of the bishops of the Church. Rather, Scheel clarified, the mission of the board of inquiry was to examine "the style and method whereby some faculty members expressed personal dissent from Papal teaching". Scheel expressed hope that the work of the board of inquiry could possibly "result in an historic statement for the entire field of speculative theology" by addressing the relationship between religious faith and authentic speculative investigation.

The board of inquiry met some twenty times over the course of the 1968–1969 academic year. It held hearings for a total of eight days and received over three thousand pages of testimony.[13] The board of trustees had entirely handed oversight of the inquiry to the CUA faculty and could do nothing but wait for the process to take its course. As the board of inquiry consulted other prominent members of Catholic academia regarding the situation at CUA, it encountered overwhelming support for the dissenting theologians and their manner of acting in issuing the "Statement of Dissent". For example, Bernard Lonergan[14] submitted testimony to the board of inquiry expressing his total

---

of Dissent, 208–11. Scheel, a Xaverian Brother and physicist, was president of Xaverian College in Silver Spring, Maryland, from 1960 to 1966. He came to CUA in the fall of 1967 as executive assistant to Father Whalen after serving as principal of Nazareth High School in Brooklyn for one year.

[13] Statistics given in Cardinal Krol's evaluation, box 20, folder 42, ACK.

[14] Bernard Lonergan, S.J. (1904–1984), professor of theology at the Gregorian University, had been one of the formative professors in Curran's experience as a seminarian in Rome, especially regarding "the importance of historical consciousness and its effects on all of theology". See Curran, *Loyal Dissent*, 10.

endorsement of the "Statement of Dissent": "I agree that the above mentioned statement can be defended on principles that are acceptable in Catholic theology."[15]

Likewise, University of Notre Dame president Theodore Hesburgh contributed his written testimony to the board of inquiry. The man who had been the driving force behind the "Land O'Lakes Statement" was confident that the "Statement of Dissent" had satisfied the AAUP norms for extramural expression, because the dissenting professors did not in any way identify themselves as speaking for their institutions when they signed the statement. The mode of dissent was also entirely appropriate, said Hesburgh, because "it was an emergency situation" and there was "no indication that they made overtures to the press". Hesburgh hoped that the difficult situation at CUA would result in a better understanding of the relationship between the Church and her universities. "The one ray of hope in the cloudy situation", he wrote, "is that it has given rise to most urgent motivations and has produced masses of material useful for clarification. It is essential that the complexities of this 'unique relationship' be worked out as quickly as possible for the benefit of both Church and theology."[16] Hesburgh's words offer a good indication of the board of inquiry's thoughts as it formulated its final report: the principles of the AAUP were to be reconciled with the principles of Catholic theology through a compromise of the latter, not the former.

The Report of the Board of Inquiry

On April 1, 1969, the faculty board of inquiry released its long-awaited report.[17] In the words of C. J. Nuesse, "The subject professors could hardly have asked for a more favorable verdict than was rendered unanimously in the report."[18] Simultaneous with its release, the report was unanimously approved by the entire CUA faculty senate. The board of inquiry issued both a summary report as well as a longer, more detailed report, both of which made the same specific recommendations

---

[15] Lonergan to Hunt, March 5, 1969, box 144c, ACK.

[16] Hesburgh to Hunt, March 11, 1969, box 144c, ACK. This last sentence was underlined by Krol in his personal copy of the letter.

[17] *Report of the Faculty Board of Inquiry*, Cardinal Shehan papers, AAB.

[18] Nuesse, *The Catholic University of America*, 406.

and conclusions regarding how to address the situation of the dissenting professors. The report's introductory remarks detailed the mandate given to the board of inquiry by the board of trustees in September 1968 as well as the clarification of the specific task of the board of inquiry, which had been made through the letter of Brother Scheel on December 23, 1968. The report observed that this letter had "placed considerable emphasis on investigation of the 'style and method' and 'mode' of the manifestation of public dissent to the encyclical" by the dissenting professors, and it also spoke of "the opportunity which the board of inquiry had to appraise or recommend norms or standards which might assist the faculty, the administration, and the board of trustees" in making CUA a place of both intellectual excellence and fidelity to the teachings of the Church.[19] The report noted that the procedural norms followed by the board of inquiry included hearing testimony from those who disagreed with the position taken by the faculty members. There had also been a conscious effort to follow the "traditional standards of fair academic procedure as enunciated by the American Association of University Professors".[20]

The report detailed how the board of inquiry had divided the issues into two categories, the first concerning the conduct of the faculty members and the second concerning the public expression of their opinions, including opinions dissenting from the teaching of the Magisterium. The board had considered six specific questions regarding the conduct of the subject professors (questions 1–6):

I. Whether the statement [of dissent] represents an untenable position in Roman Catholic Theology and is incapable of reasonable and appropriate scholarly support?

II. Whether the style, mode and manner of the statement itself exceeded the bounds of academic propriety?

III. Whether the mode and manner of the release of the statement to the public was not in accord with responsible academic procedure as practiced in American universities?

IV. Whether the statement, or the manner of issuance of the statement, violated any valid and currently enforceable statute or bylaw,

---

[19] *Report of the Faculty Board of Inquiry*, 3.
[20] Ibid., 5.

or any written regulation or policy of The Catholic University of America?

V. Whether the statement, or manner of release of the statement, violated any special commitment of the professors as teachers of theology or other sacred sciences?

VI. Whether the statement, or the manner of release of the statement, violated the "spirit" of Catholic University?

The board of inquiry had also considered four specific questions regarding the norms for public dissent by faculty members (questions 7–10):

VII. What general norms should apply to extramural statements of faculty members in an American university?

VIII. What specific norms should apply to the extramural statements made by teachers of Roman Catholic theology in a Catholic university?

IX. What additional norms should apply, if any, when these statements manifest a public dissent from a non-infallible but authoritative teaching of the Magisterium?

X. What additional norms, if any, should apply because of the pontifical character of this University?

These ten questions had formed the framework of the investigation of the board of inquiry. The answer at which it arrived after its months of holding meetings, considering evidence, and receiving testimony was quite simple: the dissenting subject professors had *in no way acted inappropriately* in their role either as professors or as theologians. Furthermore the heart of the problem at Catholic University lay entirely in the statutes of the university and in *the conduct of the board of trustees*, neither of which were in accord with what it meant to be a fully American university as defined by the AAUP. The specific content of the report of the board of inquiry merits detailed attention, because more than any other document, the report gives a rationale for the position of the dissenters and their own justification of their theological and academic position.

First, the report of the board of inquiry found that dissent against *Humanae Vitae* was without question a "tenable theological position".

It declared that the encyclical was "clearly non-infallible"; in fact, the encyclical's appeal for obedience in paragraph 28 actually seemed to anticipate dissent, indicating that the pope himself understood the encyclical to be a noninfallible statement.[21] The report invoked *Human Life in Our Day* as having clearly stated that dissent on this topic was possible in its explanation of the norms for licit dissent.[22] The interpretative dissent that existed in the statements of other national hierarchies as well as the large number of respected American theologians who had signed the "Statement of Dissent" were also presented as evidence of the theological legitimacy of the dissenting theologians' position. In a confused and confusing statement, the board of inquiry protested its theological incompetence in the same breath that it judged the dissenting professors to be theologically competent: "It is not within the competence of the board to judge the theological correctness or incorrectness of the position taken in the statement [of dissent]. However, in light of the above factors it is the conclusion of the board that the statement expresses a tenable theological opinion."

---

[21] Pope Paul VI's words in paragraph 28 of *Humanae Vitae*: "You [priests] must be the first to give an example of that sincere obedience, inward as well as outward, which is due to the Magisterium of the Church. For, as you know, the pastors of the Church enjoy a special light of the Holy Spirit in teaching the truth. And this, rather than the arguments they put forward, is why you are bound to such obedience. Nor will it escape you that if men's peace of soul and the unity of the Christian people are to be preserved, then it is of the utmost importance that in moral as well as in dogmatic theology all should obey the magisterium of the Church and should speak as with one voice." Whatever one may think about the teaching of the encyclical, it seems a bit far-fetched to cite this paragraph as a rationale for dissent against it!

[22] The bishops' letter *Human Life in Our Day* explicitly supported *Humanae Vitae* but also opened the door to ambiguity about the legitimacy of theological dissent against the encyclical: "There exist in the Church a lawful freedom of inquiry and of thought and also general norms of licit dissent. This is particularly true in the area of legitimate theological speculation and research. When conclusions reached by such professional theological work prompt a scholar to dissent from non-infallible received teaching the norms of licit dissent come into play. They require of him careful respect for the consciences of those who lack his special competence or opportunity for judicious investigation. These norms also require setting forth his dissent with propriety and with regard for the gravity of the matter and the deference due the authority which has pronounced on it. . . . The expression of theological dissent from the magisterium is in order only if the reasons are serious and well founded, if the manner of the dissent does not question or impugn the teaching authority of the Church and is such as not to give scandal" (*Human Life in Our Day*, in Hugh J. Nolan, ed., *Pastoral Letters of the United States Catholic Bishops*, vol. 3 [Washington, D.C.: United States Catholic Conference, 1983], 164–99).

Having thus declared the "Statement of Dissent" itself legitimate, the *Report of the Faculty Board of Inquiry* went on to declare that the "style, mode and manner" of the statement were likewise entirely appropriate and in accord with the norms of the 1940 AAUP statement regarding extramural utterances. The report judged the statement to have been "dignified, grave, and measured". It was "temperate" compared with other criticisms of the encyclical that had been issued, and it had been "prudently" given to the public. In fact, said the report, it would have been highly imprudent for the professors *not* to have issued a statement of dissent, for the media would have sought for comment from individual theologians, and their individual statements "would have been possibly less prepared with uncontrollable conditions of release." Far from the statement's being a scandal to believers, it would have caused greater scandal had there been no statement, the board of inquiry affirmed, for this would have generated "a suspicion that an opinion affecting the lives of millions had been self-suppressed through fear or silenced by authority", and this suspicion "would have strongly and adversely affected the credibility of the theologians and the hierarchical magisterium." The board of inquiry found nothing in the "Statement of Dissent" or in its manner of release and dissemination that was not "in accord with responsible academic procedure as practiced in American Universities today". Furthermore, there was no evidence whatsoever of any pressure being used in obtaining signatures for the "Statement of Dissent". The report's conclusion proclaimed the dissenters to be entirely justified: "The board of inquiry therefore finds that the style, mode and manner of the statement did not exceed the bounds of academic propriety."

With regard to the question of whether the statutes of Catholic University had been violated, the board of inquiry found it difficult to make an evaluation because the statutes were under revision, and it found the current statutes to be "in some degree inconsistent with modern American practice in higher education". This inconsistency was seen in numerous places where the CUA statutes were in conflict with the standards of the AAUP and the American Civil Liberties Union (ACLU). In each instance, the board of inquiry found that, in light of the AAUP position, the CUA statutes could not be considered to have binding force. Thus the report found article 66 of the CUA statutes, which Cardinal O'Boyle had invoked in his meeting with the dissenting professors on August 20, 1968, to be problematic: it stip-ulated that any alleged "offense against Catholic doctrine" would be submitted to three bishops for investigation, whereas, noted the report, "all modern procedural standards would provide for investigation by academic peers." The report invoked the "position of all American authorities" that there was no obligation for professors to refrain from extramural utterances that might be embarrassing to their institution.

But did not the canonical mission given by the Church to profes-sors of the sacred sciences call for a certain deference and restraint on their part in expressing themselves? By no means, declared the board of inquiry's report. It declared that the norms agreed to at the meeting of the School of Theology with the board of trustees on May 20, 1967 (in the aftermath of the faculty strike supporting Curran), had aban-doned the notion of a canonical mission. Even if the university statutes referred to such a mission, *these statutes could not be enforced by the board of trustees*, because "otherwise 'canonical mission' would have to be un-derstood in a way incompatible with American university practice". Furthermore, the statutes were not readily available to the faculty and had never been given to them in writing; thus, they could in no way be regarded as binding, declared the report. Once again the conclusion was stated categorically: "The board of inquiry, therefore, concludes that the subject professors have not violated any university statute or regulation applicable in this case."

What of the specific commitment of the professors as theologians and teachers of the sacred sciences? Here the report of the board of in-quiry sought to correct any simplistic notion that the professors owed some sort of direct obedience to the Magisterium. "The theologian is ultimately constrained only by truth itself", the report declared. This truth, said the report, could certainly not be identified with the statements of the Magisterium, which in the past had so often proved itself to have been mistaken. The report invoked *Gaudium et Spes* and Paul VI's 1964 encyclical *Ecclesiam Suam*[23] as evidence that its under-standing of the mission of the theologian was entirely in accord with and endorsed by the "ecclesiological dimensions" of the Second Vat-

---

[23] Paul VI's first encyclical, "On the Church" (August 6, 1964), called for a renewed theological dialogue both within the Church and between the Church and nonbelievers. Its emphasis on the importance of obedience within the Church received somewhat less attention.

ican Council.[24] With this understanding of truth, it was not only inevitable that dissent would occur in the Church; dissent was actually an act of *service* by the theologian:

> Finally, attention should be given to the arguments advanced concerning the usefulness of dissent by theologians within the Church community: it is a means of informing the sense of the faithful and of hastening the legitimate development of doctrine; it is a means of correcting a non-infallible statement and thus strengthening and supporting the continuity of the hierarchical magisterium; in Catholic doctrine it may be regarded as a working of the Spirit in the Church.

What to do then if this act of "strengthening and supporting" the Magisterium was the occasion of conflicting statements, as in the present situation? The solution was simply more dialogue: "In the resolution of apparent conflicts between the findings of theological science and the expression of the hierarchical magisterium, both the hierarchy and the theologians are bound to enter into dialogue." This dialogue would of necessity be public and employ the various forms of media. Such public dissent would simply embody another aspect of the service of the theologians to the Church, said the report, for if they failed to speak out, the result could only be the confused attribution of an authority to the hierarchical Magisterium that in fact it did not have: "Attention must be paid . . . to the immediate need to correct a false notion of the encyclical's precise authority and to forestall a diffuse presentation of less-informed theological opinion by the media."

Not only did the report claim that there was no compromise of the professors' mission to support the hierarchy; it declared that the "Statement of Dissent" was in fact an act of *assistance* to that same hierarchy's mission to teach the Catholic faith. Nor did the statement in any way violate the profession of faith, said the report, for the Tradition of the Church clearly acknowledged the possibility of dissent from noninfallible teachings. The professors had in no way violated the infallible teaching of the Creed or ecumenical councils. In light of all of these considerations, the board of inquiry concluded that the dissenting professors had performed a great service to Catholic University by their courageous action:

---

[24] *Report of the Faculty Board of Inquiry*, response to q. 5, Cardinal Shehan papers, AAB.

Acknowledging the legitimacy of theological dissent by way of evaluation and interpretation of non-infallible teaching of the hierarchical magisterium and in the light of the above considerations, the board recognizes the right of the professors to act as they did, in their capacity as Roman Catholic theologians, and it accepts their conviction that they had a duty so to act. It therefore finds that the professors acted responsibly as theologians.

Did the "Statement of Dissent" violate "the spirit of Catholic University"? The report said that nothing inappropriate had been done by the dissenting professors, and it actually invoked the board of trustees' own statement of objectives as providing justification for the professors' dissent. In that statement of objectives, which had been issued on July 27, 1968, the board of trustees had defined CUA as "a free and autonomous center of study, . . . a community of scholars" that sought "to discover, preserve, and impart truth in all its forms". In pursuit of this truth, it was the mission of the university to create "an atmosphere of academic competence where freedom is fostered and where the only constraint upon truth is truth itself". While CUA was committed to "adherence to Christian faith", the statement of objectives also made clear that it was no less committed to the "standards and procedures of American institutions". This commitment, observed the report, "would require that any disciplinary action rest on the determination by his peers as to the teacher's continued fitness for his position". Based on the board of trustees' professed commitment to the best American ideals, the report of the board of inquiry found that the dissenting professors had not violated the spirit of the university but rather had notably and admirably advanced the prestige of CUA in the eyes of the American academic community:

> The board finds no evidence of any lack of conformity with the spirit of the University as discernible from its stated objectives. On the contrary, the board finds impressive the sincerity of their varied concerns for the place of Christian values and the role of the Church in the intellectual community and in human society—concern for the ecumenical movement, for a meaningful articulation of Christian values in the mission countries, for the integrity of theology as a profession, for the reception of the teaching of the Church by the faithful, indeed for the office of the Holy Father himself.

The "free pursuit of truth" was the only spirit acceptable at an American university, said the report, and it was this free spirit that animated the "sincerity" of the dissenting professors. Legitimate norms could serve only to enhance this free pursuit of truth, whereas any spirit that was "restrictive" had no place in higher education. "It is repugnant to suggest", declared the board of inquiry, "that conformity is even desirable."

It was regrettable, said the report, that in the past the administration of the university had made attempts to curb intellectual controversy; this censorship by the university administration had been greatly damaging to the reputation of CUA. Whenever such intervention occurred, CUA became less fully a university, for it "effectively loses its neutral position, and to that extent ceases to be an open academic community". In contrast with embarrassing moments of the not-so-distant past, the courageous action of the dissenting professors had immeasurably helped to increase the esteem with which Catholic University was regarded in the eyes of the American academic establishment. This rise in prestige had occurred thanks to the courageous and united action of the "Statement of Dissent", and the report of the board of inquiry could only summarize its findings with a paean of gratitude to the dissenting professors:

> In the light of the testimony presented, the board finds that, apart from any considerations of the substance and circumstances of the declarations and actions of the subject professors, the bold statement of their convictions is consistent with the best elements of the spirit of the Catholic university and in fact has had the effect of enhancing the integrity of the University in the eyes of the academic world.

The board of inquiry report ended with a list of "conclusions and recommendations" representative of its unanimous judgment.[25] These included first and foremost that Catholic University would officially recognize that the dissenting professors had in no way violated their commitments to the university and that norms ensuring the fullness of academic freedom, judgment by peers, and due process would swiftly be enacted so as to prevent any such situation from ever recurring at

---

[25] *Summary Report of the Faculty Board of Inquiry*, box 28d, ACK.

CUA. While still paying lip service to the "ultimate canonical jurisdiction and doctrinal competence of the hierarchy", the report exhorted the trustees to "remain sensitive to the devastating effect of any exercise of power in the resolution of academic difficulties". If it had to be admitted that technically the trustees possessed authority over CUA, it was best for the smooth functioning of the university that such authority should never be used.

The report also made specific recommendations for Catholic University as a result of its proceedings. First, that the revision of the university statutes would be pressed to an early completion. Central to this revision would be the adoption of the 1940 AAUP "Statement on Academic Freedom and Tenure", but without the religious limitation clause of that statement, "as other Catholic universities already have done". Second, that "legitimate channels of theological discussion" be established that would enable the "fruitful dialogue between bishops and theologians" that had been called for by the American bishops in *Human Life in Our Day*. Finally, the board of inquiry noted that the board of trustees, by threatening to suspend the dissenting professors on September 5, 1968, had "seriously damaged [their] academic standing", had "impaired the reputation of the academic departments concerned", and had "tarnished the reputation of the University". This embarrassment, said the report, was caused mainly by the absence of due process in even mentioning the *possibility* of suspension. The board of inquiry strongly called for a guarantee that such summary action by the board would never again take place: "The board recommends that assurance be given the academic community of this university that, before even the process leading to the possibility of suspension or dismissal is initiated, such preliminary decision will be subject to due process and to the prior judgment of academic peers."

By means of all of these recommendations, the board of inquiry report sought to ensure that the academic community of Catholic University would be secure from any future intervention by the board of trustees into its inner life. Thanks to the work of the board of inquiry, Catholic University would be protected from any future violation of its academic freedom by the bishops of the United States.

Response of the CUA Faculty to the
Report of the Board of Inquiry

Although the dissenting professors had protested that the very existence of the board of inquiry was an injustice to them (because its
existence had put them under a "cloud of suspicion"), when the board
issued its findings, the professors were quick to praise its work. John
Hunt and Terrence Connelly, in their sweeping analysis of the entire
process in *The Responsibility of Dissent*, criticized the board of inquiry
because it had attempted to make a judgment as to whether the dissenting professors were innocent or guilty and had placed the burden
of proof on the faculty members, who had no choice but to accept it.[26]
Despite their misgivings about the process, however, they emphatically
endorsed the findings of the board of inquiry, which they maintained
were now definitively binding on the board of trustees. None of the
inquiry's shortcomings, they said, did anything to

> impeach the conclusion of the Inquiry Report (accepted by the
> Trustees) that the University itself could not continue to question
> that the "declarations and actions of the subject professors with re-
> spect to the Encyclical *Humanae Vitae*," . . . did not violate any of
> their obligations to Catholic University of America, did not offend
> against responsible academic procedure [and] did not depart from the
> spirit of the University.

Not only was there nothing offensive in the professors' actions, but
their dissent, said Hunt and Connelly, was actually a sign of their fidelity to the Magisterium, which had emphasized the importance of
what they called the "right to know" in the life of the Church: "In the
present ecclesiological context with its stress on co-responsibility, it
is within the pale of responsible Roman Catholic theology to say that
the theologian has an obligation to communicate his dissent to all who
have a right to know it." This obligation necessitated the communication of the dissenters' position through the mass media to all people of

---

[26] Hunt and Connelly, *The Responsibility of Dissent*, 46, 104, 133–34, 139, 172. Hunt
maintained that the professors collectively spent over $8,000 and over ten thousand hours
of labor to compile their defense.

good will, in order to respect their right to know. Had the dissenters *not* made their position public, they would have been failing in charity and justice to the countless people whom they were trying to serve by their public and vocal dissent. Wrote Hunt and Connelly: "Public silence on the part of professors who 'privately' dissent from authoritative, noninfallible teaching could be looked upon as irresponsible by many people in theological and academic circles, both Catholic and non-Catholic."

The pair also praised the service the dissenters had done to ecumenism, because their action showed that within the Catholic Church there was freedom for scholarship and "thinking" among theologians. The "Statement of Dissent" had been hailed by Union Theological Seminary, *Newsweek*, and other prominent cultural voices. It had been enormously helpful to Protestant theologians, they said, "in mitigating the appearance of the Roman Catholic Church as a monolithic institution". For all of these reasons Hunt and Connelly were convinced that the dissenting theologians were performing an immense act of service toward the good of the Catholic faithful, the good of the universal Church, and even the good of the entire human race.

What of the authority of the pope? Surely his teaching had some role to play at a Catholic university? Hunt and Connelly maintained that any such notion manifested an entirely erroneous understanding of what was meant by the authority of the pope:

"Veneration" of the Pope, rightly understood, should not restrict academic freedom. Catholics should understand the idiom well: by virtue of their faith-commitment, they believe that the Pope possesses and exercises a special ruling and teaching office in the Church. He is recognized as "supreme teacher" through the eyes of faith and in terms of the Petrine prerogative regarding the supernatural mystery of salvation, and not in the "academic" sense of the word "teacher," which is the usage in other Articles of the Statutes and in normal academic terminology. The "Apostolic Authority" enjoyed by the Roman Pontiff as "Supreme Teacher" is, therefore, a *doctrinal* authority, not a juridic or jurisdictional authority.

Consistent with their assertion, Hunt and Connelly criticized the CUA statutes for the way in which they gave such juridical authority to the American bishops. They described article 66 as "a most blatant offense against academic due process, specifically because by its terms it cedes the power of 'final adjudication' to nonpeer 'authorities' extrinsic to the University." Their objection was not to the *process* by which they had been investigated but rather to the *fact* that an authority that claimed the power to investigate and pass judgment upon them *existed at all.*

By completely ratifying the views of the dissenting professors, the report of the board of inquiry turned the tables on the board of trustees. Having been constituted to investigate the actions of the dissenting professors, it concluded by indicting the board of trustees for the supposed injustice of its attempt to interfere in the academic freedom of the university. If there was any danger to the identity of Catholic University, it was not to be found in the teaching of the School of Theology, said the report of the board of inquiry. It was rather to be found in the very existence of the board of trustees.

10

The Response of the CUA Board of Trustees to the Report of the Board of Inquiry: April–June 1969

The Krol Evaluation of the Report of the Board of Inquiry

Two weeks after the board of inquiry report was issued, the CUA board of trustees received it at its regularly scheduled meeting on April 13, 1969, in Washington. The board called for a five-man committee to evaluate the report. This committee was named by board chairman Carroll Hochwalt on April 16, 1969, and included three bishops (Cardinal Krol as chairman, Bishop Zaleski, and Bishop Shannon) as well as Brother Gregory Nugent and Mr. Laurence Hickey of the board of trustees.

Krol's committee submitted its "Evaluation of the Report of the Faculty Board of Inquiry" to the board of trustees at its general meeting on June 16, 1969.[1] Beginning with an account of the mandate given to the board of inquiry by the board of trustees, the Krol evaluation acknowledged the hard work of the board of inquiry that had been headed by Dr. Marlowe, undertaking an unprecedented work while "safeguarding the non-adversary nature of the inquiry, as directed by the board of trustees". The evaluation noted that the board of trustees had clarified (through the letter of Brother Scheel on December 23, 1968) that it was making no accusations against the faculty, that all doctrinal judgments in the matter could be made only by the bishops, and that the board of inquiry was to make its investigation solely from an academic viewpoint. The evaluation further praised the "commendable diligence and manifest sincerity" with which the board of inquiry had undertaken its vast and laborious effort.

---

[1] "Evaluation of the Report of the Faculty Board of Inquiry", June 16, 1969, box 20, folder 42, ACK.

Having attended to all the necessary preliminaries, the Krol evaluation proceeded to analyze the report of the board of inquiry. The evaluation acknowledged that there were many specific factual findings made by the report of the board of inquiry concerning the dissenting professors that found "some support in the record" and recommended that the board of trustees should accept those findings, without thereby agreeing or concurring with them. However, the evaluation also criticized the report of the board of inquiry for having gone beyond the scope of its mandate. It crossed over into the realm of "matters of policy", which were the exclusive prerogative of the board of trustees. It had not been asked to evaluate the rector or the board's performance, yet it proceeded to do just that. It had been charged with examining the conduct of the professors under the statutes of the university, yet it proceeded to find fault with the statutes themselves. It claimed to have no theological competence but then repeatedly made judgments that were explicitly theological in nature. It made a specific judgment that *Humanae Vitae* did not constitute infallible teaching.

In response to the board of inquiry report, Krol's committee recommended that the board of trustees establish a special committee to consider some of the recommendations made by the faculty, "in order that the board of trustees could seek the assistance of those bodies competent in the questions of Church doctrine, theology, and discipline." It also stated for the record that the unprecedented procedure of calling a faculty board of inquiry should not now be considered as normative: "this approach should not be viewed as a binding precedent for the handling of any similar situation which may arise in the future."

The evaluation of the Krol committee manifested a clear judgment that the faculty board of inquiry had overstepped its bounds. The crux of the issue was addressed in the paragraph concerning the statutes of the university: the board of trustees wished to determine whether the dissenting faculty members had acted in a way inconsistent with those statutes (which required that all faculty adhere to the profession of faith). This task had been entrusted to the faculty board of inquiry, but the board of inquiry had instead declared that it did not recognize the university statutes as legitimate because "in some degree they are inconsistent with modern American practice in higher education". The chief concern of the board of trustees, that the faculty of CUA be fully Catholic, was in direct conflict with the chief concern of the faculty board of inquiry, that the procedures of CUA be fully American. The board of inquiry had essentially told the CUA administration that it needed to accept dissent from the Magisterium as part of academic freedom. Krol's committee replied that it was not the faculty's place to tell the board of trustees what sort of dissent from the Magisterium was permissible, if any.

Once again the two conflicting groups spoke past each other, because each had an a priori certainty that its interpretation of the central issue in the matter was correct, and this central issue was the authority of the Magisterium. And once again a "solution" that did not solve anything was proposed: another committee, another investigation, another study to be made about when dissent from the Magisterium was proper within the community of Catholic higher education. The concluding paragraph of Krol's evaluation, designed to prevent any future repetition of the board of inquiry, was an acknowledgment that, from the point of view of the board of trustees, it had been completely ineffective.

The board of trustees, constrained by the demands of AAUP norms, had handed over the task of judging the conduct of certain faculty members to the faculty. To use the analogy of a court of law, the defendants' family and friends had been given the right to judge the defendants' course of action. Not surprisingly, the defendants had been completely vindicated by their peers, and in the process their sympathetic judges had taken the chance to tell the plaintiffs (the board of trustees) that the plaintiffs needed to make major adjustments to their own behavior. Not only did the final report of the board of inquiry not condemn the dissenting faculty; it actually contained an indictment of the very board of trustees that had initiated the inquiry. The Krol committee's analysis effectively said that the board of trustees had been foolish to have passed over the power of judgment in the case to the dissenting faculty's peers, and it should make certain that such a course of action would never be taken again.

Krol presented his committee's evaluation at the meeting of the board of trustees on June 16, 1969, in Washington.[2] Before doing so, Krol had the meeting moved into executive session, and thus the faculty

---

[2] The account of this meeting comes from the minutes of the CUA board of trustees, June 15–16, 1969, box 30c, ACK.

representatives were asked to leave the room before he presented his report. Brother Scheel objected to this move, reminding the board of its own resolution of November 12, 1967, that faculty representatives be allowed to participate in matters relating to the faculty that were on the board's agenda. Bishop Zaleski replied that Krol's business was not technically a faculty matter: Krol was speaking as the chairman of a committee that the board had itself commissioned to formulate an evaluation of the report of the board of inquiry. Archbishop Hannan then made a motion to accept Zaleski's interpretation, and the motion passed with unanimous approval, with the exception of that of Brother Scheel.

After the faculty representatives had left the room, the board of trustees accepted the Krol evaluation unanimously. Krol then read aloud a "suggested statement" affirming that the board of trustees had "never doubted" the commitment of the faculty of CUA "to present in a scholarly manner the authentic teaching of the Church". It declared that the board of trustees accepted the report of the board of inquiry insofar as it evaluated the conduct of the faculty members in question, but cautioned that in no way did it approve the theological positions expressed by the report. Krol's suggested statement then declared that the board of trustees was fully committed, in this "unprecedented situation", to "constructive collaboration between theologians and those responsible for authentic teaching in the Church". The suggested statement concluded by invoking the principles that had been adopted at the meeting of the International Federation of Catholic Universities (IFCU), sponsored by the Sacred Congregation for Catholic Education in April 1969, without any specific quotation of those principles. It seems that Krol wanted to give the most positive response he could to the faculty and to hope optimistically for collaboration in the future. After some discussion, however, Krol's proposed statement was not approved.

Cardinal McIntyre proposed a quite different response, along the same lines as the resolution he had introduced at the September 5, 1968, meeting of the board: that the report of the Krol committee be sent to the dissenting members of the faculty, offering them an immediate choice of either withdrawing their dissent or having their contracts terminated.[3] As had happened the previous September, McIn-

---

[3] The minutes themselves do not identify who made this motion, but in Cardinal McIntyre's letter to O'Boyle of June 19, 1969 (box 30a, ACK), he states that he did.

tyre's motion failed to garner much support; in fact, this time there was not even discussion because the motion immediately "died for want of a second".

It seems that at this June 1969 meeting, the board of trustees sensed that the time for dealing in such a direct way with the dissenting professors had passed. Having commissioned the board of inquiry to undertake its enormous labor and having received the report of the board of inquiry exonerating the faculty of any inappropriate behavior, the board of trustees felt it could not now respond with an ultimatum that entirely ignored the findings of the board of inquiry. To do so would have made the board of trustees (and by extension the American hierarchy) the object of ridicule from the entire American academic community, and by the summer of 1969 the American bishops lacked the resolve to endure or even initiate such a battle.

Having ended their confidential discussion of the Krol evaluation, the board of trustees invited the faculty representatives to return to the meeting. Upon returning, they made a formal protest at having been excluded from the deliberations. The board's decision was explained to the faculty representatives in the light of Bishop Zaleski's interpretation of the nature of Krol's committee. But the frustration of the faculty representatives at this exclusion and secrecy seems understandable.

An alternate resolution was now proposed by two of the board's lay members: that the board of trustees issue a statement declaring its acceptance of the report of the board of inquiry insofar as it dealt with academic procedures, but rejecting "as unacceptable that portion which goes beyond the mandate given to the faculty board". This resolution also directed that all matters of doctrine would be referred to the Doctrinal Committee of the NCCB for further review and evaluation.

In the debate that followed, support for Krol's original suggested statement reemerged, especially because it had already been reviewed by legal counsel. It was finally unanimously decided that Krol's statement should be "refined by suggestions" and then adopted as the board of trustees' official response to the board of inquiry report. In the end, the only significant modification to Krol's original statement was the addition of a quotation from the recommendations made at the April 1969 meeting of the IFCU that called for the theologian to accept and teach the authentic teaching of the Church. An addendum was also placed at the end of the statement quoting the June 5, 1969, resolution of the academic senate, whereby it declared that in accepting the board of inquiry report, it in no way intended to endorse the theological position of the dissenting faculty.

Doctrinal Investigation Approved—
Objections of Legal Counsel

At the June 16 meeting, a further motion was approved by the board of trustees, supporting O'Boyle in his wish to refer the professors' "Statement of Dissent" to Cardinal Dearden, president of the NCCB, so that its Doctrinal Committee could give a theological and doctrinal evaluation of the statement. This action would raise a serious objection from the legal counsel of the dissenting professors. On July 14, 1969, Terrence R. Connelly of Cravath, Swain, and Moore[4] of New York, legal counsel for the dissenting professors, wrote to Stephen A. Trimble of Hamilton and Hamilton[5] of Washington, legal counsel to the board of trustees, and expressed outrage at the decision to refer the matter to the NCCB Doctrinal Committee. Connelly maintained that, in accepting the report of the board of inquiry, the board of trustees had accepted the theological positions it expressed.[6] By further referring the matter to the NCCB Doctrinal Committee, Connelly said, the board of trustees was violating the "accepted American principles of academic freedom" to which the board had made a commitment. Krol had anticipated this objection and had written to Trimble on June 27, 1969, instructing him to inform John F. Hunt of Cravath, Swain, and Moore that the board of inquiry had no doctrinal competence whatsoever, even though it seemed to have assumed that it did possess doctrinal competence when it declared that no further investigation of the dissenting professors was necessary. Krol strenuously objected to the position taken by Hunt (who was in constant communication with the AAUP) that the acceptance of the report of the board of inquiry had taken any further judgment by the bishops out of the equation. Krol wrote:

> It is my opinion that Mr. Hunt is equivalently saying that the board of trustees cannot defer to the Bishops—not even in the matter of

---

[4] Second-oldest law firm in the United States.
[5] Oldest law firm in Washington.
[6] Connelly to Trimble, July 14, 1969, box 30a, ACK.

doctrine—and that the Bishops' right and duty in this matter has been forfeited by a recommendation of the Faculty board of inquiry.[7]

Krol accurately understood that the position of Hunt and the dissenting faculty was simply postconciliar theology put into practice: the magisterium of the theologians had superseded and replaced the Magisterium of the bishops, making the involvement of the hierarchy in any investigation of the theologians no longer necessary. By insisting on the bishops' right to undertake a doctrinal investigation, Krol laid his finger on the heart of the issue and called the dissenting faculty's tactic for what it was: a move to replace the teaching authority of the bishops with their own. Once again, and not for the last time, the issue was the Magisterium.

Krol's Frustration with the Board of Trustees

A personal letter from Krol to Dean Clarence Walton shortly after the June 16, 1969, meeting reveals that Krol did not relish the role of being the one who constantly had to speak out in defense of the Magisterium, a role he felt had been thrust upon him. Walton had written Krol the day after the meeting to thank him for his "superb handling of that most delicate situation of the dissenting theologians". Walton expressed his appreciation for the many hours of work Krol's committee had put in and thanked the cardinal with hopeful words: "Your wisdom and skill have turned us hopefully from the immediate crisis to the long-term construction. You were great."[8]

Krol's reply revealed a man little interested in flattery. He offered Walton a blunt expression of his frustration with the board of trustees meetings and his fear that they were proving ineffective in accomplishing any real change in the situation at CUA:

> Your letter helps to continue my resistance to the temptation to stay away from some of the many meetings I must attend, or at least to stay out of the arena of unpleasant controversy and stay with the discreetly silent participants in such meetings.

---

[7] Krol to Trimble, June 27, 1969, box 30a, ACK.
[8] Walton to Krol, June 17, 1969, box 30b, ACK.

It is a bit disheartening to attend meetings which have the single purpose of promoting the best interests of the entire university, and to find people in attendance who would attempt to promote particular interests at the expense of the welfare of the University. We shall have to find means of eliminating—not vigorous discussions and exchange of diverse views—but the spirit of adverseness, animosity and even hostility which is surfacing in the meetings.

The trustees, the administration and the faculty cannot afford to lose sight of the imperative necessity to keep the University strong. It avails nothing to win small battles if such contribute to the loss of the war.[9]

Krol's frank assessment of the situation shows that he had no illusions about the course on which CUA was headed as long as the dissenting professors remained in control of the terms of the debate, as had been the case thus far. Each time the board of trustees attempted to use its authority in governing the university, it was told the reasons why, in fact, it could not exercise that authority. In the name of academic freedom, Krol felt that he was having his hands tied behind his back. If, in the name of the University's being American, the board of trustees had been reduced to a mere advisory committee (and a weak one at that), Krol wondered whether it was really worth his time and effort to serve on the board at all.

McIntyre's Letter of Resignation

No less frustrated by the June 16, 1969, meeting was Cardinal McIntyre, who was so disgusted with the proceedings that he sent O'Boyle a letter of resignation from the board of trustees on June 19.[10] McIntyre's position was one of simple clarity, as it had been from the beginning of the *Humanae Vitae* controversy. All faculty of CUA made the profession of faith as part of their contract, a point that even the AAUP acknowledged. This fact had been completely ignored by the

---

[9] Krol to Walton, June 20, 1969, box 30b, ACK.
[10] McIntyre to O'Boyle, June 19, 1969, box 30a, ACK.

report of the board of inquiry. Since the board of trustees retained its competence to determine the fault of the dissenters on the point of the violation of the profession of faith, the dissenting professors should be given the chance to withdraw their dissent and renew their profession of faith. If they would not withdraw, the consequence in McIntyre's mind was straightforward: "Failing in these actions, we should proceed to constitute the signed declaration [the "Statement of Dissent"] a violation of the Profession of Faith, thereby mutually dissolving a contract between the University and the signers."

McIntyre, however, realized that few if any members of the board of trustees shared his own clarity in assessing the situation:

> I was shocked that this motion did not receive a second—even for discussion. This incident, combined with other minor altercations with the advocates of the faculty dissenters, places me obviously in a minority of one advocating and proposing prompt and positive action now that would admit of time to organize a faculty with which to open in September in the event the signers continued in their obstinacy.

McIntyre thus submitted his resignation to O'Boyle: "Being a minority of one, I realize that I am an unwelcome participant, rather than a helpful member of the board." Despite his evident frustration, McIntyre included a $50,000 donation to help with the deficit in which CUA found itself. But he did not intend to turn to the Catholic faithful of the Archdiocese of Los Angeles for continued support of an institution that was tolerating rejection of the Magisterium of the Church:

> This, however, does not mean that I shall be willing to appeal to my people for a collection while the present attitude of the board of trustees prevails and fails to dismiss those not willing to abide by the Magisterium of the Church.

McIntyre concluded his letter by saying that he was unwilling to serve on the board of trustees of CUA "as long as its avowed policy is not in accordance with the teachings of the Holy Father". The issue was the Magisterium.

Lay Feedback to the Hierarchy

How were the findings of the *Report of the Faculty Board of Inquiry* perceived and interpreted by the lay faithful of the United States? Two letters written to the bishops during this period indicate that at least some of the "People of God" were none too pleased with the news coming out of CUA. A woman from Maryland wrote Krol in April 1969 to ask him whether the board of trustees had considered its obligations to those paying for Catholic education as it made its decisions:

> What consideration . . . was given to the commitment of parents who have enrolled their children in a Catholic school with the natural understanding that they will be given Catholic teaching? And what consideration has been given to the Catholic students, themselves, who have assumed that the teaching they receive will be Catholic? And, finally, what consideration has been given to the indirect but no less valid or serious commitment to other Catholic universities and colleges, to seminaries, to Catholic high schools, and to the students and parents of students who attend these schools, that their Catholic-University-trained teachers will give Catholic teaching?[11]

The writer noted that to retain the Catholic name at a university whose professors were no longer obedient to the teaching authority of the Church was "to seriously defraud both parents and students". For her the issue was simply a matter of justice. As this woman saw it, the name *Catholic* carried with it an expectation of promoting the teaching of the pope and the bishops in communion with him. To do otherwise with its influence meant that Catholic University was essentially engaging in false advertising—and deceitful fundraising. The rights of the people in the pews were being violated, and she demanded that the bishops act "quickly and decisively" to correct matters at CUA.

Another letter from the "People of God" was written to O'Boyle by the members of CREDO, "An Association of Catholic Priests, Religious, and Laity" centered in Buffalo, New York.[12] The letter offered a scathing assessment of the way in which Catholic doctrine had been

---

[11] Catherine O'Connor (Rockville, Maryland) to Krol, April 19, 1969, box 28c, ACK.

[12] CREDO to O'Boyle, June 23, 1969, box 30b, ACK. CREDO was organized in 1969 by Robert Jacobi, Rupert Ederer, and James Likoudis with the stated objectives of

sacrificed "to the god of academic freedom" championed by the faculty board of inquiry's report. It predicted that the exoneration of the dissenting professors by the board of trustees would be used "as an excuse for flagrant theological dissent throughout the nation and beyond". At issue was "the very existence of ecclesiastical authority and true Christian education".[13] For these concerned lay Catholics, the issue was the Magisterium.

The viewpoints expressed by these members of the laity in their letters to the hierarchy were shared by Cardinal Krol, as revealed in his correspondence during the same period. In August 1969, Krol wrote a letter to Archbishop Alter[14] of Cincinnati, expressing his "grave concern" for the future of the university but lamenting the fact that whenever he tried to express his concerns to the board of trustees, "these seem to be subordinated to the norms of the AAUP." In the name of academic freedom, the AAUP had denied the bishops their right to oversee their own university, replacing their Magisterium with its own.[15]

Legal Analysis of the Board of Trustees' Actions

Once again, the dissenting professors' legal counsel, John Hunt and Terrence Connelly, condemned the board of trustees for meddling in matters beyond their competence.[16] They accused the trustees of duplicity: on the one hand, they wanted to give CUA a public image as a place that upheld academic freedom and due process, while on the other hand, they attempted to please what Hunt called the "conservative" Catholic press by referring the matter to further ecclesiastical inquiry. "It is clear", wrote Hunt,

> that the Trustees intended that two different versions of the affair
> be communicated to two different audiences. Those dual intentions,
> the Trustees' methods of implementing them and the knowledge and

---

cultivating the spiritual life of its members, refuting error, and supporting the truths of the Church, as well as professing religious assent of will and mind to the "Credo of the People of God" proclaimed by Pope Paul VI.

[13] CREDO to O'Boyle, June 23, 1969.

[14] Karl J. Alter (1885–1977) was archbishop of Cincinnati from 1950 to 1969.

[15] Krol to Alter, August 11, 1969, box 34c, ACK.

[16] Hunt and Connelly, *The Responsibility of Dissent*, 174, 180, 181, 187–88, 189, 190.

values they reveal are what we find most significant in the total experience.

While other bishops and other schools throughout the United States were respectful of the autonomy of their professors, finding no need to discipline those who had signed the "Statement of Dissent", Hunt decried the CUA board of trustees for acting in a way that was nothing less than immoral: the board had attempted to "straddle" the concepts of *Catholic* and *university*, resulting in "duplicity, manipulations and falsifications" by the bishops, who were guilty of "unconscionable compromise and unethical conduct". The essence of this unethical conduct was, argued Hunt, intentional dishonesty:

> The Trustees of Catholic University from the beginning of this Inquiry paid merely verbal respect for the principles of academic responsibility and fell short of a true understanding of these principles and failed at crucial times to act in accord with them.

The bishops had been irresponsible in the way in which they used "the forms of due process to put a responsible dissent under a year-long cloud" for the sake of their own individual interests.

According to Hunt, the self-centered trustees sought to suppress dissent by weakening financial support for the university, by exerting psychological pressure as superiors, by violating the rights of the faculty of the entire university, and by embarrassing CUA in the eyes of American higher education. "In the process," said Hunt, "the autonomy of the University became a myth."

What should the members of the board of trustees have done instead? Hunt maintained that if they had honestly and openly considered the widespread presence of dissent against *Humanae Vitae* around the world, this dissent "should have convinced reasonable men that there clearly were existing differences of opinion within the Church on these questions." This dissent was legitimate, reasoned Hunt, simply because of the fact that it existed:

> The Trustees should have realized that the very fact of existing differences of views on these matters within the pale of Catholic theology precluded any question as to whether a declaration or action within that pale was irresponsible theologically.

Hunt further declared that it was unacceptable to suggest, as the board of trustees was doing, that the professors' right to dissent could be opposed by suggesting that "special religious limitations" could be placed on extramural academic expression. Any such limitation had been expressly forbidden by the 1940 statement of the AAUP. The fact that the board of trustees had even attempted to impose such limitations was the proof of CUA's "lack of functional autonomy" and its "subjugation" to the American hierarchy, said Hunt. These hierarchical members of the board of trustees were, in his judgment, "woefully ignorant" of the basic norms of academic freedom and due process. The threat of suspension they had made against the dissenting professors on September 5, 1968, had no procedural justification under AAUP norms and had created a cloud of guilt that hung over the professors for the entire academic year.

Hunt concluded his attack on the board with a threatening prophecy of what fate might befall the American bishops as a result of their course of action:

> If the price to be paid for protecting their uneducated communicants is to make the schools they sponsor irrelevant to their students, at that time in the future when virtually all are educated, their churches may be empty. As with other ambivalent institutions in our society, the days of the church-related school which attempts a "straddle" of basic issues are numbered.

The Catholic-American "straddle" that Catholic University had attempted to perform for much of her history was no longer a viable option, said Hunt. The fissure between the Church's understanding of truth and the secular culture's understanding of freedom had become too great to admit of partial allegiance to both simultaneously. It was simply no longer possible for a church with a commitment to doctrinal truth to engage in any educational enterprise that was intended to be taken seriously, nor was it realistic to suppose that bishops sworn to uphold the truth of Catholic Tradition could also be committed to observing the principles of academic freedom; there was a basic conflict of interest for a church official who attempted to be trustee of a church-sponsored university as well. While it was theoretically possible for an ecclesiastical leader to be a good university trustee, it could come only at the price of "rejection" by other church leaders who were ignorant of "the values and subtleties of academic freedom".

Churchmen who were enlightened by the principles of the AAUP would happily accept the solution of allowing faculty to be judged solely by their academic peers, who would give "due weight" to Church teaching in their considerations so as to keep both sides appeased. In Hunt's estimation the whole matter was fundamentally a question of ignorance: ignorant churchmen were protecting their "uneducated communicants" from the realities of academic debate within the Church as well as the greater academic community. Hunt predicted that this head-in-the-sand mentality would lead to the end of Catholic higher education within a very short time. If churchmen would not acquiesce to·this necessary and inevitable step toward freedom, church-run universities would face a difficult but unavoidable decision: either to become full-fledged American universities and suffer the loss of financial support from church leaders or to retain the financial stability that church leaders could offer them but at the price of being something less than fully American. The decision made in this crucial matter would, Hunt predicted, determine the fate of all church-sponsored higher education in the United States in the foreseeable future. Hunt seems not to have considered a third possibility: that church-run universities could retain their Catholic name and institutional support while simultaneously rejecting the practical authority of the Magisterium over their operations.

Father Charles Curran greeting students on the campus of
Catholic University, April 19, 1967, the day that faculty
and students resolved to strike until he was reinstated
(courtesy of Father David Endres, editor of *U.S. Catholic Historian*).

Father Walter Schmitz, S.S., dean of the School of Theology at
Catholic University, and Father Charles Curran, April 1967
(courtesy of American Catholic History Research Center and
University Archives, Catholic University of America, Washington, D.C.)

Father Charles Curran with Archbishop Patrick O'Boyle of
Washington, D.C., Catholic University chancellor, April 1967
(courtesy of Father David Endres, editor of *U.S. Catholic Historian*).

Students protest during the strike; a sign quotes the Second Vatican Council's
Constitution on the Church in the Modern World (*Gaudium et Spes*)
(courtesy of American Catholic History Research Center and
University Archives, Catholic University of America, Washington, D.C.)

Father Charles Curran addresses students at a rally on
the campus of Catholic University, April 21, 1967
(courtesy of Father David Endres, editor of *U.S. Catholic Historian*).

Students, including sisters and seminarians, picket on
the campus of Catholic University, April 21, 1967
(courtesy of Father David Endres, editor of *U.S. Catholic Historian*).

Father Charles Curran
(courtesy of American Catholic History Research Center and
University Archives, Catholic University of America, Washington, D.C.)

Two sisters picket during the strike, April 19, 1967, proclaiming,
"If there is no room for Charlie in the Catholic University of America,
there is no room for the Catholic University in America"
(courtesy of Father David Endres, editor of *U.S. Catholic Historian*).

Monsignor Eugene Kevane
(courtesy of the Association of Hebrew Catholics).

11

The Controversy over the Deanship of the
School of Theology: July–August 1969

At the same board of trustees meeting of June 16, 1969, at which the Krol report was received and Cardinal O'Boyle asked for a doctrinal study of the dissenting professors' position, the board was asked to approve the nomination of Father Roland E. Murphy, O.Carm., as the dean of the School of Theology, as was standard procedure for all deans at CUA.[1] Murphy, a widely respected Scripture scholar, had been a professor of Semitic studies in the CUA School of Theology since 1948. Ordinarily such ratification by the board of trustees of the naming of a new dean by one of the schools was a routine procedure, but the matter was complicated by the fact that Murphy was one of the professors who had signed the July 30, 1968, "Statement of Dissent". The board chose to defer the appointment until its next meeting so that a committee could investigate Murphy and determine whether the full board should confirm his election as dean. The question of Murphy's appointment to the deanship of the School of Theology was to become a large controversy that significantly added to the great tension and animosity that had dominated the atmosphere at CUA since the promulgation of *Humanae Vitae*.

Cardinal Shehan was asked to chair the committee to investigate Father Murphy, and on June 19, 1969, Shehan wrote to Cardinals Cody,

---

[1] Roland E. Murphy, O.Carm. (1917–2002), taught at CUA from 1948 to 1971. In 1971 Murphy became professor of biblical studies at Duke University Divinity School, teaching there until 1987. Murphy served as coeditor of the *Jerome Biblical Commentary* (1968) as well as president of the Catholic Biblical Association and the Society of Biblical Literature of the United States.

Cooke,[2] Krol, and O'Boyle to solicit their opinions in the matter. In his letter, Shehan explained that while he personally had voted to postpone the appointment because Murphy was one of the dissenting professors, he now wondered whether that had been a wise decision. Shehan noted that Father Walter Burghardt,[3] despite his dissent, had served on the theological commission that had advised Pope Paul VI about birth control, and he asked the other cardinals whether it might not be a bit extreme to reject Murphy's nomination as dean of the School of Theology if the only objection was his dissenting position.

The response that Shehan received from the other cardinals quite emphatically disagreed: under no circumstances should a dissenting professor at CUA be given a position of authority such as a deanship. Cody wrote Shehan to tell him that "after long and prayerful deliberation", he had decided that he could not support Murphy's nomination, noting that the board of trustees "would be severely criticized" if it appointed a public dissenter as dean of the School of Theology.[4] Cody also said that he was "reliably informed" that if the board did not accept Murphy's nomination, the School of Theology intended to name Charles Curran to the deanship.[5] "If that happens," wrote Cody, "I will be one of the ones who will be listed as a 'non-supporter' of Catholic University." Cody proposed a solution to the impasse: Murphy could publicly change his mind about *Humanae Vitae* and announce that he submitted to its principles. Cody lamented to Shehan that he had heard of a recent seminar at St. Louis University at which the theologians in attendance had declared their "duty to dissent" from

---

[2] Terence Cooke (1921–1983), was archbishop of New York from 1968 to 1983. He was named a cardinal by Pope Paul VI in 1969.

[3] Walter Burghardt, S.J., (1914–2008) taught at the Jesuit seminary in Woodstock, New York, from 1946 to 1974. He was a professor of the CUA School of Theology from 1974 to 1978 and was a senior fellow at Woodstock Theological Center, Georgetown, from 1974 to 2003. Burghardt was named to the first international theological commission by Pope Paul VI in 1968 despite his public dissent from *Humanae Vitae*.

[4] Cody to Shehan, July 7, 1969, box 34c, folder 21, ACK.

[5] It seems unlikely that the School of Theology would have attempted to name Curran as dean, since such an action would have been highly inflammatory and undoubtedly controversial. Curran himself has said that he never at any time sought to become dean of the School of Theology (author's interview with Curran, April 15, 2009). Nevertheless the fear of such a move by the School of Theology may well have influenced some of the members of the board of trustees during the dispute over Murphy.

the teaching of *Humanae Vitae*. "With such an attitude rampant," Cody said, "the Magisterium has come to an end and Catholic teaching will suffer." Cody turned the dissenters' argument back on themselves as he expressed his objection to Murphy's nomination as dean: "Like the conscientious theologians who feel a duty to dissent, I feel a conscientious obligation not to assent." Freedom of conscience could work both ways in the struggle for control of CUA.

Krol also wrote Shehan to express his fundamental agreement with Cody.[6] Krol failed to see a parallel between Murphy's situation and that of Father Burghardt's position on the theological commission, because a dean held administrative authority to direct and influence others. Krol felt it should have been obvious to the School of Theology that they should not select a dissenting professor as dean: "The board of trustees should not be asked to give public evidence of supreme confidence in a dissenter whose dissent is being questioned by the same board of trustees." O'Boyle also wrote Krol to express his unity with the judgment of the other cardinals in this matter: "I am in agreement 100%."[7]

Meanwhile, Brother Gregory Nugent, F.S.C., chairman of the Academic Affairs Committee of the board of trustees, organized the investigation ordered by the board to assess whether Murphy was qualified to accept the deanship.[8] The committee met with Murphy in New York on July 21, 1969,[9] and gave a unanimous recommendation that Murphy be appointed to a three-year term as dean of the School of Theology beginning the following September. In a memorandum to board of trustees' chairman Carroll Hochwalt describing the meeting, Nugent informed Hochwalt that the committee had "discussed with Father Murphy his ideas and attitudes toward theology and its role in The Catholic University of America and exchanged views on the possible effects on the university of either Father Murphy's refusal of

---

[6] Krol to Shehan, July 11, 1969, box 34c, folder 21, ACK. Cody had sent a copy of his letter to Krol.

[7] O'Boyle to Krol, July 15, 1969, box 34c, folder 21, ACK.

[8] Nugent, a Christian Brother, later served as a special assistant to several presidents of CUA, including Clarence Walton, Edmund Pellegrino, and William Byron.

[9] The committee included Bishop Zaleski, Brother Gregory Nugent, Brother Nivard Scheel, Mr. Andrew Maloney, and Mr. Joseph McCabe. Other members of the board of trustees were also invited to attend the meeting.

the deanship or the Trustees' failure to support Father Murphy's endorsement by the faculty and the Acting President".[10] Nugent noted that "extensive and thorough discussion" had brought the committee to a conclusive decision to affirm the nomination, based on Murphy's proven scholarship, his "sound theological attitudes", and also his "realistic notions" concerning the role of the School of Theology. All that he needed now was the support of the board of trustees.

Nugent informed Hochwalt that the Academic Affairs Committee had asked Murphy to write a brief statement explaining his vision of the School of Theology, in order to reassure the board of trustees of his theological competence. The committee also urged a swift approval for Murphy, since it considered it "imperative that the entire process be completed before September 1st". It recommended that a ballot be sent by mail to every member of the board of trustees so that they could vote immediately, even before their September meeting, to confirm Murphy as dean, "in view of the importance of the relationship between the Bishops and the School of Sacred Theology". The memorandum expressed the committee's hope that this ballot would return a unanimous approval for Murphy.

Murphy's own "Statement Concerning the School of Sacred Theology" was attached to the memorandum of the Academic Affairs Committee.[11] Murphy declared his firm conviction that the School of Theology needed to become a "distinguished theological school". He also thought it was essential that the dean be freely elected by the school's faculty: "The imposition of a leader, under the present circumstances, would be demoralizing", Murphy wrote. The students of the School of Theology rightly expected the finest courses from the finest faculty, and so the school needed to cultivate a positive image in academic circles. Murphy expressed gratitude that the board of trustees had accepted the *Report of the Faculty Board of Inquiry*, thus ending the "impasse" of the 1968–1969 school year. As a result, he wrote, "the Theology faculty looks forward to a new era of mutual understanding and of cooperation with the Trustees." This new era envisioned by Murphy would be based on the bishops' giving their full support to

---

[10] Nugent to Hochwalt, July 29, 1969, box 28d, ACK.
[11] "A Statement Concerning the School of Sacred Theology", July 24, 1969, box 28d, ACK.

the professors' pursuit of theological expertise so that they could better serve the Magisterium. Invoking the School of Theology's statement of May 1967, Murphy reiterated the declaration by which the Catholic Theological Society had asked the bishops for their full trust and support:

> We are at your service, but precisely for this reason we lay claim to your understanding support, so that we may pursue our increasing tasks free of unfounded suspicions. Unless the loyalty of the theologian to the Church is presupposed, fruitful theological endeavor will be hindered.

Roland Murphy desired to be the dean of the CUA School of Theology so that it could have the freedom to undertake its theological task without undue interference from the bishops.

In response to the request of the Academic Affairs Committee memorandum and Murphy's statement, Acting Rector Scheel and Chairman Hochwalt wrote Cardinal O'Boyle on August 5, 1969, asking his approval for a ballot to be sent by mail to all the members of the board of trustees regarding Murphy's nomination as dean. O'Boyle refused.[12] Instead he wrote Hochwalt on August 9, telling him straightforwardly that there was one simple reason why he would not approve Murphy's nomination: Murphy was a dissenter. O'Boyle declared that he held no doubt whatsoever about Murphy's theological competence. He simply could not accept Murphy's position on the encyclical:

> I want to be on record that I respect the ability and the scholarship of Father Murphy, but that is not the point at issue. I am sure all the members of the board of trustees would have voted for him if he were not listed among the dissenters from the teaching of *Humanae Vitae*.

Krol likewise wrote Hochwalt to express the "gravest concern" for CUA regarding the matter of Murphy's nomination as dean.[13] Krol expressed his consternation not only regarding the academic question of dissent but especially about the pastoral implications that were clearly involved in the matter due to the public nature of the "Statement of Dissent" by professors who were also priests:

---

[12] O'Boyle to Scheel and Hochwalt, August 9, 1969, box 28d, ACK.
[13] Krol to Hochwalt, August 13, 1969, box 28d, ACK.

I and many others are convinced that it is not merely a question of academic dissent—that it was a positive highly publicized effort to preach a contrary doctrine not in an academic but in a pastoral role.

Krol expressed amazement that the Academic Affairs Committee had not even *mentioned* the issue of dissent at its New York meeting with Murphy: "I was told there was no reference to his public dissent, no withdrawal of his name from the list of dissenters." Krol was emphatic that if Murphy was named as dean, CUA's problems with its public image would only increase. Krol warned that CUA was in danger of losing the support of the American bishops:

> They have been and are still willing to support what they consider a Catholic University; but they will not, and some already have not contributed to the support of the University which they consider less than Catholic, particularly by having faculty members who conduct a public propaganda campaign against the teachings of the Holy Father.

Krol's comments indicate unanimity among the bishops as they discussed this question: they simply would not accept a dissenter in the position of dean of the School of Theology. Even the Holy See confirmed the judgment of the board in this matter, as the Sacred Congregation for Catholic Education communicated to O'Boyle that "the action of the board of trustees was not only justified but necessary."[14] The congregation recommended that a temporary dean be named until the board of trustees had completed its doctrinal examination of the "Statement of Dissent", which was then in progress. This is in fact what eventually happened.

As had occurred in their previous disputes, both sides of the argument in the case of Roland Murphy's nomination as dean of the School of Theology were convinced that a failure to accede to their demands would be disastrous for the future of the school. Murphy and his theological peers were convinced that the school must give evidence of its freedom from the authoritative guidance of the bishops if it was to

---

[14] "The Sacred Congregation has expressed the view that the action of the board of trustees [in the matter of Father Murphy's Deanship] was not only justified but necessary in view of the fact that the question of the Declaration against *Humanae Vitae* is still under study" (Archbishop Luigi Raimondi [apostolic delegate] to O'Boyle, October 20, 1969, protocol N. 2669/69, box 34c, folder 26, ACK).

attract a top, competitive faculty; they were certain that the naming of a dissenter as dean would give unquestionable evidence that the CUA School of Theology was an entirely independent (and thus theologically competent and academically free) entity. The board of trustees, on the other hand, having only just recently been handed a crushing defeat by the report of the board of inquiry exonerating the dissenters, felt it imperative to have someone in charge at the School of Theology who supported the teaching of the Magisterium. If the board could not remove dissenting faculty from the School of Theology, at least it did not have to suffer the affront of having one of those dissenting professors in the authoritative position of dean. In addition to the opposition of the board of trustees, Roland Murphy also faced the opposition of CUA's newly appointed president, Clarence C. Walton.[15]

For the first time in its history, Catholic University was headed not by a priest-rector but by a lay president. The board had chosen him as president after a search done by a recruitment committee in direct response to the recommendations of the 1967 MSA evaluation report, which had called for an end to the requirement that the head of the university be a priest. Walton had been instructed upon his appointment that his primary mission was "to restore tranquility, confidence, and trust" at CUA.[16] No sooner had Walton arrived at CUA in the summer of 1969 than he found himself in the middle of the heated controversy over Murphy's nomination as dean.

Walton was completely united with the board in their opposition to Murphy's being named dean. In an article written some twenty years later describing the controversy over Murphy, Walton claimed full responsibility for his well-considered choice to oppose Murphy's nomination, motivated by a desire to avoid "continuation of rancorous public debate" and to allow "time for reconciliation" of the volatile

---

[15] Clarence Walton (1915–2004) served as the first lay president of CUA until 1978. His career as a professor included positions at the University of Scranton, Duquesne University, and Columbia University. He came to CUA from Columbia, where he had been dean of the School of General Studies. Walton authored numerous books and articles on business ethics and corporate governance.

[16] William J. Byron, "Clarence Walton as Academic CEO: A Fine Mind on a Fine Line", in Ronald F. Duska, ed., *Education, Leadership, and Business Ethics: Essays on the Work of Clarence Walton* (Dordrecht, Netherlands: Kluwer Academic Publishers, 1998), 218.

situation at CUA.[17] Although it may have appeared to onlookers that he rejected Murphy simply because he had signed the "Statement of Dissent", Walton was emphatic that in fact he was motivated by a concern for the "future effectiveness" of the dean, and so he worked to find an external candidate who would be acceptable to the faculty as well as the chancellor and the board of trustees. Walton secured Murphy's endorsement of two alternative persons who could serve as dean, proceeded to contact them, and even secured the permission of the diocesan ordinary of one of the candidates for him to be released so as to serve at CUA. It seemed that this delicate matter of the deanship of the School of Theology was about to be resolved.[18]

At this point, however, Charles Curran directly intervened in the affair. When Walton asked Curran to support his plan to name an alternative dean, Curran adamantly refused to support anyone other than Murphy. According to Walton, Curran informed him that he [Curran] had already identified Walton's choice for the new dean as Monsignor Myles Bourke of New York.[19] Curran called Bourke and asked him whether he knew that Murphy had turned the deanship down. Bourke had not been aware of this fact, but having been informed by Curran, he called Walton back and refused to accept the deanship. In Curran's words, "No one of stature would take it."[20] Although Father Reginald Masterson, O.P., eventually accepted the position, he stepped down after a mere six months as dean, and Walter Schmitz then returned to the post as acting dean. In any event, Roland Murphy never became the dean of the CUA School of Theology. He responded to his rejection as dean by resigning from the theology faculty and accepting a professorship at Duke University.

The controversy over Murphy in the summer of 1969 marked the first time the dissenting professors encountered a firm and united front of opposition to their course of action from the board of trustees and

---

[17] Clarence C. Walton, "Academic Freedom at The Catholic University of America during the 1970's," *Catholic Historical Review* 76, no. 3 (1990), 555–63.

[18] Walton, "Academic Freedom at The Catholic University of America", 555–63.

[19] Myles Bourke (1917–2004) was a faculty member at St. Joseph's Seminary, Dunwoodie, New York, from 1947 to 1966 and pastor of Corpus Christi Parish at Columbia University from 1966 to 1992. A noted Scripture scholar, Bourke was president of the Catholic Biblical Association in 1967 and 1968.

[20] Author's interview with Curran.

the university president, and this united strength proved insurmountable for them. Although an editorial in the *Tower* somewhat cynically attributed the strong position of the board members to the fact that they "remembered the three million dollars the University received from all those conservative bishops last year", the fact of the matter was that the board had achieved what it wanted in opposing Murphy.[21] When they put their minds to it and agreed to take a stand, the board of trustees *did* have authority over the School of Theology and *could* obtain the outcome they desired in its internal proceedings. However, this uncharacteristic show of united conviction and certainty from the American bishops during the struggle for control of CUA was not to last.

---

[21] "Controversy", *Tower*, September 26, 1969, 1.

12

The Board of Trustees Capitulates:
September–November 1969

The Board of Trustees Meeting: September 13, 1969

After a contentious summer, with the Father Murphy controversy still simmering, the CUA board of trustees met for its regular meeting in Washington on September 13, 1969.[1] The meeting was a significant turning point in the controversy over the dissenting professors, for it marked the last (failed) attempt by Cardinals O'Boyle and McIntyre to remove the dissenting professors directly. It also saw the defeat of a major intervention by O'Boyle that was intended to derail the revision of the CUA university statutes that had been in process under the supervision of Cardinal Shehan. The meeting revealed the irreparable division that existed between the various bishops who sat on the board of trustees and also marked the clear victory of those who did not desire to make any further intervention in the matter of the dissenting subject professors.

The new university president, Clarence Walton, began the meeting by describing the grave situation that had existed in the School of Theology since the previous June, when Murphy had not been confirmed by the board of trustees in his election to the deanship of that school. The matter was not in itself a question of academic freedom, said Walton, because the deanship was more than a simple professorship; however, there was now a great need for "a measure of tranquility, so it [the School of Theology] can settle down and get on with its real work". The sense of an urgent need for an end to controversy prevailed throughout the meeting, as the exhausted board tried to find

---

[1] The account of this meeting comes from the minutes of the board of trustees, September 13, 1969, box 30c, ACK.

a way to return to business as usual at CUA. The board responded to Walton by naming a search committee for a new dean and applauding Walton's handling of a difficult situation.

Shehan then reported to the board on the progress of the revision of the statutes and bylaws of the university that had been under way since 1967. It had been his great concern, he said, that the revised statutes would safeguard the role of the chancellor in overseeing doctrinal concerns at CUA. Shehan affirmed that it was the sole prerogative of the chancellor to judge the orthodoxy of professors, advised by the clerical members of the board of trustees as well as the NCCB Doctrinal Committee. He assured the board that the revised statutes would specifically acknowledge the right of the chancellor to withdraw teaching faculties from an unorthodox professor, "regardless of tenure". Shehan explained this procedure as being entirely in accord with the AAUP norms for a religiously affiliated institution:

> It is our understanding that the AAUP recognizes the right of a church-related institution of higher learning to demand orthodoxy of teaching from its faculty members, provided orthodoxy of teaching is called for in the contract.

In fact, Shehan here betrayed a faulty or at least outdated understanding of the AAUP's position. True, the 1940 AAUP "Statement on Academic Freedom and Tenure" had included a clause giving religious schools the right to limit academic freedom, but the 1967 "Statement of the AAUP Special Committee" had recommended strongly against such an exception.[2] It seems almost wishful thinking on Shehan's part, but his comments show that there still remained among the episcopal members of the board the hope of somehow reconciling their magisterial authority with the demands of academic freedom as specified by the AAUP. It is difficult to understand how, after all that had transpired, they could still have believed that the proponents of academic freedom who had engineered the Curran strike and the faculty

---

[2] "[This Committee] commends to the attention of the academic community the emerging tendency of church-related colleges and universities to waive, or drastically restrict, the use of the limitation clause" (*Report of the Special Committee on Academic Freedom in Church-Related Colleges and Universities*, in *Bulletin of the American Association of University Professors* 53 [1967]).

board of inquiry's report would countenance any vestige of authority over professors being left in the hands of the board of trustees.

Shehan was adamant, however, that the revised university bylaws would be accepted by the board. Their passage was essential, he said, to the survival of Catholic University as a university, due to the pressure of the MSA for change:

> We have what almost amounts to an ultimatum from the Middle States Association of Colleges and Secondary Schools to make some changes in our structure and operation. The fact that we do not like it or that we take exception to it does not eliminate the power which that organization has to remove our accreditation.

If accreditation was removed, the university would be in serious danger of losing the financial assistance it received from the government, threatening its continued existence. The passage of the revised statutes, said Shehan, was essential to the well-being of Catholic University and thus of the entire Catholic Church in the United States. Shehan assured his fellow board members that the role of the United States hierarchy in guiding CUA was "amply provided for" in the revised statutes. Because the revision made a stricter provision to prevent the loss of clerical control of the board of trustees, requiring a vote of three-quarters of the trustees before the number of clergy on the board could be reduced, Shehan asserted that the revised statutes were in fact "a tightening of the reins".

At this point O'Boyle introduced a lengthy memorandum that strenuously objected to the proposed revision of the university statutes and bylaws, seeking to ensure that the canonical authority of the bishops of the United States and of the Holy See would remain a central part of the constitution of CUA.[3] O'Boyle demanded that an explicit statement be inserted affirming the role of canon law in the governance of CUA. He proposed an additional statute that would require an explicit adherence to the profession of faith on the part of each faculty member, to be renewed yearly as a condition of continued employment. If any dean or member of the university administration had reason to believe that

---

[3] The text of the memorandum is given in the minutes of the board of trustees, September 13, 1969, box 30c, ACK.

a particular faculty member had violated the profession of faith, the matter was to be investigated by a committee of the clerical members of the board of trustees. The faculty member would have the right to be represented by counsel and to defend himself at a public hearing. After such a hearing, if the board still believed the faculty member had violated the profession of faith, the record of the investigation and the public hearing would be sent to the Holy See for a judgment in the case. O'Boyle called for other revisions that would retain the right of the local ordinary and the Holy See to intervene in the ecclesiastical faculties. Finally, he objected to the new "Statement of University Objectives", which avoided any mention of CUA's Catholic identity while giving an unqualified endorsement of the AAUP mantra that "the only limit on truth is truth itself."

O'Boyle asked why the new statement of objectives could not specifically identify the primary mission of CUA in the service of the Church:

> I think that a statement of objectives for a Catholic university might be a little more straightforwardly Catholic. There seems to be nothing really essentially Catholic except the source of money. This is secularization, and when that happens there is no point to provide money either.
>
> There is in this statement almost a kind of shame about what is implied by Catholicism as far as intellectual life is concerned. I wish the statement would say something straightforward, such as:
>
> "The Catholic scholar, working in the light of faith and guided by the Magisterium of the Church is freed for a more fruitful pursuit of truth. He is not constantly having to be careful to remain within the confines of mere human reason and experience, but is enabled to consider all of reality—especially man and society—in their whole meaning."

O'Boyle asked his fellow board members why the university could not offer something inspiring and noble as it presented its statement of objectives:

> This statement of objectives is also loaded with stilted jargon of the worst sort. There is nothing beautiful and inspiring about it. If I were writing a statement of objectives for Catholic University, it would begin: "The Catholic University of America tries to live up to its name." From that beginning, I would say what kind of university

it should be—one in which people can really help each other learn
—respecting distinctions of status and field, but not being afraid to
share intellectual life together. As Catholic, it should work in the
light of faith, should be guided by the Magisterium of the Church,
and should not be ashamed to claim it has something of truth that
unbelievers, alas, sadly lack. Not that we're so good—it was a gift of
grace. Can't we give God his due? And as American, it should work
with special appreciation of distinctively American ideals—tolerance,
pluralism, ordered freedom—and give special effort to service to the
whole community, local and national.

O'Boyle saw no inherent contradiction in CUA's striving to be both
fully Catholic and fully American. Rather, he was convinced that the
specifically faith-guided vision of the university contained a gift for the
wider American society that ought to be put at its service. The vision
of Catholicism, rightly understood, was at the service of the vision of
America, not opposed to it.

Upon concluding his remarks, O'Boyle asked that his memorandum
be considered before the board of trustees adopted Shehan's proposed
revisions. Cardinal McIntyre seconded, and O'Boyle's memorandum
was opened to discussion.

Board member Monsignor Clarence White responded by offering
some "reflections" on O'Boyle's memorandum. He opposed the proposals that the chancellor had offered. There was no need to restate
what was already clearly in the *Code of Canon Law*, said White, nor
should the board of trustees be made the judge of orthodoxy in the
case of faculty members. It was not desirable for the board of trustees
to enter into the specific details of the academic life of the individual
schools, and so White thought it best that the academic senate han-
dle the detailed administration of the schools, especially in light of the
Congregation for Catholic Education's desire that pontifical schools
be more fully integrated into the life of the university. With regard
to the statement of objectives, White noted that it had already been
adopted by the board of trustees earlier that year, and its revision was
not within the competence of the committee on the revision of the
statutes and bylaws of the university. And there was certainly no need,
said White, to "clutter up the bylaws with inspirational statements".
As for the removal of faculty members, so long as due process was
observed, the AAUP would have to accept it, so there was no need for

any special clause regarding the removal of a faculty member by the Holy See. Lastly, there ought to be no conflict between the chancellor of the university and the local ordinary in his role as supreme ruler and teacher in his diocese. White thus summarily dismissed any need for O'Boyle's memorandum to merit the further consideration of the board.

O'Boyle proposed, with McIntyre seconding, that a secret ballot be taken: Should Shehan's proposal to revise the statutes and by-laws of the university be tabled, so as to amend them according to O'Boyle's recommendations? Out of twenty-two ballots, seven voted for O'Boyle's adjustments, fourteen voted against, and one abstained. Chairman Hochwalt thus declared the motion lost.

Next Cardinal Cody seconded Shehan's proposal, and so the formal revision of the CUA bylaws, which required a two-thirds majority, was brought to a vote of the board of trustees. The revision passed by just one vote, fifteen to seven.

O'Boyle's intervention at the September 13, 1969, meeting of the board of trustees was prescient in identifying the heart of the matter regarding the revision of the statutes and bylaws of CUA. His intervention amounted to a direct objection to the incorporation of AAUP norms into the governing statutes of the university. His criticism of the revised statutes as a capitulation to secularism, as well as his taking issue with the statement of objectives as a compilation of "stilted jargon", were indicators of O'Boyle's deep frustration with the loss of Catholic identity at CUA. He remained committed to the end to his conviction that the authoritative guidance of the Magisterium provided the essential foundation that gave Catholic education its unique and inspiring nature.

Even after O'Boyle's major intervention and two significant votes, the September 13 meeting had not seen the end of controversy. Bishop Zaleski gave a report to the board about the progress of the work of the NCCB Doctrinal Committee, which had been charged in June with the investigation of the orthodoxy of the dissenting faculty. Although the work of the committee was still in progress, Zaleski was in a position to propose a list of reasonable guidelines for the appropriate style of public dissent in the Church, which he listed as follows:

1) Dissent could be made to non-infallible teachings of the Church.

2) Non-infallible teachings mean that the Church may be in the process of learning the truth. There may be sound reasons for opposite positions.

3) Dissent must be of a believing person in a believing community, and must clearly embody all elements of belief.

4) Dissent must be respectful. The Pope has a special position in the Church by ordinance of Christ.

5) Dissent must be charitable to the community.

6) Dissent must be responsible, and constitute a response to the authentic teaching of the Church.

Zaleski's proposed norms were typically fluid and noncommittal. They made no clarification about what constituted a noninfallible teaching or what exactly was so "special" about the position of the pope. One can hear the dissenting theologians emphatically agreeing that they had observed all of these norms to the utmost capacity. These proposed guidelines for ongoing dialogue made no contribution to any resolution of the impasse that continued to exist between the dissenting professors and the teaching authority of the Church.

The September 13, 1969, meeting concluded with "McIntyre's Last Stand"—one final effort by the cardinal archbishop of Los Angeles to resolve the situation of the dissenting professors at Catholic University once and for all. Despite his letter of resignation, written the previous June, he was once again present at this crucial meeting of the board. Despite seeing O'Boyle's memorandum voted down, he once more proposed a direct intervention by the board of trustees. McIntyre motioned for and read aloud a resolution calling on the board of trustees to issue an ultimatum to the dissenting professors: either they would accept the teaching of the Magisterium of the Church in its entirety, or else they had, by their own action of dissent, terminated their teaching contracts. Their actions had caused "obvious embarrassment to the university and to its stature in public opinion and regard". They had violated the profession of faith that their contract required of them. Due process had been followed in investigating their theological positions.

They were to be offered for ten days "the privilege of making apology and expressing withdrawal of conflicting statements and of renewing by voice" their profession of faith. If they failed to do so, "the board hereby declares the contract existing between the University and the offending Professors as dissolved by mutual agreement and because of the absence of mutual concordance."

Cardinal O'Boyle seconded the motion, and discussion followed. When Chairman Hochwalt called for a vote by a show of hands, four voted in favor of the resolution, and seventeen against it. The chair declared the motion lost. Although the minutes do not relate who were the four board members who voted in favor of McIntyre's resolution (certainly that number included O'Boyle and Krol, but who else?), the overwhelming majority of the board stopped the resolution in its tracks.

McIntyre had anticipated that his proposal would be sharply rejected. He had written to Krol in late August 1969, "I feel that my insistence is a lost cause for the effectiveness of logic." He had been extremely apprehensive about the upcoming meeting in Washington, because he highly doubted that his fellow bishops would have the stomach to act decisively against the dissenting professors, as he wrote to Krol:

> I am afraid the board will not have the courage to dismiss the offenders. This will be a rather awkward situation. The continued disregard of the force of the Profession of Faith is extremely puzzling to me. I feel that this is the primary issue and should be insisted on. The syllogism and its conclusion may be accurate but it seems to be ineffective. The effect can be disastrous to the University both from its friends as well as its enemies.[4]

For McIntyre, the matter remained as clear and simple as a syllogism: professors at CUA were required to adhere to the profession of faith; the dissenting professors were teaching against the profession of faith; therefore the dissenting professors had by their own action terminated their teaching contracts. The "disastrous" effect he foresaw was that the enemies of CUA's true mission would take control of it, while the friends of CUA, faithful Catholics throughout the country, would no longer support an institution that had lost sight of that mission. Per-

---

[4] McIntyre to Krol, August 25, 1969, Mc 5493, AALA.

haps the most telling remark of McIntyre's proposed resolution was the opening paragraph about the "obvious embarrassment" the dissenting professors had caused CUA. The *Report of the Faculty Board of Inquiry* had given exactly the opposite interpretation of the effect of the events at CUA on public opinion. In its conclusions, the report had declared that the actions of the *trustees* had "certainly impaired the reputation of the academic departments concerned" and had "tarnished the reputation of the University".[5] The two statements were respectively concerned with two completely different audiences: the board of inquiry was primarily concerned with the reputation of Catholic University among other American academic institutions, while McIntyre was primarily concerned with the reputation of the university among the Catholic faithful. The chasm between the expectations of these two audiences did not offer much by way of a meeting point in the middle. McIntyre's loss meant the total victory of the dissenting professors and their radical agenda.

After September 13, 1969, there would be no further attempt by any member of the CUA board of trustees to put the matter of the hiring or firing of the dissenting professors to a straight up or down vote of the board. The dissenting professors, guided by the AAUP, had succeeded in convincing the board of trustees that the professors, and not the board, would dictate the terms of their employment. And because of their immense influence, the dissenting professors would dictate the fundamental tenor of American theology and Catholic academia for a generation to come.

The Zaleski Evaluation—Doctrinal Analysis of the Statement of Dissent

In October 1969, Bishop Zaleski presented Cardinals O'Boyle and Krol with a draft of the evaluation of the dissenters made by the NCCB Doctrinal Committee, as he had promised the board of trustees at its September 13, 1969, meeting.[6] Zaleski's evaluation, which attempted to shine the best possible light on the dissenters' motives, became yet another occasion of contention for O'Boyle and Krol.

---

[5] *Summary Report of the Faculty Board of Inquiry*, 6–7, box 28d, ACK.

[6] The text of Zaleski's evaluation is taken from the minutes of the board of trustees, November 8, 1969, box 30c, ACK.

The Zaleski evaluation had been prepared by a panel of three bishops[7] in response to the decision made by the CUA board of trustees at its June 16, 1969, meeting to give O'Boyle the right to request a doctrinal evaluation of the "Statement of Dissent". It essentially declared that the action of the dissenting professors had unintentionally lacked pastoral sensitivity as to the effects their action would have in the life of the entire Church. Theologians bore a "special responsibility", it said, to give "moral and spiritual guidance to the present generation of mankind", always subject to the direction of the Magisterium. It acknowledged that the relationship between these two entities, the theologians and the Magisterium, had encountered many problems of late. Disrespect and miscommunication had unfortunately become common occurrences. In a sentence that rebuked the bishops quite strongly, the evaluation called for the bishops to let go of their fear of theologians:

> The wounds inflicted by arbitrary exercise of authority need the healing comfort of a more relaxed environment, in which those who have something worth saying may not be afraid to say it, and those with ultimate authority will not be afraid of the consequences of theological growth.

However, the evaluation also affirmed that "the lines must be drawn". It was not licit for theologians to usurp the role of the hierarchy in teaching the Catholic faith. Division in the teaching of the faith could lead only to fragmentation of the moral lives of the Christian faithful and of the society at large:

> When each theologian claims the right to teach from his own chair, and each priest the right to preach from his own chapel to the wide world, the unity of faith is imperiled. With the fragmenting of revealed truth into segments of theological opinion, morality will follow the compromising and corrupting directions of permissiveness rather than the uphill paths of righteousness.

Having rebuked both parties to the argument, the Zaleski evaluation called upon theologians and bishops to work together, despite their dif-

---

[7] John M. Fearns, auxiliary bishop of New York; Thomas J. Riley, auxiliary bishop of Boston; and Zaleski.

fering perspective, with a sincere commitment to respect and dialogue. The evaluation attempted to make a gentle conclusion:

> In view of these premises, it seems to us that the dissent manifested by the theologians of The Catholic University was not sufficiently sensitive to the pastoral implications of their action. Although unintended, it led many to minimize the authority of the Pope in his teaching role and invited the formation of conscience without due consideration for authentic teaching. In this way it did not in our judgment contribute sufficiently to the learning process of the Church in its search for truth.[8]

The language of this final paragraph was carefully chosen and measured. It avoided attributing any intention on the part of the dissenting theologians of leading the faithful to disregard the teaching of *Humanae Vitae*. Furthermore it expressed its judgment only in terms of what "seemed" to be so. Even with this disclaimer, the evaluation said nothing directly negative about the "Statement of Dissent". The theologians had been "sensitive to the pastoral implications of their action" but—it *seemed*—perhaps insufficiently so. The "Statement of Dissent" had attempted to "contribute" to "the learning process of the Church", but—again only in the judgment of the bishops making the evaluation —this contribution *seemed* "not sufficient". The description of "the learning process of the Church in its search for truth" implied that *both* the Magisterium and the dissenting theologians were in a place of uncertainty with regard to what moral guidance to give the faithful. Somehow, however, through dialogue and cooperation, despite the "darkness of misunderstanding" that had come between them, the Zaleski evaluation expressed hope that the bishops and theologians together would eventually discover the truth, and so the learning process of the Church would reach a new and happy plateau. The implication was clearly that the dogma of the Church was historically conditioned and thus in need of constant evolution, a never-ending search for truth in which no one party had all the answers, least of all the Magisterium.

---

[8] This draft version of the evaluation's final paragraph, which was eventually modified, and the ensuing debate about its wording is taken from a telegram of O'Boyle to Zaleski, October 22, 1969, box 34c, folder 26, ACK.

O'Boyle and Krol could not accept such a weak statement by the NCCB Doctrinal Committee, and they attempted to get Zaleski to change the statement. On October 22, 1969, O'Boyle sent a telegram from Washington to Zaleski, who was in Lisbon, Portugal. The telegram, sent in the name of O'Boyle and Krol, demanded a revision of the final paragraph of the draft of Zaleski's evaluation. O'Boyle insisted that "it seems to us" be changed to "it is our considered judgment". He also asked Zaleski to strike the words "although unintended" out of the assessment of the effects of the "Statement of Dissent", objecting emphatically that their actions had shown a clear intention on the part of the dissenting professors. O'Boyle also asked for an addition at the end of the statement: "In this way it [the "Statement of Dissent"] did not in our judgment contribute sufficiently to the learning process of the Church in its search for truth. But it did in fact introduce a measure of confusion which retarded that process." Zaleski soon replied firmly from Lisbon to O'Boyle, also via telegram: "Regret cannot agree to proposed changes fear greater confusion Zaleski."

Despite Zaleski's refusal, the final paragraph of the evaluation, as it was entered into the November 8, 1969, minutes of the board of trustees, was ultimately amended to include O'Boyle's first two modifications: "it seems to us" was changed to "it is our considered judgment", and the words "although unintended" were removed from the assessment of the theologians' action. The final version of the evaluation avoided both proposed versions of the final sentence and instead offered a more simple statement about the consequences of the "Statement of Dissent": "It led many to minimize the authority of the Pope in his teaching role and invited the formation of conscience without due consideration for authentic teaching." This sentence made the overall conclusion of the Zaleski evaluation somewhat more straightforward in its acknowledgment that the "Statement of Dissent" had produced devastating effects on the practical moral life of American Catholics.

The Board of Trustees Meeting: November 8, 1969

The Zaleski evaluation was presented by O'Boyle to the full CUA board of trustees at its meeting on November 8, 1969, in Washington.[9] O'Boyle reminded the board that at its June 16, 1969, meeting, it had supported him in his wish to appeal to the NCCB Doctrinal Committee for a theological evaluation of the "Statement of Dissent". He asked all present to promise to keep the report he was about to share with them confidential. He immediately faced opposition from certain unnamed members of the board, who objected to the propriety of the report even being made at all. Zaleski then explained to the board that his evaluation was neither a statement nor a judgment on the part of the NCCB. It was, he said, simply the opinion of a committee that had responded to a personal request of O'Boyle. There followed vigorous discussion about whether the board was responsible for the orthodoxy of the professors of the university, and it was finally unanimously agreed—but only after several resolutions were made and withdrawn—that Zaleski's evaluation be read to the entire board of trustees. O'Boyle then read the entire evaluation.

A "prolonged argument" ensued over what, if any, action the board should take in response to the Zaleski evaluation. The board finally agreed to "receive" the evaluation; the meeting then proceeded with extended disagreement over what should be done with it further. The suggestion for a large committee to study the evaluation was rejected. A further resolution was proposed that called for the appointment of a committee to consider what should be done about the evaluation and then report back to the board of trustees at its next meeting. The proposal was withdrawn. The board of trustees was, it seems, finally exhausted by the endless cycle of committee meetings, committee reports, and evaluations of committee reports concerning the dissenting professors. The Zaleski evaluation expressed hope that difficulties would be worked out and that "a new kind of cooperation" would begin between the theologians and the bishops. Exactly how that cooperation would be created and fostered the evaluation did not say. The *Report of the Faculty Board of Inquiry*, issued the previous April, had not in any way discussed cooperation or a change of attitude but had simply vindicated the actions of the dissenting professors. That board of inquiry report remained the most prominent and defining statement in the struggle for Catholic University, and the board of trustees had

---

[9] The account of the meeting comes from the minutes of the board of trustees, November 8, 1969, box 30c, ACK.

accepted and received it. Even when the Zaleski evaluation declared that the July 30, 1968, "Statement of Dissent" had not been sufficiently sensitive to its pastoral implications, such a judgment of the action of dissent in no way called for any practical change to the situation on campus. The dissenting professors continued to be in control of the academic debate at CUA, which was no debate at all but an emphatic rejection of the teaching of the Magisterium. By the fall of 1969 the CUA board of trustees had accepted this status quo and was clearly in no mood to continue investigating and hearing reports from committees that offered little by way of progress or resolution of the situation. The board of trustees had accepted the fact that it was now powerless to change the bottom line at CUA: control of Catholic University was squarely in the hands of the dissenting professors.

Following its September and November 1969 meetings, the CUA board of trustees left matters at the university largely in the hands of the new president, Clarence Walton, and gave him time and space to breathe and act. The Holy See gave its express approval to this course of action (or rather inaction) chosen by the board. In a confidential letter dated November 27, 1969, Cardinal Garrone,[10] prefect of the Sacred Congregation for Catholic Education, wrote to Krol, urging him to prevail upon O'Boyle to avoid any further interference in the administration of CUA, so that the newly approved statutes and bylaws would have time to take effect and hopefully bring a new spirit to the university.[11] Garrone's letter indicated a clear desire on the part of the

---

[10] Gabriel-Marie Garrone (1901–1994) was prefect of the Sacred Congregation for Catholic Education from 1968 to 1980. He attended the Second Vatican Council and was named a cardinal by Pope Paul VI in 1967.

[11] Garrone to Krol, November 27, 1969, box 28c, ACK. "The reason why I am writing you, however, is that I want to confide to you in a brotherly way my fear that just at the moment when the new statutes and by-laws, which the new President and others worked on so hard, will be coming into force to rejuvenate and stimulate the progress of the University, something might happen which could upset matters there. The profoundly regrettable activity of the group of professors there at the appearance of the encyclical 'Humanae Vitae' does not seem to be a problem which is yet resolved, although I think that a number of these professors will not continue to have much to do with the University. I fear that some intervention by ecclesiastical authorities, short of a most prudent and careful kind, might serve to hurt the entire enterprise of rejuvenation and stimulation.

"I do not know the intentions of His Eminence, Cardinal O'Boyle, but I have a great deal of confidence that his necessary efforts to carry out his responsibilities will not in-

Holy See that the volatile situation on campus would calm down and that a certain stability and order would prevail at CUA and more generally within the Church in the entire United States. O'Boyle, Krol, and McIntyre certainly desired to carry out the wishes of the Holy See (and by implication the wishes of Pope Paul VI). Garrone's letter likely explains in no small part the reason why no further direct intervention against the dissenting professors was attempted by the board of trustees after the fall of 1969.

When the board of trustees met again on December 6, 1969, Brother Gregory Nugent of the board's Academic Committee presented the outcome of the committee's discussion held the previous day concerning "some disturbing problems and relationships within the University's academic community".[12] Nugent advised the board of trustees that it was of the utmost importance that the board clarify that, although it had received the Zaleski evaluation, it was in no way contemplating action based on the findings of the report:

> The [Academic] Committee thought it appropriate to suggest that *any* unilateral action based on this report would not only set off a series of public and perhaps legal responses by a given section of the Faculty affected, but would galvanize the larger "silent majority" of the Faculty into support for such an adversary posture. The harm not only to the School of Theology, but to the entire University, would be incalculable. This was, Brother Gregory added, simply and seriously—with utter conviction and without exaggeration.

The message of the CUA faculty to the board of trustees was blunt: stay out. *Any* attempt by the board to act in an authoritative way would

jure the University's new start. Nevertheless, Your Eminence, I wonder if it would be possible, given your prestige and influence, if together with the new President of the University, you could discreetly and personally contact Cardinal O'Boyle and let him know of this aspect of the serious problem there so that some solution can be found which would give the statutes and by-laws a chance to work? I would sincerely like to ask you to do this.

"In a spirit of trying to be of service to the University and certain that I enjoy the confidence of Your Eminence which enables me to write such a personal and private letter as this to you, as well as thanking you in advance for your help and assuring you of my brotherly affection, I am . . ."

[12] The account of the meeting is taken from the minutes of the board of trustees, December 6, 1969, box 30c, ACK.

be the cause of "incalculable harm" to the university. For the good of the long-term health of CUA, it was imperative that the board not attempt in any way to oversee the functioning of the ecclesiastical faculties. What the board should do instead, said Brother Gregory, was address the seriously dysfunctional relationship it had with the subject professors, a dysfunction *the board* had caused by its many meetings and endless creation of committees.

The solution the Academic Committee proposed was a series of dialogues and meetings between bishops and theologians, a symposium that would address the issues of contention. In the meantime, said the committee, any further disputes should be settled by "ordinary due process", as suggested by the May 1967 statement of the School of Theology, always keeping in mind the "scholarly calm prescribed by Pope Paul". This call for calm meant that the issue of the dissenting professors could no longer occupy the undivided attention of the board of trustees and indeed of the entire CUA community. The board had "bogged down" the life of CUA, and it was now time to turn to other "pressing concerns of the academic community".

The board of trustees was being told in no uncertain terms that it had no choice but to let the matter rest. The dissenting professors had been exonerated of any charges of inappropriate action by the *Report of the Faculty Board of Inquiry*. The board of trustees needed to accept that decision for the sake of peace and harmony. Surely there were other important matters to which the board could address its attention. The academic committee hoped that the board could stop being so disruptive so that the professors could get on with their important academic work and research. Such was the "final word" of the CUA faculty to the board of trustees after more than thirty months of tumultuous upheaval that had begun with the April 1967 strike.

O'Boyle responded to Brother Nugent with a firm defense of the Zaleski evaluation and expressed his desire that the board would "implement" it.[13] He protested that the three bishops who had composed Zaleski's committee were all "eminent theologians" and that if the board failed to implement the report "he would face embarrassing alternatives." O'Boyle now presented to the board a letter he had sent

---

[13] The Zaleski evaluation did not call for any specific action; it simply stated that the "Statement of Dissent" had lacked sufficient sensitivity to its pastoral implications.

to all the bishops of the United States on November 25, 1969, ten days before the meeting. This letter informed the American hierarchy that at the board's November meeting there had been "unanimous agreement that steps should be taken to implement Bishop Zaleski's report in so far as the dissenting priests are concerned".[14] A committee consisting of Chairman Hochwalt, O'Boyle, and President Walton had met twice in the days after the November 8 meeting, and in those meetings, O'Boyle explained, Walton had assured him that he (Walton) had initiated the "steps" of implementing the Zaleski report.

At this point Walton emphatically disagreed with O'Boyle's version of events. The board had *not* acted to appoint a special committee at its November 8 meeting, said Walton. The November 15 meeting between Hochwalt, Walton, and O'Boyle had taken place at O'Boyle's request, but it was simply not accurate to refer to the group as a "committee of three". At this meeting, Walton said, "he had expressed the view that solutions would not be achieved through confrontations with individuals, but rather through working with the faculty at large." Walton was under the impression that O'Boyle had accepted the faculty recommendation that the Zaleski evaluation would be discussed with the entire faculty and that no action against individual professors would be taken.

Hochwalt agreed with Walton's account and understanding of the November 15 meeting with O'Boyle. His impression was that the three had agreed on a delay until Walton could consult the faculty and that in the meantime no action was to be taken. In Hochwalt's opinion, the problem needed to be examined more fully by the NCCB.

Zaleski also agreed with Walton, stressing that "the good of the Catholic people, as well as the good of the university must be kept in mind." No solution would be possible, Zaleski warned, if emotions were allowed to rule. He repeated that his committee's evaluation of the "Statement of Dissent" was *not* a statement of the NCCB Doctrinal Committee, but merely a response to O'Boyle's personal request.

Such discrepancy and discord between O'Boyle and the other key members of the CUA administration indicate that by November 1969 a serious breakdown of communication had occurred within the board

---

[14] The recollection is not in accord with the record of the minutes of the November 8, 1969, meeting of the board of trustees, as recounted earlier in this chapter.

of trustees. If by this time Krol had communicated to O'Boyle the wishes of Cardinal Garrone that the university be allowed to operate without interference, his entreaty had fallen on deaf ears. In O'Boyle's mind the Zaleski evaluation, which had simply stated that the "Statement of Dissent" had been pastorally insensitive, had been transformed into something that needed to be "implemented". His insistence on taking action against the dissenting professors was finding a less and less receptive audience, and it is clear that the majority of the board of trustees was now in favor of avoiding any further interference in the internal life of CUA.

A Final Plea for Intervention and Its Rejection by the Board

The issue of how the board of trustees would deal with the dissenting professors had one final coda at the February 17, 1970, board meeting.[15] At that meeting, lay board member Philip D. Lewis[16] presented for the board's consideration a letter he had written to Chairman Hochwalt the previous November. He had not mailed the letter, however, until January, and he now wished that he "had had more courage". His letter expressed a frustrated plea for an end to the endless circle of ineffective, ambiguous, and confusing committee meetings regarding the whole situation of the dissenting theologians. "Can't we end this matter once and for all?" he pleaded. "Can't the board reprimand him?" Lewis suggested that the board of trustees have a final meeting with Curran, make its position clear, and then move forward. Lewis apologized for his layman's approach: "I know what I've suggested sounds too simplified and probably can't be done, but, we have to start somewhere."[17]

Lewis' request met with a cool response from both Hochwalt and President Walton. They opposed any new action by the board against dissent. It was important to let the new dean of the School of Theology have time and space to act, they said. This time even O'Boyle did not

---

[15] The account of the meeting is taken from the minutes of the board of trustees, February 17, 1970, box 28d, ACK.

[16] Philip D. Lewis (1929–2012) served as Florida state senator from 1970 to 1980.

[17] Minutes, board of trustees, November 8, 1969, box 30c, ACK.

join in the protest. While he confirmed his view that the board had been mistaken in the way it handled the dissenting professors, he said that he would go along with the prevailing opinion.

Once again the board agreed—with a certain measure of finality—that no further action was necessary, largely because it was unfeasible, in the matter of Father Curran and the dissenting professors. The issue of Curran's dissent would not be directly discussed by the board of trustees again. The board was shell-shocked and battle-weary after nearly three years of emotional conflict and tiring controversy. The battle for academic freedom at CUA, which had been waged fiercely since the spring of 1967, had reached an exhausted truce, whose terms left the dissenting professors firmly and squarely in control of the university. The Catholic University of America was finally a university that could stand with pride among its American peers as an institution firmly committed to the creed of the American Association of University Professors.

Conclusion

In 1979, only one year after his election as pope, John Paul II addressed Catholic educators at CUA, well aware of the university's ongoing significance for Catholic higher education throughout the United States. The Polish pontiff, himself a former university professor, shared how "at home" he felt in a university setting and expressed his "gratitude" and "encouragement" for the work of theologians, assuring them of the bishops' need and desire for their active contribution to the life of the Church: "We desire to listen to you and we are eager to receive the valued assistance of your responsible scholarship." At the same time, however, John Paul affirmed the essential and indispensable role of the guidance of the Magisterium of the Church in the theological enterprise, asserting the right of the faithful to receive from the Church the Word of God as authentically interpreted by the Magisterium:

> True academic freedom must be seen in relation to the finality of the academic enterprise, which looks to the total truth of the human person. The theologian's contribution will be enriching for the Church only if it takes into account the proper function of the Bishops and the rights of the faithful. It devolves upon the Bishops of the Church to safeguard the Christian authenticity and unity of faith and moral teaching. . . . It is the right of the faithful not to be troubled by theories and hypotheses that they are not expert in judging or that are easily simplified or manipulated by public opinion for ends that are alien to the truth.[1]

At the time, Charles Curran remained a tenured professor of the CUA School of Theology. In the years following, the Congregation

---

[1] John Paul II, "Address to the Catholic University of America", Washington, D.C., October 7, 1979, http://www.vatican.va/holy_father/john_paul_ii/speeches/1979/octobe r/documents/hf_jp-ii_spe_19791007_usa_washington_univ-catt_en.html.

for the Doctrine of the Faith, led by Cardinal Joseph Ratzinger, undertook an extensive examination of Curran's teaching. This investigation ultimately led to the congregation's 1986 declaration that Curran was not eligible to be a teacher of Catholic theology. CUA subsequently dismissed Curran from his professorship.[2] In 1990, John Paul issued his apostolic letter on Catholic universities, *Ex Corde Ecclesiae*, calling for a renewed fidelity within Catholic higher education to the teaching of the Magisterium in matters of faith and morals and directing bishops to use their juridical authority to ensure such fidelity. Curran and others maintained that the approach taken by John Paul and Ratzinger showed that they had erroneously interpreted the Second Vatican Council, undoing the healthy developments of the initial postconciliar years by their "restorationist" tendencies.[3] Ratzinger's election as Pope Benedict XVI in 2005 dealt a further blow to the hopes of Curran and his sympathizers for a return to the "good old days" of the late 1960s and early 1970s, when their theological outlook was in firm control of developments in American Catholic higher education.

Benedict also visited CUA in 2008 and met with Catholic educators, encouraging them in their specific and important mission within the Church. He spoke of the Christocentric mission of Catholic education and reflected on the particular duty of the Catholic educational institution to lead its students to encounter the truth revealed by God in Jesus Christ.[4] This search for the truth, said Benedict, is one that can be carried out only in an atmosphere of freedom and respect for the vocation of the professor:

---

[2] Curran subsequently filed a lawsuit against CUA. In 1989, the District of Columbia Superior Court ruled that CUA had the right to fire Curran because of the school's religious commitment.

[3] Author's interview with Curran, April 15, 2009. Daniel Maguire's interpretation of *Ex Corde Ecclesiae* was typical: "To me, it seems surpassingly naïve not to recognize that the spirit and purpose of *Ex Corde* is to reverse the freedom that came to Catholic theology before and during the Second Vatican Council. . . . Its mission, as I see it, is thought control and a denial of the legitimacy of the theological *magisterium*." See Maguire, Open Letter to Archbishop Rembert Weakland, January 25, 2002, *Academe*, v88 n3 pp. 46–50 May–June 2002.

[4] Benedict XVI, address at a meeting with Catholic educators at the Catholic University of America, April 17, 2008, http://www.vatican.va/holy_father/benedict_xvi/speeches/2008/april/documents/hf_ben-xvi_spe_20080417_cath-univ-washington_en.html.

I wish to reaffirm the great value of academic freedom. In virtue of this freedom you are called to search for the truth wherever careful analysis of evidence leads you.

Benedict's straightforward endorsement of academic freedom was accompanied by a clear warning to those who would make such freedom an absolute entity:

> Yet it is also the case that any appeal to the principle of academic freedom in order to justify positions that contradict the faith and the teaching of the Church would obstruct or even betray the university's identity and mission; a mission at the heart of the Church's *munus docendi* and not somehow autonomous or independent of it. Teachers and administrators, whether in universities or schools, have the duty and privilege to ensure that students receive instruction in Catholic doctrine and practice. This requires that public witness to the way of Christ, as found in the Gospel and upheld by the Church's Magisterium, shapes all aspects of an institution's life, both inside and outside the classroom. Divergence from this vision weakens Catholic identity and, far from advancing freedom, inevitably leads to confusion, whether moral, intellectual or spiritual.

Such confusion, said Benedict, ultimately destroys rather than promotes authentic freedom.

The papal addresses given at Catholic University by both John Paul II and Benedict XVI, in union with *Ex Corde Ecclesiae*, may be read as the response of the Magisterium to the controversies that engulfed CUA and Catholic higher education in the United States in the generation following Vatican II. They declare that although academic freedom is important to the Catholic educational and theological enterprise, it may never be asserted at the expense of the authoritative role of the Magisterium of the Church in guiding the faithful, including theologians, to an authentic understanding of the truth revealed to the Church in Jesus Christ. Whenever academic freedom claims absolute autonomy, the resulting confusion causes the faithful to be troubled; it turns public opinion against the Church and the truth and thus harms the good of the entire society.

In contrast, dynamic fidelity to the Magisterium of the Church *enables* the Catholic university to impart to its students the authentic freedom that is contained in the person of Jesus Christ. This self-understanding of Catholic education as an "encounter with the person of Jesus Christ" has been an essential aspect of the Magisterium's call for the renewal of Catholic higher education at the dawn of the third millennium. Far from being an obstacle to freedom (which would be inherently un-American), the authority of the Magisterium is in fact the foundation of a Catholic university's freedom to be itself (and hence entirely in accord with American values). It is in this sense that the Magisterium can unhesitatingly affirm, as Benedict did, "the great value of academic freedom".

When asked how he thinks Catholic higher education should resolve the tension between being Catholic and American, Charles Curran emphatically maintained his belief that it should strive to be both fully Catholic *and* fully American.[5] Eugene Kevane likewise believed that Catholic University should strive to be fully at the service of American society. The fact that these two men disagreed so completely on the course that CUA should take during the critical years from 1967 to 1969 indicates a radical difference between what each of these men meant by "American and Catholic."

Curran sought to harmonize "American and Catholic" by striving to eliminate from the Catholic understanding of authority the elements that he felt violated human rights and individual liberty. He understood the hierarchical Magisterium as a fundamentally unjust structure, which "traditionally has failed to give enough importance to human freedom and the active participation of the citizen in government".[6] In Curran's interpretation, fear of individualism had made the Catholic Church very hesitant to support human rights fully. Curran thus saw himself as a crusader for the American values of freedom and democracy, which he felt the traditional Catholic understanding of authority had opposed and even destroyed. Catholic University would become fully American, in Curran's view, on the day it threw off its vestigial attachment to the hierarchical Magisterium.

In contrast, Kevane believed that a union of "American and Catholic" identities could be achieved by giving Catholic University the "freedom to be itself," that is, to be a pontifical university fully and

---

[5] Author's interview with Curran.

[6] Charles Curran, *Loyal Dissent: Memoir of a Catholic Theologian* (Washington: Georgetown University Press, 2006), 230.

unashamedly subject to the theological authority of the pope and the American bishops. Kevane found his inspiration in one of the most cherished American values affirmed by the Founding Fathers: the right to religious liberty. Academic freedom as an ideology had, in Kevane's view, undermined the authentic pluralism that was the fruit of religious liberty and had replaced it with a monolithic uniformity that took away individual liberty. Kevane was convinced that the narrow-minded insistence of the AAUP that all American education employ the methodology of the empirical sciences was eliminating the richness of methodological diversity that made the American tradition of higher education so uniquely valuable. Freedom and truth, both prized highly by the American academic tradition, would, in Kevane's opinion, be better served if Catholic University possessed the freedom to employ the diverse and distinct methodology proper to Catholic theology, a methodology founded on the authoritative guidance of the Magisterium. Kevane was firmly convinced that his openness to diversity was inherently American and that the insistence of Curran and the AAUP on a uniform ideology manifested a closed-mindedness that was not in accord with the best that the American educational tradition had to offer.

Curran's interpretation emerged victorious at CUA. In that interpretation, embraced and amplified by a sympathetic secular press, July 30, 1968, was a date in American history akin to July 4, 1776. The "declaration of independence" that Curran and his fellow theologians made in their "Statement of Dissent" from the teaching of Pope Paul VI in *Humanae Vitae* was hailed as a victory for liberty and freedom. Their cause was consistently portrayed as one that no true American could fail to sympathize with and support.

The wave of victory carried Charles Curran to national and international prominence and fame while consigning Eugene Kevane to obscurity and the proverbial dust heap of history. Curran became a hero and media star of American Catholicism, while Kevane's name was seemingly never mentioned again by anyone who was a respected intellectual embracing "the accepted understanding of academic freedom". Kevane's role in the events at CUA has been all but omitted in most scholarly studies of the years investigated here. Nevertheless, regardless of one's evaluation of the relative merits of the respective cases of Curran and Kevane, it must be acknowledged that Kevane accurately and with great foresight placed his finger on the exact nature of the effects that developments at CUA were to have on the entire Catholic Church in the United States. His January 1968 letter of defense to the board of trustees predicted the breakdown in doctrinal fidelity to the teaching of the Magisterium that would come to be a defining mark of American Catholic higher education, as well as parochial and secondary education, in the years to follow. What Kevane described as the spread of "doubt" and "confusion", however, was affirmed and embraced by many Catholic educators as "promoting academic freedom" and "independence". Those educators understood themselves to be following the path of the "American tradition of autonomy" that had been explicitly set forth by the "Land O' Lakes Statement" the summer before Kevane's precipitate removal.

Beginning in 1968, the vast majority of Catholic education in the United States, from the university level down to parochial schools, came to be guided by the teaching authority, not of the pope and bishops, but of the "American Catholic" theologians who successfully took control of Catholic University in 1967. The alternative magisterium of these professors would, for the space of a generation or more, silence or at least relegate to the sidelines the voice of the Magisterium of the pope and the bishops in Catholic higher education. This victory of the monolithic ideology of the AAUP over the authentic pluralism of the Catholic educational tradition took place through the acquiescence of the bishops who composed the CUA board of trustees. When confronted by the AAUP's insistence on its definition of academic freedom as being normative for all of American higher education, including Catholic universities, the American bishops failed to find an effective language with which to present the Catholic commitment to freedom and the pursuit of truth as inherently in accord with the most cherished American values. In this failure lay the key to the victory of Charles Curran and the dissenting theologians as self-defined apostles of authentic American freedom.

A prominent professor of history at one of the United States' top nominally Catholic universities recently concluded a study of the history of Catholics in America with a confident prediction: "The twenty-first century will see American Catholics continue their ambivalent relationship to the papacy."[7] The fact that such a prediction could be made forty years after *Humanae Vitae*, together with a passing mention of a "lingering conflict" over Catholic higher education that the American bishops were frankly "too preoccupied" to address with any energy or effectiveness in defending their position, may be attributed in no small part to the way the American hierarchy chose to respond to dissent against the teaching of the Magisterium during the critical years 1967 to 1969 at Catholic University. The fact that the status quo of the vast majority of Catholic higher education in the United States has been embodied since 1967, with little change, in the tenets of the "Land O' Lakes Statement" is likewise largely attributable to the way events played out at CUA in the first months and years after the appearance of that declaration. The years 1967 to 1969 at CUA were a time of enduring consequence for the entire Catholic Church in the United States. Cardinal O'Boyle was well aware of this when he spoke to the board of trustees in April 1969:

> Whatever we do may be taken as a precedent by many other Catholic institutions in the United States, and even throughout the world. The outcome of this affair will be of the highest importance for Catholic theology and for the future of Catholic education in general.[8]

That outcome has been what Eugene Kevane accurately predicted in January 1968: "Religious doubt, doctrinal confusion, and outright crisis in Faith" have become the status quo for successive generations of American Catholics.

The key to the dissenters' victory was a united, focused, and brilliant strategy: to paint themselves as fighting for freedom and the bishops as opponents of freedom. By contrast, the bishops' defensive response to dissent was one of constant compromise, accepting silence rather than clarification from the dissenters. The bishops created a situation in which professors of theology at their own universities would simply not speak, at least publicly, about the most widely discussed and

---

[7] James M. O'Toole, *The Faithful: A History of Catholics in America* (Cambridge, Mass.: Belknap Press of Harvard University Press, 2008), 292. O'Toole is Clough Millennium Professor of History at Boston College.

[8] "Presentation to the Trustees of Catholic University regarding the Report of the Board of Inquiry concerning the Dissenting 'Theologians'", April 1969, box 32a, ACK.

controversial topics of the day. The stage was thus set for both sides to become extremely frustrated: on the one hand, the dissenting professor felt that he was being unjustly accused and unjustly judged, while on the other hand, the American bishops begrudgingly settled for a situation in which there was absolutely no defense of the Church's teaching by American Catholicism's leading intellectuals. The dissenters evasively refused to give a straightforward explanation of their theological position. The bishops clearly felt that the dissenters were undermining their authority at their own universities, yet they hesitated to remove or otherwise discipline them for fear of repercussions within the wider academic community. On the one occasion when the board did act decisively (its April 10, 1967, decision to allow Curran's contract to lapse), it rescinded its decision within two weeks and thus displayed a weakness and lack of resolve that would only be further exploited by the dissenters as time passed. The short-term victory of the dissenters (being allowed to continue teaching despite their direct opposition to the teaching of the Magisterium) was expanded to a long-term victory: they could now teach with the security of tenure and form their students—and eventually their students' students—as disciples of postconciliar theology. By using the appealing rhetoric of freedom and rights, the dissenters convinced their audience (the press and, through the press, the American public) that they were committed to American values and were in fact being unjustly persecuted because of that commitment.

Cardinal Krol's strategy of maintaining a strict silence about the reason for Curran's dismissal also seriously backfired. Krol's declaration that Curran was not really being fired or dismissed may have been in some sense technically correct, but the board's silence was very difficult to explain to an American public that was already deeply suspicious of authority, to say nothing of intellectuals who were frustrated by the repressively authoritarian culture then existing within Catholic academia. The common understanding—both within the Church and in the secular media—of what had happened at CUA on April 17, 1967, was that Curran was dismissed by the bishops for teaching moral theology in a manner of which they disapproved. Had the board of trustees said this straightforwardly, explained it simply and directly, and remained firmly united in its position, events might have turned out very differently for all involved. Had the board allowed Curran a public hearing in which he could have had the chance to defend himself, it likewise might have protected itself from the accusation that it had been unjust and un-American by not following due process. As it was, Krol's suggested course of taking action without warning or explanation, followed by silence on the part of the board, led to serious accusations of injustice from across Catholic academia. The bishops allowed the dissenters to take control of the public spin on the story. As one historian has observed, "the bishops left themselves wide open to charges, being leveled by Curran, that their actions were authoritarian and arbitrary and ultimately irrational."[9]

The board of trustees appeared in the public eye to be unprepared, divided, and poorly equipped to respond to the crisis at CUA.

It was ultimately the immense pressure generated by the accusations of injustice, fueled by the widespread frustration that the faculty and students had with the university's administration, that led the other bishops to part ways with Krol in deciding to reinstate Curran and give him tenure. Thus, Krol's strategy of public silence during the crucial week of April 17 to 24, 1967, enabled the School of Theology to garner widespread support for its position, which it defended adamantly from start to finish as one of human rights, educational excellence, and academic freedom—all values that Americans understood as essential to their national identity. The story line was presented as a case of young versus old, relaxed versus rigid, open and tolerant versus closed and fearful, moderately liberal versus archconservative, modern and "cool" versus old-fashioned and out of touch. Americans saw their own self-image reflected in the dissenting theologians and were decidedly turned off by the image of the American hierarchy presented by the media. The prominence the dissenters gained through this sympathetic portrayal, together with their tenacious solidarity and organization, obtained for them a lasting influence on the public face of the Catholic Church in the United States.

By maintaining that a choice had to be made between American and Catholic identity, the dissenters successfully formed the understanding of the Catholic laity and the wider American public with regard to ecclesiastical matters and dogmatic teaching, not only during the

---

[9] E. Michael Jones, *John Cardinal Krol and the Cultural Revolution* (South Bend, Ind.: Fidelity Press, 1995), 389.

specific years considered by this work but throughout the post-Vatican II era. The generation that came of age in this era remains largely influential in and characteristic of the Church in the United States to the present day. The opposing images of *American* and *Catholic* presented in the press became the essential foundation for the argument supporting dissent from *Humanae Vitae* the following year. The same dichotomy became the basis for the position of those who professed their faith in an Americanized Catholic Church, which no longer needed to heed the moral teaching of the Magisterium in the decades following the Second Vatican Council.

Although CUA may have remained America's premier Catholic university in name, after April 24, 1967, it could no longer be said to be so in fact. The hierarchy of the United States had effectively ceded control of the university to the School of Theology, adopting a policy of accommodation to the dissenters' demands. The successful campaign during the 1967–1968 academic year to oust Monsignor Kevane from his deanship, despite the protestations of the bishops on the board of trustees, demonstrated the full extent of the power the theologians now possessed. The extensive restructuring of the board of trustees and the rewriting of the statutes and bylaws of the university that occurred during this same critical year was likewise driven and guided by those faculty members who embraced the ideological position of the AAUP, the same individuals who had been instrumental in organizing and leading the 1967 strike to its successful conclusion.

Having capitulated to the demands made in the name of academic freedom in 1967, the board of trustees found its hands tied during the tumultuous summer of 1968. The board was unable to discipline Curran or any of the dissenting professors for fear of seeing a repeat of the fiasco of the 1967 strike—or worse. Although a few of the more determinedly principled bishops, namely, Cardinals McIntyre, O'Boyle, and Krol, sought to force the dissenters either to recant or to consider themselves fired, their proposal to make a direct ultimatum was never embraced by the full board. Following the precedent it had set in 1967, the board allowed itself to be guided by the principles of the AAUP in commissioning the faculty board of inquiry. Each day of the 1968–1969 academic year saw the dissenters ever more securely established in their position of total control of CUA. The board of inquiry's report

completely exonerated the dissenters, an absolute triumph for the proponents of the AAUP's vision of academic freedom as well as for the
advocates of a postconciliar theology that had severed itself from the
Catholic Tradition up to Vatican II. The board of inquiry's April 1969
report marked the clear and unquestioned ascendancy of the dissenting
theologians' interpretation of the meaning of "American and Catholic" within American academia, a far greater achievement for the dissenters than Curran's 1967 reinstatement. Curran had been restored to
his position with little official explanation or exoneration of his cause,
but the faculty report was an official university statement endorsing
the dissenters' position. The report was superlative in its praise for the
actions of the dissenters as entirely virtuous and selfless. Not only did
the report clear the dissenting professors of any wrongdoing; it effectively canonized them as martyrs in the cause of academic freedom and
American values. Their witness had finally made Catholic University
an institution that did not need to be ashamed of or embarrassed by its
episcopal oversight; rather it could proudly raise its head as an institution that embodied the ideals of the AAUP. Despite its Catholic name,
CUA could now enjoy the approval and benediction of the supreme
ideological authority of American academia, the AAUP.

The 1969 *Report of the Faculty Board of Inquiry* further constituted a
scathing rebuke not only of the board of trustees but even of the very
governing principles of Catholic University. By its bold rejection of the
existing statutes of the university as being incompatible with American
practices, by its flat denial of the validity of the term *canonical mission*,
and by its use of the board of trustees' very own statement of objectives
to justify its findings, the report firmly and unambiguously declared
that there was no place for ecclesiastical authority in the administration
and operation of the university. It demanded that the bishops maintain
an agnostic position in dealing with any kind of academic controversy.
This denial of the practical authority and oversight of the Magisterium
was seen by the faculty as the essential condition for the preservation
of the American identity of Catholic University. It was the board of
trustees, not the dissenting professors, who needed to amend their
ways. There was simply no place for any juridical authority at CUA,
in American higher education, or in the American Catholic Church in
general, other than that of the dissenting theologians.

The aftermath of the 1969 report of the board of inquiry was that the board of trustees essentially abandoned any further attempt to discipline the dissenting theologians. Although the board of trustees united in opposing the nomination of Roland Murphy as dean of the School of Theology in the summer of 1969, it found itself incapable of doing anything further about the presence on the CUA faculty of professors who openly showed contempt for its authority and that of the Magisterium. While there were a few isolated efforts to revive the debate in the fall of 1969, these proposals fell on deaf ears when presented to the entire board, which by now was tired of the fight and ready to "move on". Moving on, however, meant that the dissenting theologians were allowed to remain permanently and unassailably in their position controlling Catholic University. Thus, the American bishops, having sacrificed victory in the battle over Curran's dismissal in 1967, supposedly for the sake of winning the greater war to preserve faithful teaching and Catholic identity at CUA, found by the end of 1969 that they had lost the struggle for the identity of CUA and with it the identity of Catholic higher education throughout the country.

The struggle at CUA never strayed far from a recurring theme, identified by Eugene Kevane in the first days of the 1967 strike: "The issue is the Magisterium." The central issue of the debate was the specific nature of the authority of the pope and the bishops. Both the dissenters and the board of trustees agreed that the proper functioning of the bishops was essential to the university's success in its mission. In the dissenters' view, the bishops needed to remove themselves from making any theological judgment whatsoever about the content of their teaching. The bishops, in contrast, expected that their definitive teaching would be promoted and defended by the professors they commissioned to teach. The clash of these two incompatible understandings of the Magisterium lay at the heart of the entire story as it unfolded. The so-called compromise between the two that was eventually reached was in fact a settlement entirely deferential to the demands of the dissenters.

In effect, the CUA School of Theology told the bishops, who made up the Magisterium, that they had a faulty understanding of the nature of the Magisterium. With bold confidence in their inevitable victory, the dissenters, led by Curran, directly challenged and denied the bishops' understanding of their own authority. They made it their life's work to ensure that the Christian faithful, and most of all the bishops of the Church, properly understood the true nature of the bishops' own authority. Closely linked to this question was the question of the precise role of a Catholic university as part of the mission of the Church to proclaim the gospel. The dissenting theologians saw little if any connection between the purpose of a university and the mission of the Church, while the board of trustees believed that a Catholic university was a direct instrument by which the Church teaches the saving truth of the gospel. The idea of a mission to teach unchanging truth embarrassed these intellectuals as they sought to win recognition as equals in the halls of American academia. Despite professing their commitment to dialogue with the Magisterium, the dissenters repeatedly and categorically dismissed the bishops as uneducated amateurs. They had but one goal in their interactions with the bishops: to demonstrate the self-evident intellectual and theological superiority of postconciliar theology and the ideals of the AAUP over the teaching of the Magisterium. It was impossible that even an exponential number of dialogues, commissions, and committee meetings would bring about any sort of mutual agreement. Their only goal was to eliminate from CUA the practical authority of the bishops as the alleged enemies of the American ideal of freedom.

This elimination of the bishops' authority would have profound consequences for the entire program of Catholic education, at every level, throughout the United States. Once the ideology of the AAUP had been embraced at the top of the educational system, it would not be long before dissent and the rejection of dogma would come to be par for the course at many of the nation's Catholic secondary and parochial schools. The overwhelming tide of postconciliar theology would sweep an entire generation of American Catholics away from the traditional Catholic faith that their immigrant grandfathers had taken great pains to preserve intact and pass on faithfully as they came to the New World. The handing over of this faith, which had occurred from generation to generation for centuries, would be all but entirely undone within the space of the one modern, relevant, media-savvy, "fully American" post-Vatican II Catholic generation that came of age in 1968.

The coup at Catholic University by the dissenting professors led by Curran marked the beginning of the formation of an entire generation of undergraduate and graduate students at Catholic universities throughout the United States who were thoroughly indoctrinated in postconciliar theology's understanding of Catholic identity: a teacher of the Catholic faith could freely disagree with the authoritative teaching of the Magisterium, all the while affirming his respect for what was called the opinion of the pope and bishops. For nearly twenty years Curran taught at CUA, despite his positions openly contradicting the teaching of the Magisterium. The takeover of CUA in 1967 was the single most significant cause of the widespread dissent from Church teaching among the Catholic laity in the United States after the Second Vatican Council.

The ongoing importance of the debate over the meaning of academic freedom in Catholic higher education in the United States is unquestioned. As one commentator on the Curran controversy has written:

> The fact is, though, that the resolution of the Curran case will have substantial impact on the definition of the role of the theologian in the Roman Catholic Church, on American Roman Catholic higher education, on the interpretation of academic freedom in confessional colleges and universities of any religious persuasion, and for American society more broadly.[10]

The Catholic Church in America remains in need of a more fully informed awareness of the issues that lie at the root of much of the turmoil and difficulty of her recent past. The postconciliar Magisterium has emphatically called American Catholic universities to unite a strong commitment to the best of the American tradition of academic freedom with an unwavering witness to the authentic Catholic identity gained by fidelity to the definitive teaching of the Church. *Catholic* and *American* need not be mutually exclusive adjectives in higher education. In fact, Eugene Kevane was convinced that it was precisely because of the American commitment to religious freedom that CUA could be entirely and unwaveringly faithful to the Magisterium without apology or compromise. The Church in the United States should then be encouraged by Kevane's great hope that, in the ongoing quest for authentic academic freedom united with authentic fidelity to the Magisterium of the Church at America's Catholic universities, "the battle may not be lost."

---

[10] William W. May, ed., *Vatican Authority and American Dissent* (New York: Crossroad, 1987), 1.

APPENDICES

AAUP Statement of Principles on Academic Freedom and Tenure (1940)

The purpose of this statement is to promote public understanding and support of academic freedom and tenure and agreement upon procedures to ensure them in colleges and universities. Institutions of higher education are conducted for the common good and not to further the interest of either the individual teacher or the institution as a whole. The common good depends upon the free search for truth and its free exposition.

Academic freedom is essential to these purposes and applies to both teaching and research. Freedom in research is fundamental to the advancement of truth. Academic freedom in its teaching aspect is fundamental for the protection of the rights of the teacher in teaching and of the student to freedom in. It carries with it duties correlative with rights.

Tenure is a means to certain ends; specifically: (1) freedom of teaching and research and of extramural activities, and (2) a sufficient degree of economic security to make the profession attractive to men and women of ability. Freedom and economic security, hence, tenure, are indispensable to the success of an institution in fulfilling its obligations to its students and to society.

Reprinted with permission from the *Bulletin of American Association of University Professors* 1 (1940): 49–51.

Academic Freedom

1. Teachers are entitled to full freedom in research and in the publication of the results, subject to the adequate performance of their other academic duties; but research for pecuniary return should be based upon an understanding with the authorities of the institution.

2. Teachers are entitled to freedom in the classroom in discussing their subject, but they should be careful not to introduce into their teaching controversial matter which has no relation to their subject. Limitations of academic freedom because of religious or other aims of the institution should be clearly stated in writing at the time of the appointment.

3. College and university teachers are citizens, members of a learned profession, and officers of an educational institution. When they speak or write as citizens, they should be free from institutional censorship or discipline, but their special position in the community imposes special obligations. As scholars and educational officers, they should remember that the public may judge their profession and their institution by their utterances. Hence they should at all times be accurate, should exercise appropriate restraint, should show respect for the opinions of others, and should make every effort to indicate that they are not speaking for the institution.

Academic Tenure

After the expiration of a probationary period, teachers or investigators should have permanent or continuous tenure, and their service should be terminated only for adequate cause, except in the case of retirement for age, or under extraordinary circumstances because of financial exigencies.

In the interpretation of this principle it is understood that the following represents acceptable academic practice:

1. The precise terms and conditions of every appointment should be stated in writing and be in the possession of both institution and teacher before the appointment is consummated.

2. Beginning with appointment to the rank of full-time instructor or a higher rank, the probationary period should not exceed seven years, including within this period full-time service in all institutions of higher education; but subject to the proviso that when, after a term of probationary service of more than three years in one or more institutions, a teacher is called to another institution, it may be agreed in writing that the new appointment is for a probationary period of not more than four years, even though thereby the person's total probationary period in the academic profession is extended beyond the normal maximum of seven years. Notice should be given at least one year prior to the expiration of the probationary period if the teacher is not to be continued in service after the expiration of that period.

3. During the probationary period a teacher should have the academic freedom that all other members of the faculty have.

4. Termination for cause of a continuous appointment, or the dismissal for cause of a teacher previous to the expiration of a term appointment, should, if possible, be considered by both a faculty committee and the governing board of the institution. In all cases where the facts are in dispute, the accused teacher should be informed before the hearing in writing of the charges and should have the opportunity to be heard in his or her own defense by all bodies that pass judgment upon the case. The teacher should be permitted to be accompanied by an advisor of his or her own choosing who may act as counsel. There should be a full stenographic record of the hearing available to the parties concerned. In the hearing of charges of incompetence the testimony should include that of teachers and other scholars, either from the teacher's own or from other institutions. Teachers on continuous appointment who are dismissed for reasons not involving moral turpitude should receive their salaries for at least a year from the date of notification of dismissal whether or not they are continued in their duties at the institution.

5. Termination of a continuous appointment because of financial exigency should be demonstrably bona fide.

1940 Interpretations

At the conference of representatives of the American Association of University Professors and of the Association of American Colleges on November 7–8, 1940, the following interpretations of the 1940 *Statement of Principles on Academic Freedom and Tenure* were agreed upon:

1. That its operation should not be retroactive.

2. That all tenure claims of teachers appointed prior to the endorsement should be determined in accordance with the principles set forth in the 1925 *Conference Statement on Academic Freedom and Tenure*.

3. If the administration of a college or university feels that a teacher has not observed the admonitions of paragraph 3 of the section on Academic Freedom and believes that the extramural utterances of the teacher have been such as to raise grave doubts concerning the teacher's fitness for his or her position, it may proceed to file charges under paragraph 4 of the section on Academic Tenure. In pressing such charges, the administration should remember that teachers are citizens and should be accorded the freedom of citizens. In such cases the administration must assume full responsibility, and the American Association of University Professors and the Association of American Colleges are free to make an investigation.

Land O' Lakes Statement on the Nature of the Contemporary Catholic University (July 23, 1967)

1. The Catholic University: A True University with Distinctive Characteristics

The Catholic University today must be a university in the full modern sense of the word, with a strong commitment to and concern for academic excellence. To perform its teaching and research functions effectively the Catholic university must have a true autonomy and academic freedom in the face of authority of whatever kind, lay or clerical, external to the academic community itself. To say this is simply to assert that institutional autonomy and academic freedom are essential conditions of life and growth and indeed of survival for Catholic universities as for all universities.

The Catholic university participates in the total university life of our time, has the same functions as all other true universities and, in general, offers the same services to society. The Catholic university adds to the basic idea of a modern university distinctive characteristics which round out and fulfill that idea. Distinctively, then, the Catholic university must be an institution, a community of learners or a community of scholars, in which Catholicism is perceptibly present and effectively operative.

2. The Theological Disciplines

In the Catholic university this operative presence is effectively achieved first of all and distinctively by the presence of a group of scholars in

In Neil G. McCluskey, ed., *The Catholic University: A Modern Appraisal*, (Notre Dame, Ind.: University of Notre Dame Press, 1970), 336–41. Reprinted with permission.

all branches of theology. The disciplines represented by this theological group are recognized in the Catholic university, not only as legitimate intellectual disciplines, but as ones essential to the integrity of a university. Since the pursuit of the theological sciences is therefore a high priority for a Catholic university, academic excellence in these disciplines becomes a double obligation in a Catholic university.

3. The Primary Task of the Theological Faculty

The theological faculty must engage directly in exploring the depths of Christian tradition and the total religious heritage of the world, in order to come to the best possible intellectual understanding of religion and revelation, of man in all his varied relationships to God. Particularly important today is the theological exploration of all human relations and the elaboration of a Christian anthropology. Furthermore, theological investigation today must serve the ecumenical goals of collaboration and unity.

4. Interdisciplinary Dialogue in the Catholic University

To carry out this primary task properly there must be a constant discussion within the university community in which theology confronts all the rest of modern culture and all the areas of intellectual study which it includes.

Theology needs this dialogue in order:

A) to enrich itself from the other disciplines

B) to bring its own insights to bear upon the problems of modern culture; and

C) to stimulate the internal development of the disciplines themselves.

In a Catholic university all recognized university areas of study are frankly and fully accepted and their internal autonomy affirmed and guaranteed. There must be no theological or philosophical imperialism; all scientific and disciplinary methods, and methodologies, must be given due honor and respect. However, there will necessarily result from the interdisciplinary discussions an awareness that there is a philo-sophical and theological dimension to most intellectual subjects when they are pursued far enough. Hence, in a Catholic university there will be a special interest in interdisciplinary problems and relationships.

This total dialogue can be eminently successful:

A) if the Catholic university has a broad range of basic university disciplines;

B) if the university has achieved considerable strength in these disciplines; and

C) if there are present in many or most of the non-theological areas Christian scholars who are not only interested in, and competent in their own fields, but also have a personal interest in the cross-disciplinary confrontation.

This creative dialogue will involve the entire university community, will inevitably influence and enliven classroom activities, and will be reflected in curriculum and in academic programs.

5. The Catholic University as the Critical Reflective Intelligence of the Church

Every university, Catholic or not, serves as the critical reflective intel-ligence of its society. In keeping with this general function, the Cath-olic university has the added obligation of performing this same ser-vice for the Church. Hence, the university should carry on a continual examination of all aspects and all activities of the Church and should objectively evaluate them. The Church would thus have the benefit of continual counsel from Catholic universities. Catholic universities in the recent past have hardly played this role at all. It may well be one of the most important functions of the Catholic university of the future.

6. The Catholic University and Research

The Catholic university will, of course, maintain and support broad programs of research. It will promote basic research in all university fields but, in addition, it will be prepared to undertake by preference, though not exclusively, such research as will deal with problems of greater human urgency or of greater Christian concern.

7. The Catholic University and Public Service

In common with other universities, and in accordance with given circumstances, the Catholic university is prepared to serve society and all its parts, e.g., the Federal Government, the inner-city, etc. However, it will have an added special obligation to carry on similar activities, appropriate to a university, in order to serve the Church and its component parts.

8. Some Characteristics of Undergraduate Education

The effective intellectual presence of the theological disciplines will affect the education and life of the students in ways distinctive of a Catholic university.

With regard to the undergraduate—the university should endeavor to present a collegiate education that is truly geared to modern society. The student must come to a basic understanding of the actual world in which he lives today. This means that the intellectual campus of a Catholic university has no boundaries and no barriers. It draws knowledge and understanding from all the traditions of mankind; it explores the insights and achievements of the great men of every age; it looks to the current frontiers of advancing knowledge and brings all the results to bear relevantly on man's life today. The whole world of knowledge and ideas must be open to the student; there must be no outlawed books or subjects. Thus the student will be able to develop his own capabilities and to fulfill himself by using the intellectual resources presented to him.

Along with this and integrated into it should be a competent presentation of relevant, living, Catholic thought.

This dual presentation is characterized by the following emphases:

A) a concern with ultimate questions; hence a concern with theological and philosophical questions;

B) a concern for the full human and spiritual development of the student; hence a humanistic and personalistic orientation with special emphasis on the interpersonal relationships within the community of learners;

C) a concern with the particularly pressing problems of our era, e.g., civil rights, international development and peace, poverty, etc.

9. Some Special Social Characteristics of the Catholic Community of Learners

As a community of learners, the Catholic university has a social existence and an organizational form.

Within the university community the student should be able not simply to study theology and Christianity, but should find himself in a social situation in which he can express his Christianity in a variety of ways and live it experientially and experimentally. The students and faculty can explore together new forms of Christian living, of Christian witness, and of Christian service.

The students will be able to participate in and contribute to a variety of liturgical functions, at best, creatively contemporary and experimental. They will find the meaning of the sacraments for themselves by joining theoretical understanding to the lived experience of them. Thus the students will find and indeed create extraordinary opportunities for a full, meaningful liturgical and sacramental life.

The students will individually and in small groups carry on a warm personal dialogue with themselves and with faculty, both priests and laymen.

The students will experiment further in Christian service by undertaking activities embodying the Christian interest in all human problems—inner-city social action, personal aid to the educationally disadvantaged, and so forth.

Thus will arise within the Catholic university a self-developing and self-deepening society of students and faculty in which the consequences of Christian truth are taken seriously in person-to-person relationships, where the importance of religious commitment is accepted and constantly witnessed to, and where the students can learn by personal experience to consecrate their talent and learning to worthy social purposes.

All of this will display itself on the Catholic campus as a distinctive style of living, a perceptible quality in the university's life.

10. Characteristics of Organization and Administration

The total organization should reflect this same Christian spirit. The social organization should be such as to emphasize the university's concern for persons as individuals and for appropriate participation by all members of the community of learners in university decisions. University decisions and administrative actions should be appropriately guided by Christian ideas and ideals and should eminently display the respect and concern for persons.

The evolving nature of the Catholic university will necessitate basic reorganizations of structure in order not only to achieve a greater internal cooperation and participation, but also to share the responsibility of direction more broadly and to enlist wider support. A great deal of study and experimentation will be necessary to carry out these changes, but changes of this kind are essential for the future of the Catholic university.

In fine, the Catholic university of the future will be a true modern university but specifically Catholic in profound and creative ways for the service of society and the people of God.

NOTE: Position paper adopted, July 20–23, 1967, at Land O' Lakes, Wisc., by the seminar participants: Gerard J. Campbell, S.J., President, Georgetown University; John Cogley, Center for the Study of Democratic Institutions, Santa Barbara, Calif.; Charles F. Donovan, S.J., Academic Vice President, Boston College; Most Rev. John J. Dougherty, Chairman, Episcopal Committee for Catholic Higher Education and President, Seton Hall University, South Orange, N.J.; Thomas R. Fitzgerald, S.J., Academic Vice President, Georgetown University; Rev. F. Raymond Fowerbaugh, Assistant to the President, Catholic University of America; Most Rev. Paul J. Hallinan, Archbishop of Atlanta; Robert J. Henle, S.J., Academic Vice President, Saint Louis University; Theodore M. Hesburgh, C.S.C., President, University of

Notre Dame; Howard J. Kenna, C.S.C., Provincial, Indiana Province, Congregation of Holy Cross, Robert D. Kidera, Vice President for University Relations, Fordham University; Germain-Marie Lalande, C.S.C., Superior General, Congregation of Holy Cross, Rome, Italy; Felipe E. MacGregor, S.J., Rector, Pontificia Universidad Catolica del Peru, Lima, Peru; Right Rev. Theodore E. McCarrick, President, Catholic University of Puerto Rico, Ponce; Neil G. McCluskey, S.J., Secretary of the Seminar, University of Notre Dame; Leo McLaughlin, S.J., President, Fordham University; Vincent T. O'Keefe, S.J., Assistant General, Society of Jesus, Rome, Italy; Right Rev. Alphonse-Marie Parent, Laval University, Quebec, Canada; Paul C. Reinert, S.J., President, Saint Louis University, M. L'abbe Lorenzo Roy, Vice Rector, Laval University; Daniel L. Schlafly, Chairman, board of trustees, Saint Louis University; George N. Shuster, Assistant to the President, University of Notre Dame; Edmund A. Stephan, Chairman, board of trustees, University of Notre Dame; M. L'abbe Lucien Vachon, Dean, Faculty of Theology, University of Sherbrook, Canada; John E. Walsh, C.S.C., Vice President for Academic Affairs, University of Notre Dame; Michael P. Walsh, S.J., President, Boston College.

APPENDIX C

Statement of Dissent

Washington, D.C., July 30, 1968

As Roman Catholic theologians we respectfully acknowledge a distinct role of hierarchical Magisterium (teaching authority) in the Church of Christ. At the same time Christian tradition assigns theologians the special responsibility of evaluating and interpreting pronouncements of the *magisterium* in the light of the total theological data operative in each question or statement. We offer these initial comments on Pope Paul VI's Encyclical on the Regulation of Birth.

The Encyclical is not an infallible teaching. History shows that a number of statements of similar or even greater authoritative weight have subsequently been proved inadequate or even erroneous. Past authoritative statements on religious liberty, interest-taking, the right to silence and the ends of marriage have all been corrected at a later date.

Many positive values concerning marriage are expressed in Paul VI's Encyclical. However, we take exception to the ecclesiology implied in the methodology used by Paul VI in the writing and promulgation of the document: they are incompatible with the Church's authentic self-awareness as expressed in and suggested by the acts of the Second Vatican Council itself. The Encyclical consistently assumes that the Church is identical with the hierarchical office. No real importance is afforded the witness of the life of the Church in its totality; the special witness of many Catholic couples is neglected; it fails to acknowledge

In John F. Hunt and Terrence R. Connelly, *The Responsibility of Dissent: The Church and Academic Freedom* (New York: Sheed and Ward, 1969), 203–205. Reprinted with permission.

the witness of the separated Christian Churches and Ecclesial Communities; it is insensitive to the witness of many men of good will; it pays insufficient attention to the ethical import of modern science.

Furthermore, the Encyclical betrays a narrow and positivistic notion of papal authority, as illustrated by the rejection of the majority view presented by the Commission established to consider the question, as well as by the rejection of the conclusions of a large part of the international Catholic theological community.

Likewise, we take exception to some of the specific ethical conclusions contained in the Encyclical. They are based on an inadequate concept of natural law: the multiple forms of natural law theory are ignored and the fact that competent philosophers come to different conclusions on this very question is disregarded. Even the minority report of the papal commission noted grave difficulty in attempting to present conclusive proof of the immorality of artificial contraception based on natural law.

Other defects include: overemphasis on the biological aspects of conjugal relations as ethically normative; undue stress on sexual acts and on the faculty of sex viewed in itself apart from the person and the couple; a static worldview which downplays the historical and evolutionary character of humanity in its finite existence, as described in Vatican II's *Pastoral Constitution on the Church in the Modern World*; unfounded assumptions about "the evil consequences of methods of artificial birth control"; indifference to Vatican II's assertion that prolonged sexual abstinence may cause "faithfulness to be imperiled and its quality of fruitfulness to be ruined"; an almost total disregard for the dignity of millions of human beings brought into the world without the slightest possibility of being fed and educated decently.

In actual fact, the Encyclical demonstrates no development over the teaching of Pius XI's *Casti Connubii* whose conclusions have been called into question for grave and serious reasons. These reasons, given a muffled voice at Vatican II, have not been adequately handled by the mere repetition of past teaching.

It is common teaching in the Church that Catholics may dissent from authoritative, noninfallible teachings of the magisterium when sufficient reasons for so doing exist.

Therefore, as Roman Catholic theologians, conscious of our duty and our limitations, we conclude that spouses may responsibly decide according to their conscience that artificial contraception in some circumstances is permissible and indeed necessary to preserve and foster the values and sacredness of marriage.

It is our conviction also that true commitment to the mystery of Christ and the Church requires a candid statement of mind at this time by all Catholic theologians.

Notes on Possible Courses of Action
at CUA (September 4, 1968)

The notes on the following pages were written by Germain Grisez on the pros and cons of various courses of action regarding the future of CUA. They were presented by Cardinal O'Boyle on September 4, 1968, at an informal meeting of the bishops on the CUA board of trustees prior to the meeting of the full board on September 5, 1968.

Doing Nothing

This possibility explains itself.

Pro

1) Avoids problems with A.A.U.P. and with the law.

2) In the short run, at least, this is the cheapest and easiest course.

3) Few who have significant influence will complain.

4) Other Catholic institutions do not seem to be doing anything; why should we?

5) The positions taken by the Dutch and Belgian hierarchies would not demand any drastic action in a case like this. The Pope isn't doing anything about their positions. Should we be more loyal to the Pope that he's being to himself?

From the papers of James Cardinal McIntyre, Archives of the Archdiocese of Los Angeles. San Fernando Mission, Mission Hills, California. Used with permission.

Con

1) Nothing in Catholic theology can justify the present sort of dissent. This dissent is an offense against Catholic doctrine. The offense must be rectified.

2) Failure to act means that the Catholic Church in America is sponsoring an outright rejection of papal teaching.

3) Theologians who do not adhere to the proper criterion of faith are not functioning as competent theologians. Catholic theologians accept the magisterium of the Church as the criterion. Whatever the technical skill of the dissenters and however vehement their verbal professions of loyalty to the teaching authority of the Church, their dissent has made them incompetent to teach Catholic theology; an analogous argument applies to the other discipline concerned. It is necessary to act for the sake of maintaining academic respectability as a truly Catholic university.

4) The dissent is scandalous to the faithful whom it leads away from the teaching of the Church. The University was established precisely to promote the teaching of Catholic truth.

5) Doing nothing is particularly unacceptable at Catholic University because of the Pontifical character of the institution and because this case will set a pattern for all others.

A Merely Symbolic Reaction

In practice this course could take on many different forms. For example, the board of trustees might issue an admonition to the dissenting theologians. Or a public statement might be made indicating that the views of the dissenters represent private opinions, not the teaching of the Church. The Trustees might affirm their own assent to the teaching of the Church. Several such symbolic acts might be combined in one statement, or there could be several acts over a period of weeks.

Pro

1) This course has all the advantages of doing nothing.

2) It registers the displeasure of the Trustees, and shows at least that they do not fully support the dissent. This might mitigate the scandal to the faithful caused by the appearance that Catholic University of America does not accept the Catholic Church's authentic teaching.

3) This course leaves all other options open. This could be the first act in a crack-down, or it could be the neatest way of doing nothing while seeming to do something.

Con

1) All the reasons against doing nothing apply here too.

2) An ineffectual gesture on the part of the Trustees probably will do more harm than good in the long run; it will further undermine their authority by making their impotence evident.

3) The dissenters probably are expecting the Trustees to act in this manner. If their expectations are fulfilled, they will consolidate their position. The possibility of doing anything except secularizing the University or watching it go secular will be lost.

4) There is dishonesty and evasion of responsibility in meeting an extremely important issue with a mere gesture. If one means to do nothing, why not be honest with oneself and with others about it?

Try to Get Rid of the Offenders and Carry On

One naturally thinks of this as the proper course of action. But it must be done in a legal way. A member of the university faculty who has a contract or its legal equivalent has a certain status in the institution. He is not merely an employee. One needs just cause and adherence to due process or the final situation is liable to be worse than the initial one.

There are several ways for Trustees to get rid of faculty members. In the cases of priests, one might ask their bishops to reassign them. But not all bishops will cooperate and not all men will obey. Again, the Trustees or the Rector might veto faculty recommendations to renew contracts of undesirable faculty members. This would take years and it would never touch the Professors who have permanency.

The method that is envisaged in the General Statutes of the University is: "Statute 66—If a teacher offends against Catholic doctrine or is guilty of grave misconduct, the whole matter should be brought to the board of trustees, who shall submit the whole case to three Bishops for the investigation and final adjudication, with due regard for the rules of the University, and, in the case of a cleric, for the regulations of Canon Law."

Pro

1) This is the method that seems to be envisaged by law.

2) Even to begin this process would greatly mitigate scandal to the faithful.

3) If the process were carried through successfully, the offense of the open dissent from papal teaching would be excluded within this University.

4) This course offers some hope of preserving the University and restoring it fully to the service of its original objectives.

5) Less damage to innocent individuals is involved in this course than in the next possibility—closing down parts of the University for the time being.

Con

1) This method means that the dissenters will occupy their chairs for this year. (The spirit if not the letter of Art. 66 demands careful hearings in regard to each individual case.)

2) During the year, pressure will develop against carrying through. This could involve something worse than Columbia University last spring.

3) The board of trustees probably would give in somewhere along the line.

4) This course would be costly in time and effort, as well as in money (e.g., paying off contracts).

5) Probably it would be difficult to find good professors or students in the future.

6) If the procedure "succeeded," affected schools almost certainly would close next year anyhow.

7) Dissenters will argue that Art. 66 does not apply. First, because they claim it is common teaching in the Church that there is a right and obligation to dissent as they are doing. Second, because they claim the teaching on contraception is not infallible and will argue that Art. 66 applies only to cases of outright heresy.

Third, because they will claim that the University would infringe their personal freedom if it interested itself in the positions they take outside of the classroom.

Close the Ecclesiastical Schools and the Department of Religious Education

From time to time the Trustees of a University are faced with insuperable problems (usually financial) which lead them to close down one or more sections of a university. Normally this would be done in an orderly way—i.e., with plenty of advance notice to students and faculty. Usually there is no expectation that the affected sections will ever reopen.

In the present situation, the board of trustees could simply close the affected sections of Catholic University. The reason would be that these programs no longer serve the purposes for which the institution was founded. However, since the College program includes required courses in philosophy and religion, and since these could not be supplied if these schools were closed, the College also would have to be closed.

Pro

1) The affected sections could be closed at once, by a simple decision of the Trustees.

2) This course would immediately end the scandal arising from dissent within the University.

3) There would remain some hope of keeping the property and reforming the University for its original purposes.

4) This course would avoid the long process implied by the previous possibility.

5) The example of closing the affected segments of the University would be an extremely effective way to teach that the present form of dissent is irreconcilable with Catholic doctrine.

Con

1) This course would be extremely expensive, e.g. in paying off contracts.

2) Where would you get the money to operate the remaining fragments of the University?

3) Probably other students and faculty would leave.

4) It is doubtful whether reorganization of the affected sections could ever be accomplished. The rest of the University might be forced to close and even the property might revert to the District of Columbia.

5) Innocent individuals, e.g., students planning to appear for classes shortly, would be harmed. There might well be a series of lawsuits to recover damages for such harm.

Separate the University from the Church

The trend in Church-related institutions has been toward secularizing. This process already has advanced a certain way at Catholic University. What this course amounts to is simply pressing secularization to its limit immediately in order to end the absurdity of the Catholic Church officially sponsoring the undermining of its own teaching.

This course can be carried out administratively, if need be, even against the wishes of the majority of the Trustees. E.g. Chancellor can deprive dissenters of their canonical mission to teach (General Statutes Statute 21e), as well as of the faculties of the Archdiocese. The American Bishops as a whole could pass a declaration that the University is no longer Catholic, and could ask Rome to revoke the Pontifical charter.

If the board of trustees wishes, the University might be *given* to the District of Columbia and, perhaps with the help of a special Act of Congress, it might be arranged that the Bishops would be allowed to remove religious articles, materials on ecclesiastical subjects in the library, and certain collected items such as manuscripts and objects of art.

Pro

1) This course merely formalizes what already is largely accomplished fact.

2) By clarifying the situation, this course would mitigate the scandal to the faithful.

3) It can be argued plausibly that it is impossible to operate a genuinely religious university in the midst of our modern secular American culture.

4) This course would be much cheaper and easier than trying to reform the University.

5) This course would evoke the least adverse reaction from the public in general and would leave "liberal Catholics," including the faculty, happy.

6) Would not harm the innocent.

Con

1) The work and sacrifices of faithful Catholics have built the University to serve the faith. This course makes an outright gift of it to the faithless.

2) If this course is followed here, probably all major Catholic institutions of higher education will be secularized very quickly.

3) The bad influence of the University would not be ended by secularizing it. It will serve as a powerful center for teaching against the Church's teaching.

Summary Report of the Faculty Board of Inquiry (April 1, 1969)

In the pursuit of this inquiry, the board held 20 meetings, including 8 days of hearings, received 70 exhibits, examined 38 witnesses and studied over 3,000 pages of exhibits, testimony and background material.

The controlling documents were the September 5, 1968 and December 23, 1968 communications from the Trustees, and the Procedures for the Conduct of Inquiry adopted by the Senate on October 17, 1968.

The conclusions and recommendations which follow in this summary report represent the unanimous judgment of the board of inquiry.

Recommendations

That the University recognize that the commentary made by the subject professors in their July 30, 1968 statement is adequately supported by theological scholarship, and that their actions in composing, issuing and disseminating this statement did not violate the professors' commitments to the University or to the academic or theological communities.

That no further proceedings be instituted which would question the fitness of subject professors to teach at Catholic University of America

---

From the Archives of the Archdiocese of Baltimore. St. Mary's Seminary and University, Baltimore, Maryland. Used with permission.

based upon those declarations and actions with respect to the Encyclical "Humanae Vitae."

That the University proceed quickly to incorporate in its statutes, bylaws and regulations, those norms of academic freedom and academic due process recommended in this report.

That the University reassure the academic community that in the future it will not resort even to a threat of suspension, much less actual suspension, of faculty members without first affording the professor involved academic due process. In particular, the University should recognize that any judgment regarding the acceptability of the results of theological scholarship always should be made, in the first instance, by the professors' academic peers.

That, while acknowledging the ultimate canonical jurisdiction and doctrinal competence of the hierarchy, the Trustees remain sensitive to the devastating effect of any exercise of power in the resolution of academic difficulties.

Conclusions Regarding Subject Professors

The 30 July statement of the subject professors represents a responsible theological dissent from the teaching of the Encyclical "Humanae Vitae" and this dissent is reasonably supported as a tenable scholarly position.

There is no convincing reason to regard this statement as a "Catholic University of America statement." The subject professors took adequate precautions to make it clear that this was their personal statement, and no evidence exists to the contrary. Indeed, other signatories to the statement indicated that they would resent any such implication.

The content and style of the statement are well within the bounds of academic propriety. The right of a faculty member to determine the content of his public statement, without fear of reprisal, even though such statement may embarrass his institution in its relationship with its various constituencies, cannot be challenged. The right of a theological scholar to dissent from non-infallible teachings of the magisterium is well documented, most recently in the 15 November 1968 pastoral letter from the American Bishops.

From the perspective of the Church, there well may be novel elements in the use of the public media which must be resolved in the future, but the release of this statement cannot be regarded as contrary to the accepted norms of academic procedure. Neither the timing, the content, nor the means of securing circulation and concurrence of colleagues are to be regarded as extraordinary or improper in the light of current academic practices. The alternatives of either repressing the statement or of adopting a policy of concerted silence would have been more truly improper. Given the realities of the public media, the extensive theological dissent on this issue and the possibility of such dissent were certain quickly to become matters of widespread public knowledge. All allegations of surprise, confusion, scandal and related concerns must be judged in the light of this certain public knowledge. The subject professors were compelled to some kind of honest response, and we conclude that the statement thus may have averted at least as much harm as it is alleged by some to have caused.

The statement does not conflict with the Profession of Faith taken by subject professors, and this is the only portion of the current Statutes which could be considered as applicable. All other statutory admonitions are inapplicable, either being not germane, not enforced in practice, or not made known to the subject professors at the time of their appointment. Further, some provisions of the Statutes are patently incompatible with modern American university practice. Above all, the positive exhortation of Article 1 should take precedence, namely "to search out truth—and to apply it to the molding—of both private and public life."

Conclusions Regarding the Norms of Licit Dissent

Although the current inquiry was the result of a specific instance of dissent, it should be realized that it is inevitable that such instances will arise, rather frequently, in any university worthy of the name. The board recommends as the basic norms of academic freedom to be observed in such cases:

1940 Statement of Principles on Academic Freedom and Tenure, of the AAUP

1958 Statement on Procedural Standards in Faculty Dismissal Proceedings, of the AAUP

1964 Statement of Committee A on Extramural Utterances, of the AAUP

1967 Report and Draft Recommendation of a Specific Committee on Academic Freedom in Church-Related Colleges and Universities, of the AAUP

The board has considered other formulations, similar both in content and scope, of theses norms, (such as those of the ACLU, the AAU, the IFCU, etc.), but is of the opinion that careful adherence to the norms listed above would be adequate.

The 1960 norms of the American Association of Theological schools, which incorporate the AAUP 1940 norms for academic freedom, and which consider both classroom teaching and extramural expression, are the most suitable norms currently available to academic institutions at which theology is taught. These norms provide adequate guides for specifying the grounds of alleged professional incompetence with respect to theology and other sacred sciences by reference to the confessional commitment of the particular school.

If the professional competence of a teacher of Roman Catholic theology is seriously questioned, (whether on grounds of deviation from the Roman Catholic faith commitment, or on any other scholarly grounds), the presumptive judgment regarding the teacher's fitness for his position must be the province of his academic peers, made under conditions which assure academic due process. The Trustees should attach such weight to this judgment as is set forth in the AAUP 1958 statement of Procedural Standards in Faculty Dismissal Proceedings. A determination of doctrinal orthodoxy may, under AATA norms, be made by a public ecclesiastical tribunal. When such a determination is made, it is still for the academic community to render judgment concerning competency to teach.

No grounds other than fitness to teach . . . may be invoked as grounds for dismissal proceedings. As applied to extramural utterances, the AAUP 1965 Statement on this subject is the best available and is fully adequate. Even opinions which constitute dissent from official, but non-infallible, teach of the magisterium need no special norms. The existing, generally accepted norms may be fairly read to require only that

The opinion be tenable Roman Catholic teaching.

The opinion be supportable by solid scholarship, if support is requested.

The official teaching of the magisterium is recognized.

Due consideration be given to the effect on the lives of all, particularly of those who have made a faith commitment.

No special norms are required because of the pontifical character of the University or of any of its schools. The commitment of the Roman Catholic teacher in a pontifical university or school to the Catholic faith differs in no way whatever from the commitment of a Roman Catholic teacher in any other institution. The profession of Catholic faith and the context of the faith commitment are not affected by the canonical status of the institution.

Conclusions on Other Matters

The current efforts of the University to revise its Statutes, and to update and improve its Bylaws and Regulations, particularly with regard to tenure, academic freedom and due process, should be pressed to an early completion. The ambiguities of the existing documents, and the failure to make them readily available to faculty, (particularly to new appointees), are potential sources of new crises. As part of this effort, the University should consider adoption of the 1940 AAUP statement without the "limitation clause" of that statement, as other Catholic universities already have done.

There is immediate need for adoption of a detailed set of procedures implementing the Report of the School of Theology of June 15, 1967 regarding possible conflict between any member of that School and any member of the American Episcopate. We presume that this would be part of the "fruitful dialogue between bishops and theologians" called for in the 1968 pastoral letter of the American Bishops. Establishment of the International Committee of Theologians, called for by the Synod of Bishops, is also urgently required. Existence of such legitimate channels of theological discussion might have avoided the crisis which gave rise to this inquiry.

This board finds that the actions of the Trustees on 5 September, in threatening suspension of subject professors and in giving public circulation of this threat, may have seriously damaged the academic standing of the professors, have certainly impaired the reputation of the academic departments concerned and, in some circles, have tarnished the reputation of the University. Even recognizing the "danger of immediate harm" rule, it appears to the board that it is essential that the elements of academic due process should have been invoked and the threat of suspension should never have been made a matter of public knowledge. The seriousness was compounded by Rector Whalen's request to subject professors to sign a statement regarding opposition to the encyclical and the obligation to silence, even though this request was later withdrawn.

The board recommends that assurance be given the academic community of this university that, before even the process leading to the possibility of suspension or dismissal is initiated, such preliminary decision will be subject to due process and to the prior judgment of academic peers.

Bibliography

Archives

Archives of the Archdiocese of Baltimore. St. Mary's Seminary and University, Baltimore, Maryland.

Archives of the Archdiocese of Los Angeles. San Fernando Mission, Mission Hills, California.

Archives of the Catholic University of America. American Catholic History Research Center and University Archives, Catholic University of America, Washington, D.C.

Archives of Monsignor Eugene A. Kevane. St. Gregory the Great Seminary Library, Seward, Nebraska.

Archives of John Cardinal Krol. Philadelphia Archdiocesan Historical Research Center, Philadelphia, Pennsylvania.

Archives of Father Carl J. Peter. Boys' Town, Nebraska.

Sources

American Association of University Professors. "Faculty Participation in College and University Government: Statement of Principles Approved by the Council, October 26, 1962". *Bulletin of the American Association of University Professors* 48 (1962): 4, 321–23.

———. "General Declaration of Principles". *Bulletin of the American Association of University Professors* 1 (1915): 21; 40 (1954–1955): 90–112.

———. *General Report of the Committee on Academic Freedom and Academic Tenure. Bulletin of the American Association of University Professors* 1 (1915): 36.

————. *Report of the Special Committee on Academic Freedom in Church-Related Colleges and Universities.* In *Bulletin of the American Association of University Professors* 53 (1967): 4, 369.

————. "Statement of Principles on Academic Freedom and Tenure". *Bulletin of the American Association of University Professors* 26 (1940): 1, 49–51.

————. "Statement on Procedural Standards in Faculty Dismissal Proceedings". *Bulletin of the American Association of University Professors* 50 (1964): 1, 69–71.

————. "Statement on Professional Ethics". *Bulletin of the American Association of University Professors* 52 (1966): 1, 57–58.

Annarelli, James John. *Academic Freedom and Catholic Higher Education.* New York: Greenwood Press, 1987.

Beaumont, Tom. "Senate Conceives Special Inquiry". *Tower,* September 27, 1968, 1.

Benedict XVI. Address at a meeting with Catholic educators at the Catholic University of America, Washington, D.C., on April 17, 2008. http://www.vatican.va/holy_father/benedict_xvi/speeches/2008/april/documents/hf_ben-xvi_spe_20080417_cath-univ-washington_en.html.

————. Address at the welcoming ceremony of the pope's apostolic journey to the United States, Washington, D.C., April 16, 2008. http://www.vatican.va/holy_father/benedict_xvi/speeches/2008/april/documents/hf_ben-xvi_spe_20080416_welcome-washington_en.html.

————. Christmas address to the Roman Curia. December 22, 2005. http://www.vatican.va/holy_father/benedict_xvi/speeches/2005/december/documents/hf_ben_xvi_spe_20051222_roman-curia_en.html.

"Bid to Oust Strike Foe Tests New CUA Rector". *National Catholic Reporter,* November 22, 1967.

"Birth Control Not Issue". *Tablet,* April 27, 1967, 1.

Brannan, Tom. "Report Will Brief Board of Trustees". *Tower,* November 10, 1967, 1.

Bull, George. "The Function of the Catholic Graduate School". *Thought* 13 (1938): 364–80.

Burghardt, Walter J. "American Church and American Theology: Response to an Identity Crisis". *Proceedings of the CTSA* 28 (1973): 1–14.

———. "Freedom and Authority in Education". *Theology Digest* 16 (1968): 310–16.

———. "Presidential Address: Towards an American Theology". *CTSA Proceedings* 23 (1968): 20–27.

Bush, George W. "President Bush Welcomes Pope Benedict XVI to U.S." Transcript of address given at welcoming ceremony in Washington, D.C., on April 16, 2008. FoxNews.com. http://www.fox news.com/story/0,2933,351467,00.html.

Byron, William J. "Clarence Walton as Academic CEO: A Fine Mind on a Fine Line". In *Education, Leadership, and Business Ethics: Essays on the Work of Clarence Walton*, edited by Ronald F. Druskay, 211–23. Dordrecht: Kluwer Academic Publishers, 1998.

Capece, Victor A. "Fight for Freedom". *Tower*, April 25, 1967, 4.

Cardozo, Manuel. "With Dignity". *Tower*, April 27, 1967, 2.

"Catholic U. Strike Backed by Rector". *New York Times*, September 30, 1967, 1.

Catholic University of America Faculty Board of Inquiry. *Report of the Faculty Board of Inquiry*. April 15, 1969. Cardinal Shehan Papers. Archives of the Archdiocese of Baltimore.

Cogley, John. "The Future of an Illusion". *Commonweal*, June 2, 1967, 310–16.

Congar, Yves. "Magisterium and Theologians". *Theology Digest* 25 (Spring 1977): 17.

"Controversy". *Tower*, September 26, 1969, 1.

Crosson, Frederick. "Personal Commitment as the Basis of Free Inquiry". In *Academic Freedom and the Catholic University*, edited by Edward Manier and John W. Houck, 87–102, Notre Dame: Fides Publishers, 1967.

"CU Classes are Empty". *Washington Daily News*, April 20, 1967, 2.

Curran, Charles E. "Academic Freedom: The Catholic University and Catholic Theology". *Furrow* 30 (December 1979): 739–54.

———. *Loyal Dissent: Memoir of a Catholic Theologian.* Washington, D.C.: Georgetown University Press, 2006.

———. "Ten Years Later." *Commonweal*, July 7, 1978, 427.

"Curran—'No Monopoly on the Spirit' ". *National Catholic Reporter*, September 21, 1966, 1–2.

Deferrari, Roy J., *Memoirs of the Catholic University of America: 1918–1960.* Boston: St. Paul Editions, 1962.

Donahue, Charles. "Freedom and Education: The Pluralist Background". *Thought* 27 (1952): 542–60.

———. "Freedom and Education: The Sacral Problem". *Thought* 28 (1953): 209–33.

———. "Freedom and Education: Catholicism and American Freedom". *Thought* 29 (1954): 555–73.

———. *Washington Perspective: A Newsletter for Superintendents*, reprinted and distributed on campus by Curran's steering committee, "CUA Controversies" box, "Curran Controversy, 1967" folder, ACUA.

"Double-Edged Issue: Freedom and Authority". *National Catholic Register*, May 7, 1967, 1.

Ellis, John Tracy. "American Catholics and the Intellectual Life". *Thought* 30 (1955): 351–88.

———. *The Formative Years of the Catholic University of America.* Washington: American Catholic Historical Association, 1946.

"Father Curran: Symbol of Bishops' Problem". *National Catholic Reporter*, April 26, 1967, 5.

Fellman, David. "Academic Freedom and the American Political Ethos". In *Academic Freedom and the Catholic University*, edited by Edward Manier and John W. Houck, 60–86. Notre Dame: Fides Publishers, 1967.

Fialka, J., "CUA Reinstates Father Curran, Shutdown Ends". *Evening Star*, April 25, 1967, 1.

Fitzgerald, Margaret M., "Rev. Msgr. Michael Eugene Kevane". *The Hebrew Catholic* 64 (Winter 1997): 11–15. http://hebrewcatholic.org /TheHebrewCatholic/64winter1997.html.

Geiger, Louis G., *Higher Education in a Maturing Democracy*. Lincoln: University of Nebraska Press, 1963.

Gleason, Philip. "Academic Freedom". *NCEA Bulletin* 64 (August 1967): 67–74.

———. "Academic Freedom and the Crisis in Catholic Universities". In *Academic Freedom and the Catholic University*, edited by Edward Manier and John W. Houck, 33–56. Notre Dame: Fides Publishers, 1967.

———. *Contending with Modernity: Catholic Higher Education in the Twentieth Century*. New York: Oxford University Press, 1995.

Grant, Gerald. "Fight for Academic Freedom Still Wide Open at Catholic U." *Washington Post*, April 23, 1967, 1.

Hailey, J. R. "Catholic U. Rebellion Laid to Faculty". *Washington Post*, April 22, 1967, 1.

Hennessey, James. "American History and Theological Enterprise". *CTSA Proceedings* 26 (1971): 91–115.

Herzfeld, N. K. "Blow Up at Catholic U." *Commonweal*, May 5, 1967, 190–91.

Hesburgh, Theodore. *God, Country, Notre Dame*. New York: Doubleday, 1990.

———. Preface to *The Catholic University: A Modern Appraisal*, edited by Neil G. McCluskey, vii–xiii. Notre Dame: University of Notre Dame Press, 1970.

Hunt, John F. and Terrence R. Connelly. *The Responsibility of Dissent: The Church and Academic Freedom*. New York: Sheed and Ward, 1969.

Hunt, Robert."Panel Discussion". *CTSA Proceedings* 23 (1968): 245–67.

"The Jig Is Up". *Tower*, April 25, 1967, 2.

John Paul II, "Address to the Catholic University of America". Washington, D.C., October 7, 1979. http://www.vatican.va/holy_father/john_paul_ii/speeches/1979/october/documents/hf_jp-ii_spe_1979100 7_usa_washington_univ-catt_en.html.

———. *Ex Corde Ecclesiae* (apostolic constitution on Catholic universities). August 15, 1990. http://www.vatican.va/holy_father/john_pau l_ii/apost_constitutions/documents/hf_jp-ii_apc_15081990_ex-corde -ecclesiae_en.html.

Jones, E. Michael. *John Cardinal Krol and the Cultural Revolution*. South Bend, Ind.: Fidelity Press, 1995.

Kahn, Journet. "The Threat to Academic Freedom". *Proceedings of the American Catholic Philosophical Association* 30 (1956): 160–70.

Kearns, Francis E. "Academic Freedom". In *The Shape of Catholic Higher Education*, edited by Robert Hassenger, 223–49. Chicago: University of Chicago Press, 1967.

Knight, D. M., "What Happened at Catholic U." *America*, May 13, 1967, 725.

"Krol on Carpet". *Tower*, April 25, 1967, 4.

"Land O' Lakes Statement on the Nature of the Contemporary Catholic University" (1967). In *The Catholic University: A Modern Appraisal*, edited by Neil G. McCluskey, 336–41. Notre Dame, Ind.: University of Notre Dame Press, 1970.

Manier, Edward and John W. Houck, eds. *Academic Freedom and the Catholic University*. Notre Dame: Fides Publishers, 1967.

Macelwane, James B. "Place of the Association in a Catholic University". *Bulletin of the American Association of University Professors* 26 (1940): 366–67.

MacGregor, Morris J. *Steadfast in the Faith: The Life of Patrick Cardinal O'Boyle*, Washington, D.C.: Catholic University of America Press, 2006.

Mahoney, John. "The American College and the Faith". *Thought* 39 (1964): 239–52.

Manier, Edward. Introduction to *Academic Freedom and the Catholic University*, edited by Edward Manier and John W. Houck, 1–27. Notre Dame: Fides Publishers, 1967.

MacKaye, William R., "Impact of Vatican II Is Seen in Walkout". *Washington Post*, April 22, 1967, 1.

Massa, Mark S. *The American Catholic Revolution: How the Sixties Changed the Church Forever*. New York: Oxford University Press, 2010.

May, William W., ed. *Vatican Authority and American Catholic Dissent: The Curran Case and Its Consequences*. New York: Crossroad, 1987.

McCluskey, Neil G. "This Is How It Happened". In *The Catholic University: A Modern Appraisal*, edited by Neil G. McCluskey, 1–28. Notre Dame, Ind.: University of Notre Dame Press: 1970.

McCormick, Richard A. "The Teaching of the Magisterium and the Theologians". *CTSA Proceedings* 24 (1969): 239–54.

McKenzie, John L. "The Freedom of the Priest-Scholar". In *Academic Freedom and the Catholic University*, edited by Edward Manier and John W. Houck, 164–76. Notre Dame, Ind.: Fides Publishers, 1967.

Mill, John Stuart. *On Liberty*. New York: P. F. Collier, 1910.

Moran, Gabriel. "The God of Revelation". *Commonweal*, February 10, 1967, 499–503.

Morris, Charles R. *American Catholic*. New York: Times Books, 1997.

"Multiple Efforts Under Way to End Catholic U. Shutdown". *Washington Evening Star*, April 22, 1967, 1.

Nuesse, C. Joseph. *The Catholic University of America: A Centennial History*. Washington: Catholic University Press, 1990.

O'Brien, David J. "The Historical Context of North American Theology: The United States' Story". *CTSA Proceedings* 41 (1986): 3–21.

"Of Many Things". *America*, May 6, 1967, 663.

O'Toole, James M. *The Faithful: A History of Catholics in America.* Cambridge, Mass.: Belknap Press of Harvard University Press, 2008.

"Ouster of Liberal Priest Spurs CUA Boycott Threat". *Washington Post*, April 19, 1967, 1.

Paul VI. *Humanae Vitae.* San Francisco: Ignatius Press, 1998.

Pierce, Albert C. *Beyond One Man* (Washington, D.C., 1967).

"Priest for Students: Charles Edward Curran". *The New York Times*, April 25, 1967, 1.

Quinn, John R. "The Magisterium and Theology". *CTSA Proceedings* 24 (1969): 255–61.

Rock, Augustine. "Panel Discussion: Academic Freedom and the Theologian". *CTSA Proceedings* 23 (1968): 245–67.

Schaefer, J. R. "These Were the Real Issues at C.U." *Catholic Review*, April 8, 1967, 1.

"Shehan Backs Fired Priest-Professor". *Baltimore Evening Sun*, April 21, 1967, 1.

Spalding, Thomas W. *The Premier See: A History of the Archdiocese of Baltimore, 1789–1989.* Baltimore: Johns Hopkins University Press, 1989.

"Statement of Dissent". July 30, 1968. In *The Responsibility of Dissent: The Church and Academic Freedom*, edited by John F. Hunt and Terrence R. Connelly, 203–5, New York: Sheed and Ward, 1969.

"This Time, Catholic U". *Commonweal*, May 5, 1967, 187.

Thomas, Samuel J. "A 'Final Disposition . . . One Way or Another': The Real End of the First Curran Affair". *Catholic Historical Review* 91, no. 4 (October 2005), 714–42.

Tillich, Paul. "The Significance of the History of Religions for the Systematic Theologian". In *The History of Religions: Essays on the Problem of Understanding*, edited by Joseph M. Kitagawa, 241–55. Chicago: University of Chicago Press, 1967.

"Time for Boy Scouts?" *Time*, April 28, 1967, 62.

Townsend, Robert B., "Culture, Conflict, and Change: The '67 Strike at Catholic University", unpublished paper written in 1990.

United States Catholic Conference. *Human Life in Our Day*. In *Pastoral Letters of the United States Catholic Bishops*. Vol. 3, edited by Hugh J. Nolan, 164–99. Washington, D.C.: United States Catholic Conference, 1983.

"Victory at C.U." *Time*, May 5, 1967, 84.

Wall, A. E. P., "Fr. Curran Says Catholics Should Talk to Each Other". *Catholic Review*, April 28, 1967, 1.

Walsh, John E., "The University and the Church". In *Academic Freedom and the Catholic University*, edited by Edward Manier and John W. Houck, 103–18. Notre Dame: Fides Publishers, 1967.

Walton, Clarence. "Academic Freedom at the Catholic University of America during the 1970's". *Catholic Historical Review* 76 (July 1990): 555–63.

Weigel, George. *The Courage to Be Catholic: Crisis, Reform, and the Future of the Church*. New York: Basic Books, 2002.

"Wrapup of Catholic U.—Curran Case". *National Catholic Register*, May 14, 1967, 3.

Index

of, 251–52; on source of CUA controversies, 117–19

Kevane, Eugene (replacement controversy): Academic Senate motion, 141–42; board meetings about, 129–31; faculty defenders, 132–35, 144–45; faculty opponents, 128–29, 133–34; re-election as dean, 128, 134; removal of, 143; response to special committee, 135–41; special committee actions, 131, 134–35, 141, 142–43

Krol, John: AAUP's letter of concerns, 41; background, 33; cardinal appointment, 128n4; on Curran's writing style, 156; in Kevane replacement controversy, 128–29, 130, 132–33, 143–45; in Murphy deanship controversy, 218, 219, 221–22; on Survey and Objectives Committee, 111n2

Krol, John (in Curran controversy): contract nonrenewal recommendation, 26–27, 35–36; investigative committee work, 32, 34–35; Kevane's communications about, 109–10; O'Boyle's negotiations, 51–52; opposition to reinstatement, 52–53, 54; Vagnozzi's letter, 51; Villanova University's letter, 48–49

Krol, John (in Dissent controversy): committee appointment, 178; communication with legal counsel, 208–9; evaluation of *Report of Faculty Inquiry*, 203–7; frustration about, 209–10; Garrone's letter about, 240–41; Kevane's letter, 187; lay comments to, 212–13; McIntyre's communications, 234; response to Doctrinal Committee report, 238–39; in trustee discussions, 173n1, 175

Küng, Hans, 37n31

Kurland, Jordan, 161

"Land O' Lakes Statement", 18, 84–88, 267–73

Leo XIII, 16n, 42–43

Lewis, Philip D., 244

Likoudis, James, 212n12

Linford, Alton A., 145n32

Lonergan, Bernard, 188–89

Long Range Planning Committee, 42

Lovejoy, Arthur, 73

loyal dissenters. *See* "Statement of Dissent"

Magisterium's role: overview of conflict consequences, 15–19, 251–60; AAUP's opposition, 33–34, 70; in accreditation report, 120, 121–25; Curran's interpretation, 29–31, 82–83, 250; in *Ex Corde Ecclesiae*, 248; faculty frustrations with, 40; Hunt's interpretations, 31n12, 89–90; Kevane's interpretation, 250–51; media coverage, 58–59, 61; papal addresses about, 247, 249–50; School of Education's position, 104–8; in School of Theology's *Report*, 97–102; in statutes revision debate, 229–33; and *Tentative Working Paper*, 113, 115–16, 118–19; tradition of education oversight, 15, 16. *See also* board of trustees *entries*

Magner, James, 25n1

Maguire, Daniel, 45, 155, 157–58, 163, 248n3

Maloney, Andrew P., 42, 135n17, 219n9

Maloney, Charles P., 111n2

Marlowe, Donald E., 111n2, 112, 116, 141–42, 186n9, 187–88

Marthaler, Berard, 159–60, 164–65